RAY-CENTERED ASTROLOGY

RAY-CENTERED ASTROLOGY

by
Ruth Mierswa
in collaboration with Richard Mierswa

First Edition

Library of Congress Catalog No. 84-90404

Copyright © 1986 by Ruth Mierswa in collaboration with
Richard Mierswa

Libra Publishers, Inc.
4901 Morena Blvd., Suite 207
San Diego, CA 92117

Manufactured in the United States of America

ISBN 0-87212-185-2

To Richard
    without whose collaboration
    this book could not have been

CONTENTS

CHARTS

Acknowledgement

I am indebted to the Lucis Trust for permission to quote from the works of Alice A. Bailey. These quotations from Alice A. Bailey's books cannot be reproduced without special permission from the Lucis Trust which holds copyright.

Although sexist language is not intended, in order to avoid excessive verbiage, the masculine gender, as used by the author, has not been changed.

RAY-CENTERED
ASTROLOGY

INTRODUCTION

"Who am I?" "Why am I here?" "What is the purpose of my life?" People in ever-increasing numbers are asking these questions to which there are presently few meaningful answers. Ray-Centered Astrology is a revolutionary way of optimally understanding and using Astrology, based on a new application of the Ancient Wisdom which offers pathways to the answers to these questions. It also gives a depth of knowledge and understanding of one's strengths, developed and latent abilities, weaknesses with new and better ways of overcoming them, and an uplifting of consciousness. A Tibetan Master of Wisdom said at the beginning of this century, that before its close there would be an Astrology of the Rays that would be used by humanity. Its time is now.

An increasing number of people do not know why they are here on earth. They do not know their unique ability for successfully contributing to others. They do not know their purpose in this life. They are increasingly bewildered, they want to reach out for answers but do not know where to reach; they have lost their moorings.

There are a number of reasons for this difficult state. One has its origin in the development of colonial empires all over the world in the early twentieth century. By 1910 the major European powers had divided most of Africa, Indonesia, the Malay Archipelago, and the islands of the South Seas, and had established enclaves in many of the Asian powers. These foreign colonies required extensive military establishments, ostensibly for protection, but in truth, were intended for eventual conquest, due to the second growth factor, the industrial revolution. This resulted in the outbreak of World War I in 1914. At the end of the war, vast areas of the world were redivided through treaties. This was followed by large population dispersions and worldwide depression. Even though recovery was relatively rapid in America and Europe as a result of the growth of huge industrial enterprises, the treaties had not brought peace to the minds and hearts of millions. It was in-

1

evitable that as industrial growth expanded, with technology changing every industrial nation, that the pressures of international geopolitics would have two results—increased armaments and spreading restlessness. Then came the fiasco of Chamberlain's meeting with Hitler and the start of the Second World War which involved every country on the globe and placed the nuclear capacity to destroy the earth in the hands of the military.

The second reason for the difficult conditions in which we find ourselves has to do with the time period through which we are passing. The present is the outcome of eons of time in which people became more and more involved in selfish concerns. Although we now should be on the evolutionary upward, spiritual climb, we are moving downward. This is a time of dichotomy when multitudes of people who are the products of the long upward struggle, the slow changing growth called evolution, have reached a point in cosmic time from which logically their progression should accelerate, but as a result of character weaknesses of many combined with greater intellectual strengths, which combination led them to greed, deviousness, and lust for power, civilization can easily slide back perilously closer to the abyss from which in the Ages following Lemuria it has painfully crawled. We can prevent this if we can spread an awareness through the minds of the masses of what is happening. Humankind once understood through the esoteric knowledge of Astrology why they were here on earth. This astrological knowledge was the key to their future. Regrettably, most of this understanding was lost in the carnage that swept away race after race and civilization after civilization, leaving only a small handful to guard and nurture the fragments of knowledge they were able to salvage. Through the Dark Ages these Guardians were thwarted in their efforts to place this knowledge into the hands of those who sought it.

The third reason for the bewilderment of people today is that Aquarian energies are pouring down on humanity at an accelerating rate; we are now in the transition stage from the Piscean to the Aquarian Age. Although these new Aquarian energies are what we need at this stage of our evolutionary progress, it is never easy to make the transition from one Age to another. It does not happen too often because each Age lasts approximately twenty-one hundred years. We can equate this transition with the change from childhood to adolescence; both changes are needed for eventual growth but it is not an easy process. To understand this process, we must introduce the concept of Reincarnation, which is a belief accepted by more than two thirds of the world's population—that each of us lives many lives, learning and progressing from one to the next. For many lifetimes during the Piscean Age, the majority were, comparatively speaking, like children who needed the guidance of leaders, especially religious leaders who told us what to believe, what to do, and what not to do. We were emotionally polarized in that we followed these leaders out of blind faith. Evolutionarily speaking we are now adolescents. We have had enough lives in the Piscean Age to begin to become independent beings. The Aquarian energies flowing through our minds urge us to reverse the polarity of our lives. We are urged to change Piscean dependency of thinking and acting according to what others tell us, to Aquarian independence and freedom to think and act according to our own conscience. We are urged to rely less on our emotions and more on our understanding. So it is the evolutionary order of things that people in ever-increasing numbers are no longer emotionally and blindly following concepts handed down from the Piscean Age. They are searching for understanding and reasonable answers to such questions as, "Why am I here?" The churches, by and large, have not kept pace with these new Aquarian energies and new needs. The result, of course, is that people are leaving the churches in large numbers. Now, as evolutionary adolescents, we no longer need or want the type of security and guidance that organized religions offered us in the Piscean Age. We are now eager and ready for real understanding which Aquarian energies now offer us.

People are searching for something that will help them understand who they are, why they are here, and how they can attain a sense of accomplishment, a sense of self-realization. Where can they turn now to give their lives real meaning?

Some are turning to psychology. Though some help can be found in this discipline, it is minimal as compared to what it could be if combined with "Ray-Centered Astrology." That "Ray-Centered Astrology" and psychology working hand-in-hand can become the dominant science of the future is the opinion of the Master Djwhal Kuhl, and is the basic premise upon which this book is based. "Psychology is only just come into its own, and only now is its function beginning to be understood; in one hundred years' time, however, it will be the dominating science; and the newer educational systems, based on scientific Psychology, will have completely superseded our modern methods. The emphasis in the future will be laid upon the determining of a man's life purpose. This will be brought about through an understanding of his Ray, through an analysis of his equipment (and of this, vocational Psychology is the faint first beginning), through a study of his horoscope, and through giving him a sound grounding in mind control, as well as training his memory to the impartation of information."* The basis of this impartation of information is the determination of his Soul Ray from which he becomes aware of his Soul's purpose for entering life on the earth.

Although present-day Astrology offers the seeker a number of helpful answers, it fails to provide satisfying solutions to the problems, and answers to the questions that bring increasing numbers of clients to the astrologer; nor has it succeeded in becoming what it once was. There is an urgent need for Astrology to be raised once more to the level where, in spite of smog and atmospheric contamination created by the greed of humanity, it can read the meanings of the heavens in a manner that will uplift the minds and hearts of people. This can be accomplished by Ray-Centered Astrology by helping people attain two major goals—finding purpose in life and eradicating weaknesses.

None of us come into this earth plane with the same life purposes or capacities; each of us is a unique person. Because no one else has had the identical past lives and experiences, no two persons can contribute to humanity in the same way. No one else is equipped to perform successfully another's life

*Bailey, Alice A. *Esoteric Psychology.* 1936, London: Lucis Trust, pp. 293, 294.

service. The challenge is to find our special niche. No techniques learned in my undergraduate or graduate study in psychology or in my many years of Astrological study and practice have contributed as much to the successful meeting of this challenge as does Ray-Centered Astrology.

The second goal of this book is to help others eradicate weaknesses, not only in helping them to become aware of them, especially those which give the most trouble, but also by pointing out particular strengths needed and how they can be acquired.

When a weakness has been eradicated, the energy that formerly was used in that weakness, especially at cyclic astrological periods when a particular energy is at its peak, will be used for one's life purpose. As a result, one will then experience an accelerating Soul evolvement and the joy of finding oneself possessed of additional benefits. It has been widely observed that as Soul development progresses, the psychic centers and glandular system function more efficiently. The physical and emotional health will then definitely improve.

All disease whether physical or emotional is the result of inhibited Soul life. As one begins to operate on a Soul level, one begins to live in harmony with the rhythm of the universe and fellow workers. In rhythm and harmony, there is no disease but ease of physical and emotional function.

True lasting success in one's life's work can be attained only if it is attuned to the Soul's purpose for incarnating. By-products of this success are monetary compensation if needed, self-realization, and joy.

Ray-Centered Astrology deals with the understanding of the Seven Rays—their meanings, origin, manifestation, and application to our lives so that we can know why we are here and how we can successfully use the time allotted to us.

Chapter One

NATURE AND FUNCTION OF THE RAYS

Flowing from certain stars to the zodiacal signs, the sun, the planets, and ultimately into the consciousness of all humanity, are Seven distinct Rays of energy. It is upon these Rays—their powers, functions, and effects that Ray-Centered Astrology is based. Every person has a Soul Ray and a Personality Ray among seven which determine the Soul's purpose or life plan, and the special type of personality through which the Soul's purpose is carried out. This chapter deals with the source and use of the Rays.

The Rays are forms of energy. Scientists have proved that everything in this universe is energy. Matter is energy at its lowest vibration, and spirit is energy at its highest vibration. A number of gradations of energy fall into groups. We know that the lowest vibratory energies are solids; the next higher are liquids; and finally gases. The ether of space is of a higher vibration than any of these.

It is in the ether, the energy fields that pervade stars, planets, and human beings, that Astrological Rays of energy are found. The Seven Rays are each distinct kinds of very high vibrational energies that enter and leave the etheric fields of stars, planets, and ultimately individuals on earth.

> "A Ray confers, through its energy, peculiar physical conditions, and determines the quality of the astral-emotional nature; it colours the mind body; it controls the distribution of energy; for the Rays are of differing rates of vibration, and govern a particular center in the body (differing with each Ray) through which that distribution is made. Each Ray works through one center primarily, and through the remaining six in a specific order. The Ray predisposes a man to certain strengths and weaknesses, and constitutes his principle of limitation, as well as endowing him with capacity. Certain attitudes of mind are easy for one Ray type and difficult for another."*

* Bailey, Alice A., *Esoteric Psychology,* Volume I, p. 128.

To understand the Rays it is important to be aware that each star, each planet, and each person is controlled by its spirit. Each one of us, though uniquely different, is controlled by the spirit within us; yet we all contribute to the whole of humanity—diversity in unity. And so it is with the planets and stars—as above, so below; the macrocosm of the heavens operates in the same way as the lesser microcosm of humanity. Each physical planet and each physical star is the manifestation of a great spiritual life, each differing from the other but in harmony with all others, again exemplifying diversity in unity. All energy that we receive on earth comes from the Seven Rays, and has its source in these great entities. In ages past, Astrology gave to humanity a truer picture of the Divine Plan than it does at present. Through the study and use of the Rays, Astrology again can become what it once was long ago—the most important science of the Age.

In the words of the Tibetan Master,

> "Astrology is a science which must be restored to its original beauty and truth before the world can gain a truer perspective and a more just and accurate appreciation of the Divine Plan, as it is expressed at this time through the Wisdom of the Ages. Astrology is essentially the purest presentation of occult truth in the world at this time, because it is the science which deals with those conditioning and governing energies and forces which play through and upon the whole field of space and all that is found within that field. When this fact is grasped and the sources of those energies are better comprehended and the nature of the field of space is correctly understood, we shall then see a far wider and at the same time, a more closely related horizon; the relationships between individual, planetary, systemic, and cosmic entities will be grasped, and we shall then begin to live scientifically. It is this scientific living which is the immediate purpose of Astrology to bring about."*

It is imperative that we live more scientifically now because we are no longer in the Piscean Age in which faith in the workability of Astrology and other sciences was sufficient; we are now in the Aquarian Age of enlightenment and of science in which a greater and deeper understanding of Astrology is

*Bailey, Alice A. *Esoteric Astrology,* p. 5.

paramount for scientific living. To attain a greater and deeper understanding of Astrology, we must know the sources of Ray energies, their transmission, their meanings, and the implication of the particular Rays for each of us.

The Seven Rays of energy originate in the consciousness of the Seven Great Entities controlling the seven stars of the Great Bear, known as Ursa Major or the "Big Dipper." The Great Bear as a unit emanates Ray One energy which is will, power, and creativity. Every Ray, though manifesting primarily in accordance with its identity, also manifests the Seven Ray energies in a subsidiary capacity, called sub-rays.

All seven entities of the Great Bear send Ray One energy, but in addition to basic Ray One, each sends a specific Ray. Thus the specific Rays sent by the seven entities controlling the seven stars are as follows: star number one sends out the specific Ray One energy of will, power, and creativity; star number two sends out Ray Two energy of love and wisdom; star number three sends out Ray Three energy of intellectual creativity; star number four sends out Ray Four energy of harmony through conflict; star number five sends out Ray Five energy of concrete knowledge; star number six sends out Ray Six energy of devotion and idealism; and star number seven sends out Ray Seven energy of rhythm and order.

It must be remembered that every Ray, no matter what its degree of sub-ray, also has lesser sub-rays of all the Seven Rays. For example, star number three of the Great Bear primarily would send Rays One and Three energies, in addition to all Seven Ray energies as sub-rays.

Each of the seven Great Bear entities sends its Ray energies to the Star Sirius where there is a blending of each with the basic Ray Two energy from Sirius of love and wisdom.

From Sirius the seven specific Ray energies are then sent to the seven stars of the Pleiades, which as a unit emanates Ray Three energy of intelligent activity. Each of the specific Rays from Sirius blends not only with Ray Three, but with the specific sub-rays of the Pleiades consonant with it.

It is important to remember that the basic Ray One energy of will, power, and creativity is sent out from the seven Great Bear entities to Sirius of Ray Two energy of love and wisdom

10

and blends with it, then enters the Pleiades whose basic Ray Three of intelligent activity blends with Ray One and Two energies. At the same time, each subsidiary Ray of the seven stars of the Great Bear keeps its distinct Ray identity as it enters first Sirius, then the Pleiades.

Though there are seven distinct Ray energies flowing from the Great Bear, Sirius, and the Pleiades, the most important Rays from the great entities controlling these stars are their basic Rays—Ray One, Two, and Three. For this reason these three Rays are the most spiritual of all the Seven Rays. (See Chart 1 which will help clarify the general meaning of these three Rays.)

CHART 1

THE SPIRITUAL RAYS

RAY 1	RAY 2	RAY 3
Will & power	Love & wisdom	Intelligent activity
Great Bear	Sirius	The Pleiades
Spirit	Soul	Physical body & personality
Father	Son	Holy Spirit
Shiva	Vishnu	Brahma
Shambala	Hierarchy	Humanity
Creates divine plans	Carries out divine plans	Beneficiary of divine plans

Each of the Seven Ray energies, originating from the Great Bear and passing through Sirius and the Pleiades, is basically of the first three Rays but is differentiated one from the other by a specific subsidiary Ray.

These seven specific Rays of energy from the Great Bear of basic Ray One energy, after blending with Ray Two energy from Sirius and Ray Three energy from the Pleiades, enter the twelve zodiacal signs. Each of the Seven Rays enters three signs of the zodiac. (See Chart 2 which is basic to the study of the Rays.)

CHART 2

SIGNS EACH RAY ENTERS

Ray 1 enters	♈	♌	♑
Ray 2 enters	♊	♍	♓
Ray 3 enters	♎	♋	♑
Ray 4 enters	♍	♉	♐
Ray 5 enters	♌	♒	♐
Ray 6 enters	♓	♍	♐
Ray 7 enters	♈	♑	♋

From Bailey, Alice A., *Esoteric Astrology,* p. 489.

From the zodiacal signs, the Seven Rays enter our Sun where they blend with the basic potent Ray Two energy of the Sun. The entity controlling the Sun then sends all seven subsidiary Ray energies to the planets of its system. Each planet receives one of the Seven Ray energies, yet each Ray includes all Seven Rays in a subsidiary capacity. For Planet Earth the basic Ray is Three of intellectual activity which includes all Ray energies in a lesser amount. (See Chart 5 which shows the basic Ray that each planet revolving around the Sun receives from it. These planets are considered the rulers of the Rays that enter them from the Sun.)

Ray Three, the basic Ray of Earth and all its subsidiary Seven Rays reach the inhabitants of Earth. There is a lessening of the potencies of these Ray energies each time they enter another star, a group of stars, zodiacal signs, planets, or individuals. This reduction is very necessary because, unless they are of a diluted nature, the first three Ray energies in their purity and potency could not be handled by humanity at its present level of spiritual evolvement.

The basic Ray Three energy of Earth enables humanity, through intelligent acitivity, to learn the necessary lessons for overcoming weaknesses and for enhancing the abilities and capacities for serving others. The Earth in one's chart is positioned opposite one's Sun.

Vulcan, which is never more than a few degrees from Mercury, enables persons to reach to the very depths of their nature in order to become aware of their weaknesses, and to crystallize and destroy them through Ray One energy of power and will.

The entity, Sanat Kumara, controlling Planet Earth, sends its basic Ray Three energy and also one of its seven subsidiary Rays to each of the seven various kingdoms on Earth—the mineral, plant, animal, human, and three spiritual kingdoms. Because humanity is midway between the lowest and the highest kingdoms, the middle Ray which is Ray Four of harmony through conflict, is the specific Ray of humanity as a unit. See Chart 3 which shows the origin of the Rays and their paths of travel from the Great Bear through Sirius, the Pleiades, the zodiacal signs, the Sun, the Earth, humanity, and individuals.

Note that the Ray of humanity as a unit is Ray Four of harmony through conflict. All persons therefore must resolve their conflicts to attain harmony, the Law of Karma being an aid for hastening this process. Note further that the next basic Ray is that of the Earth—Ray Three of intelligent activity; the more successful we are in resolving our conflicts, the more time and energy we have for intellectual activity. Note that the next basic Ray is that of the Sun—Ray Two of love and wisdom. When we have gained sufficient knowledge, through intellectual activity, we receive more Ray Two energy from the Sun, which enables us to use our knowledge wisely through love for all humanity. This upward gradation of the quality of our energy illustrates the path we can follow in the use of successive Ray energies, resulting in the refinement of our Soul and mental, emotional, and physical bodies.

To understand the orderly and efficient way in which the Universe functions, it is important to know that all Ray energies flow from more highly evolved entities to less highly evolved entities. As the energy transfer is made from one entity to the next, a dilution in energy intensity takes place according to the capacity of the entity to absorb the energy received. This dilution is repeated stepwise, downward in intensity in the order pictured in Chart 3.

Just as each planet has a unique purpose for its existence, and a specific function consonant with its Ray toward the evolvement of the Universe, so does each individual have a unique purpose for existence and a specific function consonant with *his* Soul Ray toward the evolvement of humanity.

The Seven Ray energies are distributed among us in such a way that, although they are consonant with the abilities of each, there are enough recipients of each Ray energy to contribute to all the necessary functions for Soul evolvement of the human race. In addition to the Soul Ray designating the purpose of each person's Soul, each of us receives a specific Personality Ray which helps us to achieve our life plan.

In the words of the Ancient Wisdom, "As above, so below." Just as certain entities controlling planetary bodies are more spiritually evolved than others, resulting in some planets being considered sacred and others nonsacred, so it is with humans. Some are much more highly evolved than others. This is an individual process concerned with free will which is one of the fundamental laws of the Universe.

It must be remembered that no matter what the specific Rays of the Soul and Personality, Rays Two, Three, and Four are basic in each of us because they are the Rays of Sun, Earth, and human kingdom. Even though the originating sources of Ray energy from the Great Bear, Sirius, and the Pleiades are basically Rays One, Two, and Three, they are, relatively speaking, very remote, and thus extremely diluted. The Ray energies coming directly to us are from our Sun, Ray Two, as differentiated from other suns, and from the Earth, Ray Three, as differentiated from all other planets but Saturn, and from the human kingdom, Ray Four, as differentiated from all other kingdoms on Earth.

It is the destiny of each of us to receive a predominance of one of the Ray energies for the Soul's purpose or life plan for serving others. It is also secondarily the destiny of each of us to receive a predominance of one of the Ray energies for the Personality Ray. These two Rays are destined in accordance with what we have accomplished in our past lives, the weaknesses we have not yet overcome and must eradicate, and what

14

CHART 3

PATH OF RAYS TO HUMANITY

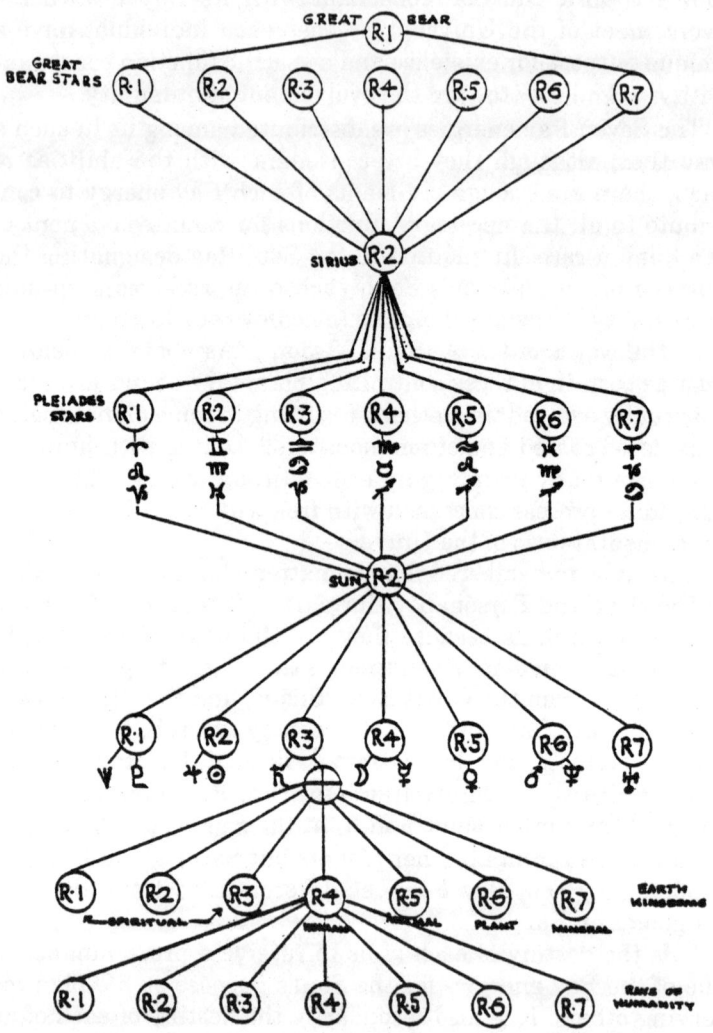

Revised from Bailey, Alice A., *Esoteric Astrology*, pp. 604, 609, 610.

our main accomplishment or Soul purpose for this life should be. When we have become aware of our Soul and Personality Rays, we can go about our mission in life, knowing that it is the one that our Soul destined for us and the one that will not only give us a sense of fulfillment, but will enable us to best serve others. Until we know what our true life's work is to be and follow it, living can be very frustrating. This work was written to help the reader reduce or avoid the years of unhappiness—years which can be enjoyable and during which others also could profit.

The identities of one's Soul Ray and Personality Ray are found in the natal horoscope. Each of us is born at a time that is synchronized with the activity of the cosmos that determines our destiny. This work shows how to calculate one's specific Soul and Personality Rays and interpret their meanings. No matter what one's Soul or Personality Ray may be, we must remember all other Rays are inherent in it in subsidiary roles.

Humanity's Ray Four of harmony through conflict is the most immediate of basic Rays, Two, Three, and Four, for two reasons. The first is because each of us is a part of humanity. The second is that we must attain a certain degree of harmony by resolving our conflicts before we have the time and energy to receive and use Ray Three energy which is devoted to intellectual creativity, and then through the intellect make use of Ray Two energy of love and wisdom.

As each person is born, the energy of one particular Ray enters his consciousness as his Soul Ray which designates his Soul's purpose. In addition, one of the Seven Rays enters his consciousness as the designator of his Personality. There are variables in one's chart that differentiate one's Soul's purpose from another who has the same Soul and Personality Rays. This is elucidated in the following chapters.

Each of us receives the particular Soul Ray we are ready for and need for evolutionary development in any one lifetime. It is the Soul's wish in a particular life to work on a Ray which supplies the energy for the type of serving for which that particular Soul is most capable. A Ray Seven Soul has a need to learn and a capability to serve through order and organization. A Ray Six Soul has a need to learn and a capacity to serve through idealism and devotion. A Ray Five Soul has a need to learn and a capability to serve through the concrete mind. A Ray Four Soul has a need to learn and a capability to serve through an integrated personality in which the mind would become the master of the emotions. A Ray Three Soul has a need to learn and a capability to serve through the abstract higher mind. A Ray Two Soul has a need to learn and a capability to serve through love and wisdom. A Ray One Soul has a need to learn and a capability to serve through will and power.

To help in the synthesis of the delineation, it is important to remember that there is a general difference between the odd- and even-numbered Rays. The odd-numbered Rays have an affinity mainly with electricity, will power, intellect, and assertiveness—positive polarity, the masculine part of our being or the animus as Jung describes it. The even-numbered Rays have an affinity with magnetism, attraction, love, emotions, and sensitivity—the negative polarity, the feminine part of our being, the anima as Jung calls it. Neither the odd-numbered or even-numbered Rays are better; they are merely different, and both are necessary to our spiritual development.

All Ray energies flow from the zodiacal signs to our solar system. Ever since Ptolemy introduced the concept of the rulership of signs by the planets, this concept has been helpful for interpretation. Ray-Centered Astrology, unlike traditional astrology which deals only with the exoteric rulers, concerns itself with three kinds of planetary rulers of the signs—the exoteric rulers which have been in use for centuries, the spiritual esoteric rulers, and the higher spiritual hierarchical rulers. Those who are not yet in contact with their Soul, and are therefore making no effort to overcome weaknesses, are manifesting on a personality level and receive the energies from the exoteric rulers only. Those who have made Soul contact receive energy from the exoteric rulers on a higher level than do their less-evolved brothers, and also receive energies from the esoteric rulers of the signs. Those who are very advanced and have made a great deal of progress in their spiritual evolvement, and are serving others in accordance with their Souls' Rays, not only receive the energies of the exoteric and esoteric rulers, but receive them at a higher level than their less-evolved brothers. In addition, they receive energies from the hierarchical rulers of the signs. For example, whatever house one's Aries is in (and, of course, this is stronger if one has an angle or planets in Aries) the energy of the exoteric ruler, Mars, is activated. This is pure physical energy which can be used unwisely in anger or in sex without love, or it can be used wisely in courage to help those in need. One who is using the exoteric ruler's energy wisely receives energy also from the esoteric ruler of Aries which is Mercury. Thus, that person's mind becomes very alert and interested in spiritual matters. If he continues to use his mind in spiritual concerns, the energy of the hierarchical ruler of Aries will also come to him. Uranus will give him intuitive capacities and interests in occult wisdoms such as astrology or original ideas and concepts in other fields that are consonant with his Soul's purpose.

Those who receive hierarchical ruling planetary energies from the signs are in contact with the hierarchy which is composed of extremely highly evolved Souls who work toward manifesting God's Plan on Earth with the help of humanity. Because more and more people are now learning to contact their Souls, Ray-Centered Astrology with the use of rulers other than the exoteric will soon become universal. (See chart 4, p. 19).

Esoteric and hierarchical rulers are necessary to calculate the Rays for each person, to set up one's Ray-Centered horoscopes, and delineate them.

Color, too, finds an important place in Ray-Centered Astrology. It is in the wearing, seeing, and/or visualizing not only the particular color that has affinity with one's Soul Ray but also the color that has affinity with one's Personality Ray, through which one's Ray energies are enhanced. This enhancement increases the probability of manifesting along the lines of one's particular Rays. Color can also be used profitably by those whose horoscopes note a definite lack of a desirable characteristic. A lack of love is helped by pink, and a lack of self-confidence is helped by white. The color having affinity with the characteristic that is lacking should be used to help bring about that characteristic in the consciousness of the person. Certain colors are used because everything in the Universe is energy, and since each color has a different flow of energy (rate of vibration), each color affects us in different ways—but always in correlation with its Ray.

Chapter Two

CALCULATING THE RAYS

The calculations of the Soul and Personality Rays are done by following clearly outlined steps: An accurate natal chart is a requirement for the calculations of the Rays; the Personality Ray requires only two steps for its determination; the Soul Ray of most horoscopes requires only one or a few steps for its determination.

In Ray-Centered Astrology, the Ascendant is equated with the Soul and the Sun is equated with the personality. You will note that this is a reversal of the traditional, personality-centered astrology, in which the Ascendant signifies one's personality and the Sun, one's Soul potential. Ray-Centered Astrology is esoteric and Soul-oriented while traditional astrology is exoteric and personality-oriented.

As we begin to contact our Soul, the Ascendant and the first house portray the Soul and its expression, and the Sun, our personality. Because we are now raising our consciousness from a former concern for self only, to concern for others as well; what was real to us previously is no longer real; we are finding a new reality. We are beginning to have more control over our life; we find that the exoteric personality-centered horoscope is becoming less and less accurate, not only in the natal interpretation of character weaknesses, but in the events and experiences that transits and progressions should indicate. When so-called difficult transits or progressions appear in our natal horoscope, we are learning to use their energies in a constructive manner. Whether we are aware of it or not, we are benefiting from Ray-Centered Astrology.

It is important for those who have reached or are reaching toward this level in their development to know exactly what their Soul and Personality Rays are, and to use them to accelerate their Soul growth. And it is equally important before calculating the Soul and Personality Rays, that their horoscopes be transformed from the Sidereal System, if it is so calculated, to the Tropical System which is used throughout this book.

Finding the Personality Ray
Step 1. Find the esoteric ruler of the Sun sign from the following chart.

CHART 4

THE ESOTERIC AND HIERARCHICAL RULERS OF THE SIGNS

SIGN	ESOTERIC RULER	HIERARCHICAL RULER
♈	☿	♆
♉	♀ (Vulcan)	♀ (Vulcan)
♊	♀	⊕
♋	♆	♆
♌	☉*	☉*
♍	☽	♃
♎	♅	♄
♏	♂	☿
♐	⊕	♂
♑	♄	♀
♒	♃	☽*
♓	♇	♇

*The Sun as an esoteric ruler veils Neptune, and as a hierarchical ruler, veils Uranus. The Moon as an esoteric ruler veils Vulcan for the average person, and Neptune for the developed person. The Moon as a hierarchical ruler veils Vulcan or Uranus, depending on the level of evolvement. When the Sun or Moon veils a planet it focuses its strength or energy on that planet.

From Bailey, Alice A., *Esoteric Astrology*, p. 68.

Step 2. Using the planet found in Step 1, find in the following chart the Ray of which it is a ruler. This is the Personality Ray.

CHART 5

RULING PLANETS OF THE RAYS

Ray 1—	♈* ♇
Ray 2—	♃ ☉
Ray 3—	♄ ⊕
Ray 4—	☿ ☽
Ray 5—	♀
Ray 6—	♆ ♂
Ray 7—	♅

*Symbol for Vulcan
Bailey, Alice A., *Esoteric Astrology,* p. 649.

Finding the Soul Ray
   It is important to take the following steps in the order given. (Use only enough steps to find the Soul Ray.)

   Step 1. Find in the following chart which Ray or Rays enter the Ascendant sign.

CHART 6

RAYS ENTERING EACH SIGN

SIGN	RAYS	SIGN	RAYS	SIGN	RAYS
♈	1 & 7	♌	1 & 5	♐	4, 5, & 6
♉	4	♍	2 & 6	♑	1, 3, & 7
♊	2	♎	3	♒	5
♋	3 & 7	♏	4	♓	2 & 6

From Bailey, Alice A., *Esoteric Astrology*, p. 86.

This step determines the Soul Ray for Taurus, Gemini, Libra, Scorpio, and Aquarius Ascendants because only one Ray enters each of these signs. For all other Ascendants, list the two or three Rays that enter the Ascendant, one of which will be found to be the Soul Ray.

Step 2. From the two or three Rays found in Step 1, list from Chart 7 the three signs each Ray enters.

Step 3. Find the esoteric ruler of the Ascendant from Chart 4. From the natal horoscope find the sign the esoteric ruler is in. If it is in one of the signs which one of the Rays (found in Step 2) enters, and that sign does not receive energy from the other Ray or Rays found in Step 2, this is the Soul Ray. If the esoteric ruler of the Ascendant is in a sign which receives energy from two of the three listed Rays, the Soul Ray must be one of these two Rays.

CHART 7

SIGNS EACH RAY ENTERS

Ray 1 enters	♈ , ♌ , ♑
Ray 2 enters	♊ , ♍ , ♓
Ray 3 enters	♎ , ♋ , ♑
Ray 4 enters	♍ , ♉ , ♐
Ray 5 enters	♌ , ♒ , ♐
Ray 6 enters	♓ , ♍ , ♐
Ray 7 enters	♈ , ♑ , ♋

From Bailey, Alice A., *Esoteric Astrology*, p. 86.

As an example, suppose one has a Capricorn Ascendant. We then list the Rays that enter Capricorn along with the other signs these Rays enter (from Charts 6 and 7)

Ray 1 enters	♈ , ♌ , ♑
Ray 3 enters	♎ , ♋ , ♑
Ray 7 enters	♈ , ♋ , ♑

Chart 4 tells us that the esoteric ruler of Capricorn is Saturn. Suppose Saturn is in Libra in the natal chart. Since Libra appears in only one of the Rays listed, namely Ray 3, the Soul Ray is Ray 3. If Saturn is in Leo, the Soul Ray is Ray 1 because that is the only Ray of the three Rays listed in which Leo is found; if Saturn is in Aries, the Soul Ray must be 1 or 7; if

Saturn is in Cancer, the Soul Ray must be 3 or 7; if Saturn is in Capricorn, the Soul Ray must be 1, 3, or 7.

Step 4. From Chart 4 find the hierarchical ruler of the Ascendant. Then from the natal horoscope find the sign the hierarchical ruler is in. In the above example the hierarchical ruler of Capricorn is Venus. Looking at the chart in Step 3, we find the following:

Saturn in Capricorn and Venus in Libra, gives a Ray 3 Soul.
Saturn in Capricorn and Venus in Leo, gives a Ray 1 Soul.
Saturn in Capricorn and Venus in Aries gives a Ray 1 or 7 Soul.
Saturn in Capricorn and Venus in Cancer gives a Ray 3 or 7 Soul.
Saturn in Aries and Venus in Leo gives a Ray 1 Soul.
Saturn in Aries and Venus in Cancer gives a Ray 7 Soul.
Saturn in Aries and Venus in Capricorn gives a Ray 1 or 7 Soul.
Saturn in Aries and Venus in Aries gives a Ray 1 or 7 Soul.
Saturn in Cancer and Venus in Libra gives a Ray 3 Soul.
Saturn in Cancer and Venus in Aries gives a Ray 7 Soul.
Saturn in Cancer and Venus in Capricorn gives a Ray 3 or 7 Soul.
Saturn in Cancer and Venus in Cancer gives a Ray 3 or 7 Soul.

If the hierarchical ruler of the Ascendant is located in a sign which receives energy from only one of the possible Soul Rays, that is the Soul Ray. If this sign receives energy from two of the possible Soul Rays, one of those two Rays must be the Soul Ray.
Example 1: Suppose one has a Capricorn Ascendant with the esoteric ruler, Saturn, in Aries, and the hierarchical ruler, Venus, in Libra. Rays 1, 3, and 7 enter Capricorn.

Ray 1 enters   ♈ , ♌ , ♑

Ray 3 enters   ♎ , ♋ , ♑

24

Ray 7 enters ♈ , ♋ , ♑

Since Saturn is in Aries and only Rays 1 and 7 enter Aries, the Soul Ray must be Ray 1 or 7. Since Venus is in Libra and only Ray 3 enters Libra, Ray 3 is not the Soul Ray. As given immediately above, the Soul Ray must be Ray 1 or 7.

Example 2: Suppose one has a Capricorn Ascendant as in Example 1, but with the esoteric ruler, Saturn, in Cancer, and the hierarchical ruler, Venus, in Capricorn. Since Saturn is in Cancer and only Rays 3 and 7 enter Cancer, the Soul Ray must be either Ray 3 or 7. Since Venus is in Capricorn, and both Rays 3 and 7 enter Capricorn, the Soul Ray has not yet been found.

Step 5. List all planets in the natal horoscope found in any signs in which the two or three possible Rays enter.

Example 1: If one has a Capricorn Ascendant, and if both Saturn and Venus are in Capricorn, and if there are more planets in the signs that Ray 1 enters than in the signs that Ray 3 or 7 enters, the Soul Ray is 1.

Example 2: Suppose with a Capricorn Ascendant, Saturn is in Capricorn and Venus is in Aries. The Soul Ray must be Ray 1 or Ray 7. Suppose the Sun is in Aries, Mercury in Taurus, Mars in Leo, Jupiter in Cancer, Uranus in Aquarius, Neptune in Leo, and Pluto in Cancer. The Sun and Mars are in the signs that Ray 1 enters; the Sun, Jupiter, and Pluto are in the signs that Ray 7 enters. Since there are more planets in the signs that Ray 7 enters than in the signs that Ray 1 enters, the Soul Ray is Ray 7.

If there are no planets in the signs which the two or three possible Rays enter, skip this step. If there are only two possible Rays, and if there are more planets found in the signs that one Ray enters than in the signs that the other Ray enters, that is the Soul Ray. If there are three possible Rays, and if there are more planets in the signs that one Ray enters than in the signs that either of the other two Rays enter, that is the Soul Ray.

Step 6. If there are no planets in the signs in which the two or three Rays concerned enter, or if there are the same number of planets in any two groups of three signs that the two or three Rays concerned enter, proceed to this step. Using Chart 4, find the esoteric rulers of all the signs in which the two or three Rays concerned enter, except the Ascendant with which we have already dealt. If more of these esoteric rulers fall in the signs that one of the concerned Rays enter than in the signs that any other concerned Ray enters, the former Ray is the Soul Ray.

Example: Suppose with a Capricorn Ascendant, Saturn and Venus both in Capricorn, there are the same number of natal planets in the signs of each of the three Rays concerned entering each group of signs. The signs, excluding the Ascendant in which Rays 1, 3, and 7 enter, are Aries, Leo, Libra, and Cancer. The esoteric ruler of Aries is Mercury found in Aries, the esoteric ruler of Leo is the Sun found in Pisces; the esoteric ruler of Libra is Uranus found in Aquarius; the esoteric ruler of Cancer is Neptune found in Leo. Only two of these esoteric rulers are in signs the concerned Rays enter—Mercury in Aries; which Rays 1 and 7 enter and Neptune in Leo which Ray 1 enters. Therefore, Ray 1 is the Soul Ray.

Step 7. Use the hierarchical rulers of signs as found in Chart 4 in the same manner as the esoteric rulers were used in Step 6.

Step 8. Use all progressed planets of a day for a year, except the progressed Moon, in the same procedure as the esoteric rulers were used in Step 6.

Step 9. Using the ephemeris, check to see if one or more progressed planets, excluding the Moon, changes signs from the present age to age of one hundred years. If so, use the same procedure as the esoteric rulers were used in Step 6. If it takes these 9 steps to determine the Soul Ray, in all probability, you will begin to fulfill your Soul purpose late in life.

Step 10. Use the North Node in the same procedure as the esoteric rulers were used in Step 6.

26

Step 11. Use the South Node in the same procedure as the esoteric rulers were used in Step 6.

Step 12. Use the M.C. in the same procedure as the esoteric rulers were used in Step 6.

Step 13. Use the Descendant in the same procedure as the esoteric rulers were used in Step 6.

Step 14. Use the I.C. in the same procedure as the esoteric rulers were used in Step 6.

Step 15. Using Chart 5, if the esoteric ruler of the Ascendant is a ruler of one of the Rays concerned, that Ray is the Soul Ray.
Example: If the Ascendant is Capricorn, Saturn is the esoteric ruler and is also a ruler of Ray 3. Because the Rays under consideration are Rays 1, 3, and 7, the Soul Ray is Ray 3.

Step 16. Using Chart 5, use the hierarchical ruler of the Ascendant following the same procedure as the esoteric ruler of the Ascendant in Step 15.
Example: If the Ascendant is Capricorn, Venus is the hierarchical ruler, and is also the ruler of Ray 5. Because the Rays under consideration are Rays 1, 3, and 7, the Soul Ray is not yet found.

Most natal horoscopes require only a few steps to find the Soul Ray. Except for the rare and most unusual horoscope, the preceding 16 procedural steps are more than enough to reveal the Soul Ray. In the unusual case in which the 16 steps do not reveal the Soul Ray, the two or three possible Rays in the following chapter should be studied with the utmost care to determine from the natal horoscope delineation with which Ray the client has the most affinity.

To find the Ascendant, it is necessary to know one's clock time of birth. Doctors who deliver babies are required to file the birth certificate with the Bureau of Vital Statistics, which is located in many cities and in the capitals of all states. For a fee, anyone can obtain a copy of his birth certificate from the Bureau. The only problem is that some certificates do not list the clock time, or if they do, there is a possibility that it is not accurate. At present it is difficult to be definitely certain of one's minute of birth. Precise birth times will be uniformly recorded when the need and importance of a true Ascendant is in the consciousness of enough people.

The time will surely come (and it is not too far off) when all school children will learn Astrology along with reading, writing, and arithmetic. Astrology is now being introduced in some schools at different scholastic levels as a part of science or sociology, and as a separate subject in others. When the astrological need of an accurate birth time is implanted in the consciousness of most people, it will be recorded.

For the present it is important for someone who wants a Ray-Centered delineation to know that his Soul Ray is determined by his time of birth, and if this is inaccurate beyond certain limits, his calculated Soul Ray will be inaccurate. It takes approximately two hours for the Ascendant to change from the beginning of one sign to the beginning of the next. It depends upon how accurate one's birth time is and how close the calculated Ascendant is to an adjacent sign in terms of degree as to whether or not the calculated Soul Ray is accurate.

Suppose a calculated Ascendant is 20° Leo. Because the Ascendant moves approximately one degree every four minutes, if the birth time was forty minutes or more later than originally calculated, the Ascendant would more than likely be in Virgo, giving it a different Soul Ray. If the true time of birth was eighty minutes or more earlier than originally calculated, the Ascendant more than likely would be in Cancer, giving it a different Soul Ray. However, if the true time was less than eighty minutes earlier or less than forty minutes later than originally calculated, the calculated Soul Ray would more than likely still be accurate. Allowance must be made for the fact that some signs are of long ascension and some are of short ascension. Thus some signs move faster than others. For that reason I used the phrase "more than likely."

After calculating the Soul and Personality Rays, you must decide through your perception of the one for whom the work is being done whether or not the two-Ray combination fits him. After calculating the Soul and Personality Rays of the seven following example cases, I found that the Soul-Personality Rays of six cases seem to fit the individuals well. One did not fit at all. This is Horoscope Example 1 with an Aries Ascendant, giving him a Ray Seven Soul. He has a Ray One Personality. If his Ascendant was accurate, both odd-numbered Rays would tend to give him a strong will, extroverted behavior, and possibly a cold, unloving manner and tone of voice. During the interview I found him to be somewhat introverted, warm, loving, and sensitive, with a pleasant, kind voice. With the time of birth given, his Ascendant calculated to twenty eight degrees Aries fifty seven minutes. I knew that he was born more than four minutes later than the time given me because one Degree of the Ascendant is equal to about four minutes of clock time. With a Taurus Ascendant, his Soul Ray would be Ray Four which fits in well with how I perceived him.

If, after calculating the Rays, you find them both to be even-numbered and you do not perceive that person to be sensitive, loving, and somewhat lacking in will-power, the birth time and the Ascendant sign are evidently wrong unless there are many planets in fire, air, or fixed signs. If you find both Rays to be odd-numbered and you do not perceive the person to be strong-willed and possibly insensitive to others' needs, the Ascendant sign is evidently wrong unless there are many planets in water or mutable signs.

If the Ascendant is wrong, the Soul Ray more than likely is inaccurate. It is imperative to use the following procedure if the Ascendant is either less than five degrees or more than twenty-five degrees of a sign after calculating the Soul and Personality Rays. If the Ascendant is less than five degrees of the sign and the Soul-Personality Rays do not fit the person, use the sign preceding the Ascendant as the new Ascendant and recalculate the Soul Ray. If the Ascendant is more than twenty-five degrees of a sign and the Soul-Personality Rays do not fit the person, use the sign following the Ascendant as the new Ascendant and recalculate the Soul Ray.

Examples of Calculating the Soul and Personality Rays

To illustrate the variances in Ascendants and to enhance this understanding of the more involved calculations required of certain horoscopes, the following example horoscopes were chosen because: (1) All seven horoscopes present more complexities in calculation than any of the other one hundred eighty-three horoscopes used for research, thus giving the reader ample opportunity to become adept at techniques of calculation. (2) These seven horoscopes illustrate all seven Ascendant signs into which more than one Ray enters. (If only one Ray enters the Ascendant, as it does in the remaining five signs, the Soul Ray is easily determined.) All horoscopes picture the natal planets in the inner circle and the progressed planets in the outer circle.

HOROSCOPE EXAMPLE 1

To Find the Personality Ray

Step 1. Find the esoteric ruler of the Sun sign in Chart 4. The esoteric ruler of the Pisces Sun is Pluto.

Step 2. Using Pluto from Step 1, find the Ray of which it is a ruler in Chart 5. Pluto is a ruler of Ray One. Thus, Ray One is the Personality Ray.

To Find the Soul Ray

Step 1. Find which Ray or Rays enter the Ascendant sign, using Chart 6. Rays One and Seven enter the Aries Ascendant. The Soul Ray is either Ray One or Ray Seven.

Step 2. Using Rays One and Seven from Step 1, find, in Chart 7, the three signs each of them enters. Ray One enters Aries, Leo, and Capricorn. Ray Seven enters Aries, Cancer, and Capricorn.

HOROSCOPE EXAMPLE 1

RAY 7 SOUL, RAY 1 PERSONALITY

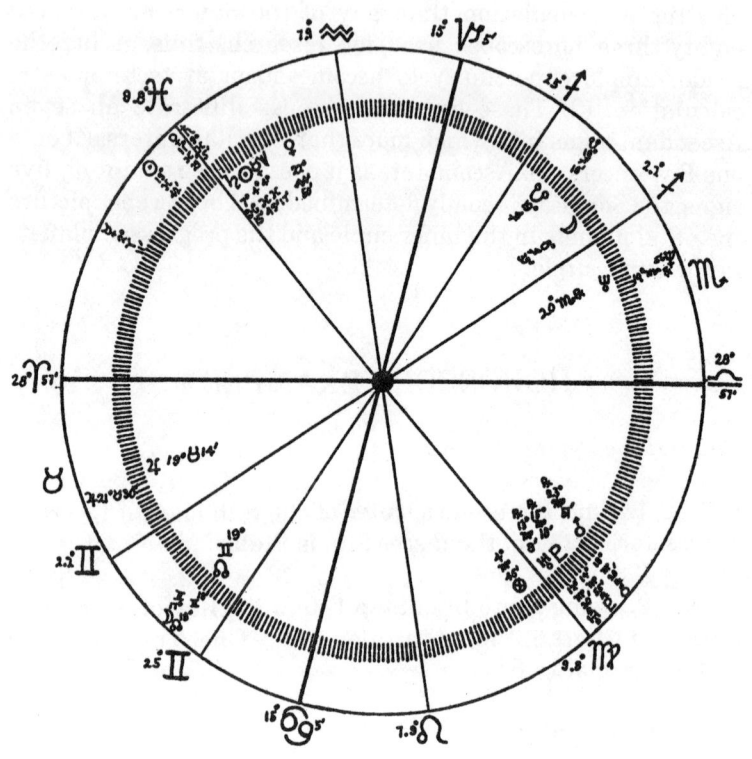

Step 3. Find the esoteric ruler of the Aries Ascendant in Chart 4. In the natal horoscope find the sign the esoteric ruler is in. If it is in a sign which only one of the Rays (found in Step 2) enters, that is the Soul Ray. The esoteric ruler of the Aries Ascendant is Mercury which is in Pisces in the natal horoscope. From Step 2 we see that Pisces is not a sign that Ray One or Seven enters. The Soul Ray is not yet found.

Step 4. Find the hierarchical ruler of the Aries Ascendant in Chart 4. In the natal horoscope find the sign the hierarchical ruler is in. If it is in a sign which only one of the Rays (found in Step 2) enters that is the Soul Ray. The hierarchical ruler of the Aries Ascendant is Uranus which is in Virgo in the natal horoscope. From Step 2 we see that Virgo is not a sign that Ray One or Seven enters. The Soul Ray is not yet found.

Step 5. Find in the natal horoscope all planets in any signs which Rays One or Seven enter. If there are more planets found in signs that Ray One enters than in signs that Ray Seven enters, Ray One is the Soul Ray. If more planets are found in the signs that Ray Seven enters than in the signs that Ray One enters, Ray Seven is the Soul Ray. There are no planets in Aries, Leo, or Capricorn which Ray One enters. There are no planets in Aries, Cancer, or Capricorn which Ray Seven enters. The soul Ray is not yet found.

Step 6. In Chart 4 find the esoteric rulers of all signs except the Ascendant which Rays One and Seven enter. If more of these esoteric rulers are found in signs that Ray One enters than in signs that Ray Seven enters, the Soul Ray is Ray One. If more of these esoteric rulers are found in signs that Ray Seven enters than in signs that Ray One enters, the Soul Ray is Ray Seven. The esoteric ruler of Leo is the Sun which is in Pisces. The esoteric ruler of Capricorn is Saturn which also is in Pisces. The esoteric ruler of Cancer is Neptune which is in Scorpio. Neither Ray One nor Ray Seven enters either of these signs. The Soul Ray is not yet found.

Step 7. Use the hierarchical rulers in Chart 4 in the same manner as the esoteric rulers were used in Step 6. The hierarchical ruler of Leo is the Sun which is in Pisces. The hierarchical ruler of Capricorn is Venus which is in Aquarius. The hierarchical ruler of Cancer is Neptune which is in Scorpio. Neither Ray One nor Ray Seven enters any of these signs. The Soul Ray is not yet found.

Step 8. Find all progressed planets except the Moon and use them in the same manner as the esoteric rulers were used in Step 6. The only progressed planet that is found in any of the signs which Ray One or Ray Seven enters is Mercury which is in Aries. Since both Rays One and Seven enter Aries, we have not yet found the Soul Ray.

Step 9. Using the ephemeris, check to see if one or more progressed planets, excluding the Moon, changes signs from the present age to one hundred years of age. If one or more planets change signs, use them in the same manner as the esoteric rulers were used in Step 6. Of all progressed planets, excluding the Moon, up to age one hundred, we find that only the Sun and Venus changed signs, putting both of them in Aries. Because both Rays One and Seven enter Aries, the Soul Ray is not yet found.

Step 10. Use the North Node of the Moon in the same manner as the esoteric rulers were used in Step 6. The North Node of the Moon is in Gemini which neither Ray One nor Ray Seven enters. The Soul Ray is not yet found.

Step. 11 Use the South Node of the Moon in the same manner as the esoteric rulers were used in Step 6. The South Node of the Moon is in Sagittarius which neither Ray One nor Ray Seven enters. The Soul Ray is not yet found.

Step 12. Use the MC in the same manner as the esoteric rulers were used in Step 6. The MC is in Capricorn which both Rays One and Seven enter. The Soul Ray is not yet found.

Step 13. Use the Descendant in the same manner as the esoteric rulers were used in Step 6. The Descendant is in Libra which neither Ray One nor Ray Seven enters. The Soul Ray is not yet found.

Step 14. Use the IC (Nadir) in the same manner as the esoteric rulers were used in Step 6. The IC is in Cancer which Ray One does not enter but Ray Seven does. Therefore the Soul Ray is Ray Seven.

HOROSCOPE EXAMPLE 2

To Find the Personality Ray

Step 1. Find the esoteric ruler of the Sun sign in Chart 4. The esoteric ruler of the Libra Sun is Uranus.

Step 2. Using Uranus from Step 1, find the Ray it rules in Chart 5. Uranus rules Ray Seven. Thus Ray Seven is the Personality Ray.

To Find the Soul Ray

Step 1. Find which Ray or Rays enter the Ascendant sign, using Chart 6. Rays Three and Seven enter the Cancer Ascendant. Therefore the Soul Ray is either Ray Three or Ray Seven.

Step 2. Using Rays Three and Seven from Step 1, find in Chart 7, the three signs each of them enters. Ray Three enters Cancer, Libra, and Capricorn. Ray Seven enters Cancer, Aries, and Capricorn.

Step 3. Find the esoteric ruler of the Cancer Ascendant in Chart 4. In the natal horoscope find the sign the esoteric ruler is in. If it is in a sign which only one of the Rays (found in Step 2) enters, that is the Soul Ray. The esoteric ruler of the Cancer Ascendant is Neptune which is in Leo. From Step 2 we see that Leo is not a sign that Ray Three or Seven enters. The Soul Ray is not yet found.

Step 4. Find the hierarchical ruler of the Cancer Ascendant in Chart 4. In the natal horoscope, find the sign the hierarchical ruler is in. If it is in a sign which only one of the Rays (found

HOROSCOPE EXAMPLE 2

RAY 7 SOUL, RAY 7 PERSONALITY

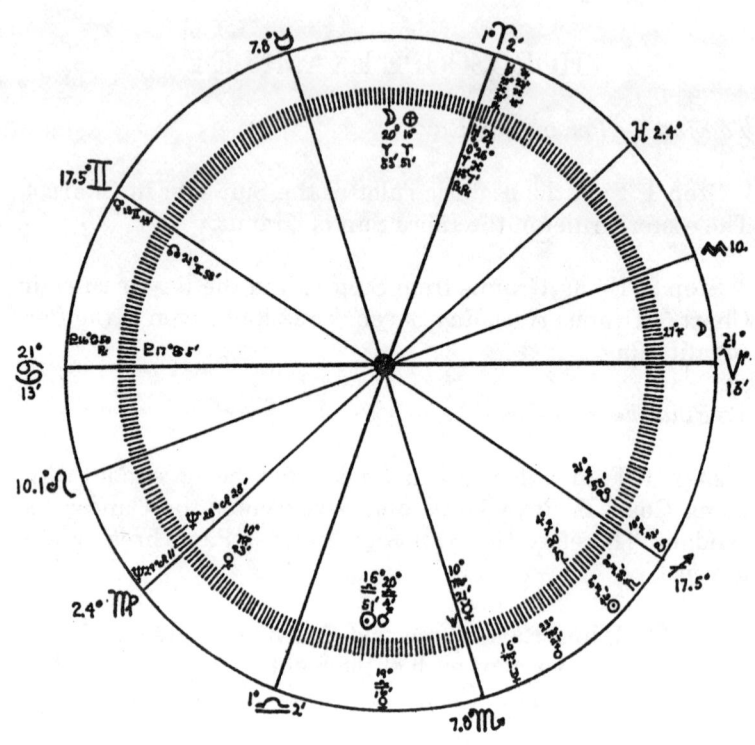

in Step 2) enters, that is the Soul Ray. The hierarchical ruler of the Cancer Ascendant is Neptune which is in Leo in the natal horoscope. From Step 2 we see that Leo is not a sign that Ray Three or Seven enters. The Soul Ray is not yet found. (Since Neptune is both the esoteric and hierarchical ruler of Cancer, this step could be skipped in this example.)

Step 5. Find in the natal horoscope all planets posited in any signs which Rays Three or Seven enter. If more planets are found in signs that Ray Three enters than in signs that Ray Seven enters, Ray Three is the Soul Ray. If more planets are found in the signs that Ray Seven enters than in the signs that Ray Three enters, Ray Seven is the Soul Ray. Ray Three—Pluto in Cancer, Sun and Mars in Libra. Ray Seven—Pluto in Cancer, Moon, Earth, and Uranus in Aries. Since there are three planets in the signs that Ray Three enters, and four planets in the signs that Ray Seven enters, the Soul Ray is Ray Seven.

HOROSCOPE EXAMPLE 3

To Find the Personality Ray

Step 1. Find the esoteric ruler of the Sun sign in Chart 4. The esoteric ruler of the Taurus Sun is Vulcan.

Step 2. Using Vulcan from Step 1, find the Ray of which it is a ruler in Chart 5. Vulcan is a ruler of Ray One. Thus, the Personality Ray is Ray One.

To Find the Soul Ray

Step 1. Find which Ray or Rays enter the Ascendant sign, using Chart 6. Rays One and Five enter the Leo Ascendant sign. The Soul Ray is either Ray One or Ray Five.

Step 2. Using Rays One and Five from Step 1, find in Chart 7, the three signs each of them enters. Ray One enters Leo, Aries, and Capricorn. Ray Five enters Leo, Aquarius, and Sagittarius.

HOROSCOPE EXAMPLE 3

RAY 5 SOUL, RAY 1 PERSONALITY

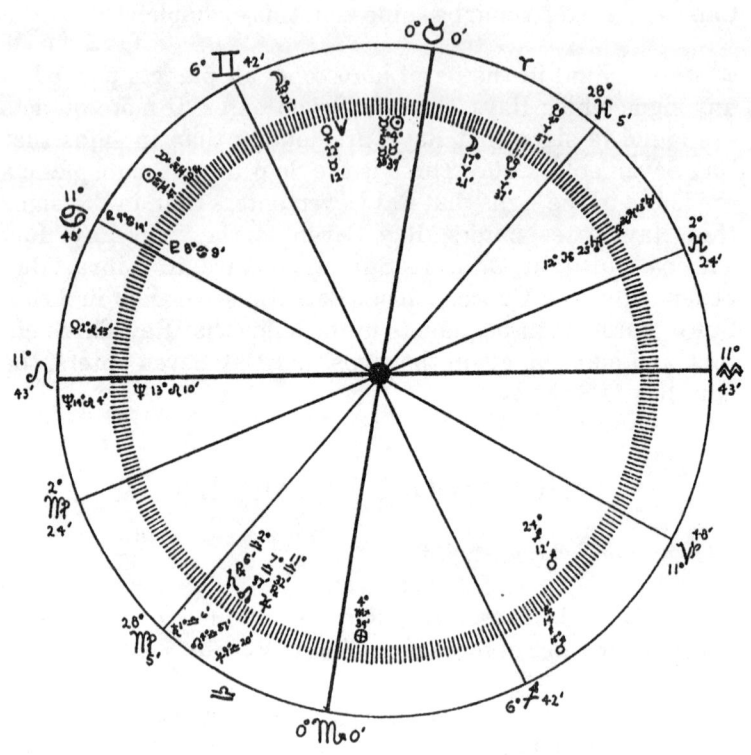

Step 3. Find the esoteric ruler of the Leo Ascendant in Chart 4. In the natal horoscope find the sign the esoteric ruler is in. If it is in a sign which only one of the Rays (found in Step 2) enters, that is the Soul Ray. The esoteric ruler of the Leo Ascendant is the Sun which is in Taurus. From Step 2 we see that Taurus is not a sign that Ray One or Five enters. The Soul Ray is not yet found.

Step 4. Find the hierarchical ruler of the Leo Ascendant in Chart 4. In the natal horoscope find the sign the hierarchical ruler is in. If it is in a sign which only one of the Rays (found in Step 2) enters, that is the Soul Ray. The hierarchical ruler of the Leo Ascendant is the Sun which is in Taurus. From Step 2 we see that Taurus is not a sign that Ray One or Five enters. The Soul Ray is not yet found. (Since the Sun is both the esoteric and hierarchical ruler of Leo, this step could be skipped in this example.)

Step 5. Find in the natal horoscope all planets in any signs which Rays One or Five enters. If more planets are found in signs that Ray One enters than in signs that Ray Five enters, Ray One is the Soul Ray. If more planets are found in signs that Ray Five enters than in signs that Ray One enters, Ray Five is the Soul Ray. Ray One—Neptune in Leo, Moon in Aries, none in Capricorn. Ray Five—Neptune in Leo, Mars in Sagittarius, none in Aquarius. Since there are two planets in the signs that Ray One enters, and also two planets in the signs that Ray Five enters, the Soul Ray is not yet found.

Step 6. Find, in Chart 4, the esoteric rulers of all signs, except the Leo Ascendant, which Rays One and Five enter. If there are more of these esoteric rulers found in signs that Ray One enters than in signs that Ray Five enters, Ray One is the Soul Ray. If more of these esoteric rulers are found in signs that Ray Five enters than in signs that Ray One enters, Ray Five is the Soul Ray. Ray One—The esoteric ruler of Aries is Mercury found in Taurus. The esoteric ruler of Capricorn is Saturn found in Libra. Ray Five—The esoteric ruler of Aquarius is Jupiter found in Libra. The esoteric ruler of Sagittarius is Earth found in Scorpio. None of these esoteric rulers are found in any signs that Ray One or Ray Five enters. Therefore the Soul Ray is not yet found.

Step 7. Use the hierarchical rulers, found in Chart 4, in the same manner as the esoteric rulers were used in Step 6. Ray One—The hierarchical ruler of Aries is Uranus found in Pisces. The hierarchical ruler of Capricorn is Venus found in Taurus. Ray Five—The hierarchical ruler of Aquarius is the Moon found in Aries. The hierarchical ruler of Sagittarius is Mars found in Sagittarius. There is only one planet, the Moon in Aries, found in a sign that Ray One enters and there is only one planet, Mars in Sagittarius, found in a sign that Ray Five enters. Because of this tie; the Soul Ray is not yet found.

Step 8. Find all progressed planets, except the Moon, in the natal horoscope and use them in the same manner as the esoteric rulers were used in Step 6. Ray One—Progressed Neptune in Leo, Progressed Venus in Leo, none in Aries or Capricorn. Ray Five—Progressed Neptune in Leo, Progressed Venus in Leo, Progressed Mars in Sagittarius, none in Aquarius. Since there are only two Progressed planets in signs that Ray One enters, but three in signs Ray Five enters, Ray Five is the Soul Ray.

HOROSCOPE EXAMPLE 4

To find the Personality Ray

Step 1. Find the esoteric ruler of the Sun sign in Chart 4. The esoteric ruler of the Sagittarius Sun is Earth.

Step 2. Using Earth from Step 1, find the Ray of which it is a ruler in Chart 5. Earth is a ruler of Ray Three. Thus, the Personality Ray is Ray Three.

To Find the Soul Ray

Step 1. Find which Ray or Rays enter the Ascendant sign, using Chart 6. Rays Two and Six enter the Virgo Ascendant sign. The Soul Ray is either Ray Two or Ray Six.

HOROSCOPE EXAMPLE 4

RAY 2 SOUL, RAY 3 PERSONALITY

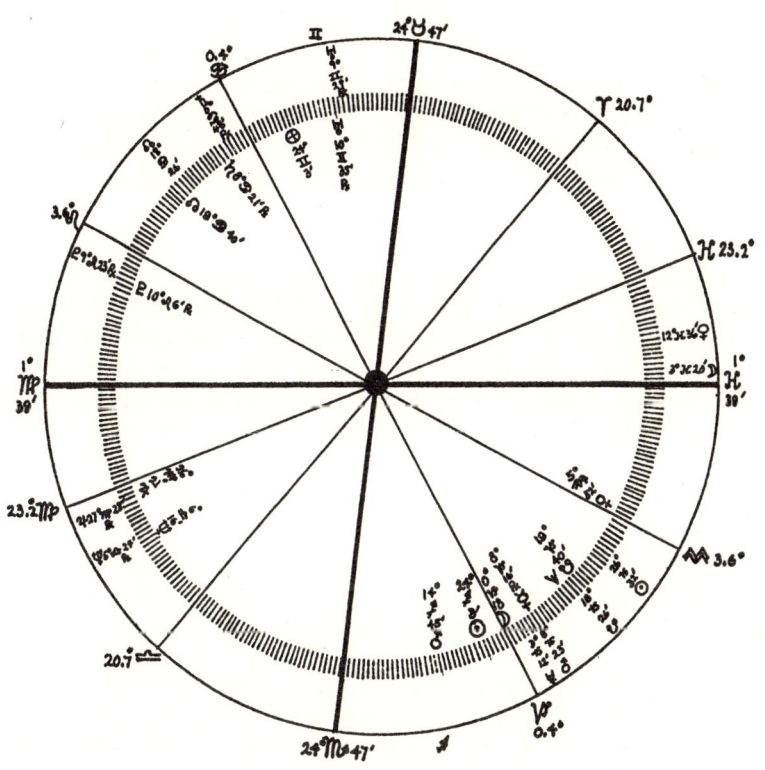

Step 2. Using Rays Two and Six from Step 1, find in Chart 7, the three signs each of them enters. Ray Two enters Virgo, Pisces, and Gemini. Ray Six enters Virgo, Pisces, and Sagittarius.

Step 3. Find the esoteric ruler of the Virgo Ascendant in Chart 4. In the natal horoscope, find the sign the esoteric ruler is in. If it is in a sign which only one of the Rays (found in Step 2) enters, that is the Soul Ray. The esoteric ruler of the Virgo Ascendant is the Moon which is in Capricorn in the natal horoscope. From Step 2 we see that Capricorn is not a sign that Ray Two or Six enters. The Soul Ray is not yet found.

Step 4. In Chart 4 find the hierarchical ruler of the Virgo Ascendant sign. In the natal horoscope, find the sign the hierarchical ruler is in. If it is in a sign which only one of the Rays (found in Step 2) enters, that is the Soul Ray. The hierarchical ruler of the Virgo Ascendant sign is Jupiter which is in Virgo in the natal horoscope. From Step 2 we see that both Rays Two and Six enter Virgo. The Soul Ray is not yet found.

Step 5. Find in the natal horoscope all planets found in any signs which Rays Two or Six enters. If more planets are found in signs that Ray Two enters than in signs that Ray Six enters, Ray Two is the Soul Ray. If more planets are found in signs that Ray Six enters than in signs that Ray Two enters, Ray Six is the Soul Ray. Ray Two—Jupiter in Virgo, Uranus and Earth in Gemini, none in Pisces. Ray Six—Jupiter in Virgo, Sun and Mars in Sagittarius, none in Pisces. Since there are three planets in the signs Ray Two enters and also the same number of planets in the signs that Ray Six enters, the Soul Ray is not yet found.

Step 6. Find in Chart 4 the esoteric rulers of all signs except the Virgo Ascendant which Rays Two and Six enter. If more of these esoteric rulers are found in signs that Ray Two enters than in signs that Ray Six enters, Ray Two is the Soul Ray. If more of these esoteric rulers are found in signs that Ray Six enters than in signs that Ray Two enters, Ray Six is the Soul Ray. Ray Two—The esoteric ruler of Pisces is Pluto found in Leo. The esoteric ruler of Gemini is Venus found in Aquarius.

Ray Six—The esoteric ruler of Pisces is Pluto found in Leo. The esoteric ruler of Sagittarius is Earth found in Gemini. None of these esoteric rulers is found in signs that Ray Six enters. One of these esoteric rulers, Earth, is found in a sign that Ray Two enters. Therefore the Soul Ray is Ray Two.

HOROSCOPE EXAMPLE 5

To Find the Personality Ray

Step 1. Find the esoteric ruler of the Sun sign in Chart 4. The esoteric ruler of the Capricorn Sun is Saturn.

Step 2. Using Saturn from Step 1, find the Ray of which it is a ruler in Chart 5. Saturn is a ruler of Ray Three. Thus the Personality Ray is Ray Three.

To Find the Soul Ray

Step 1. Find which Ray or Rays enter the Sagittarius Ascendant sign, using Chart 6. Rays Four, Five, and Six enter the Sagittarius Ascendant sign. The Soul Ray is Ray Four, Ray Five, or Ray Six.

Step 2. Using Rays Four, Five, and Six from Step 1, find in Chart 7 the three signs each of them enters. Ray Four enters Sagittarius, Taurus, and Scorpio. Ray Five enters Sagittarius, Leo, and Aquarius. Ray Six enters Sagittarius, Pisces, and Virgo.

Step 3. Find the esoteric ruler of the Sagittarius Ascendant in Chart 4. In the natal horoscope, find the sign the esoteric ruler is in. If it is in a sign which only one of the Rays (found in Step 2) enters, that is the Soul Ray. If it is in a sign that two of the three Rays enter, the Soul Ray is one of those two Rays. The esoteric ruler of the Sagittarius Ascendant is Earth which is in Cancer in the natal horoscope. From Step 2 we see that Cancer is not a sign that Ray Four, Ray Five, or Ray Six enters. The Soul Ray is not yet found.

HOROSCOPE EXAMPLE 5

RAY 4 SOUL, RAY 3 PERSONALITY

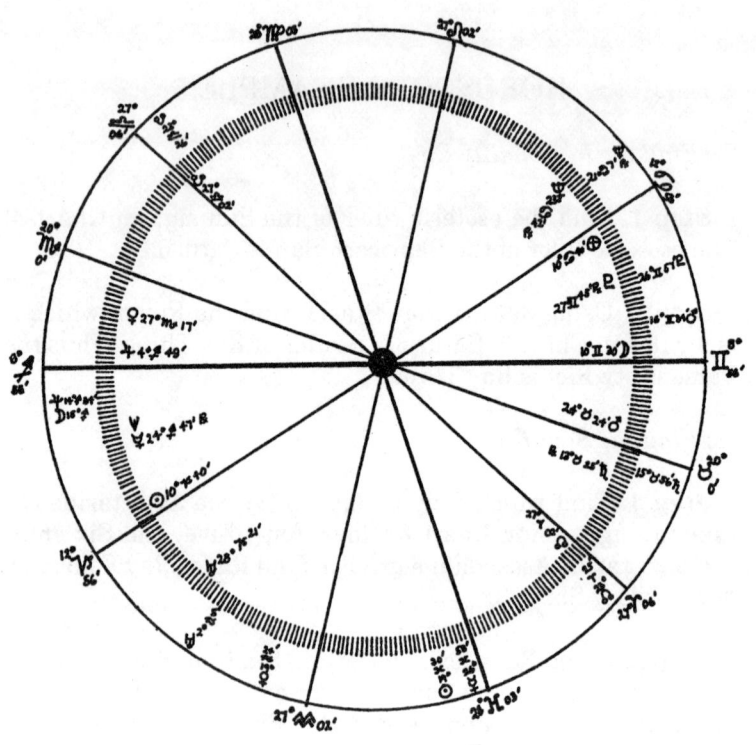

Step 4. Find the hierarchical ruler of the Sagittarius Ascendant in Chart 4. In the natal horoscope, find the sign the hierarchical ruler is in. If it is in a sign which only one of the Rays (found in Step 2) enters, that is the Soul Ray. If it is a sign that two of the three Rays enter, the Soul Ray is one of those two Rays. The hierarchical ruler of the Sagittarius Ascendant is Mars which is in Taurus. Only one of the Rays listed in Step 2, namely Ray 4, enters Taurus. Thus, the Soul Ray is Ray Four.

HOROSCOPE EXAMPLE 6

To Find the Personality Ray

Step 1. Find the esoteric ruler of the Sun sign in Chart 4. The esoteric ruler of the Virgo Sun is the Moon.

Step 2. Using the Moon from Step 1, find the Ray of which it is a ruler in Chart 5. The Moon is a ruler of Ray Four. Thus, the Personality Ray is Ray Four.

To Find the Soul Ray

Step 1. Find which Ray or Rays enter the Capricorn Ascendant sign, using Chart 6. Rays One, Three, and Seven enter the Capricorn Ascendant sign. The Soul Ray is Ray One, Ray Three, or Ray Seven.

Step 2. Using Rays One, Three, and Seven from Step 1, find in Chart 7 the three signs each of them enters. Ray One enters Leo, Aries, and Capricorn. Ray Three enters Libra, Cancer, and Capricorn. Ray Seven enters Aries, Cancer, and Capricorn.

Step 3. Find the esoteric ruler of the Capricorn Ascendant in Chart 4. In the natal horoscope, find the sign the esoteric ruler is in. If it is in a sign which only one of the Rays (found in Step 2) enters, that is the Soul Ray. If it is in a sign that two of the three Rays enter, the Soul Ray is one of those two Rays. The esoteric ruler of the Capricorn Ascendant is Saturn which is in Aries in the natal horoscope. From Step 2 we see that Aries is not a sign that Ray Three enters, but it is a sign

HOROSCOPE EXAMPLE 6

RAY 1 SOUL, RAY 4 PERSONALITY

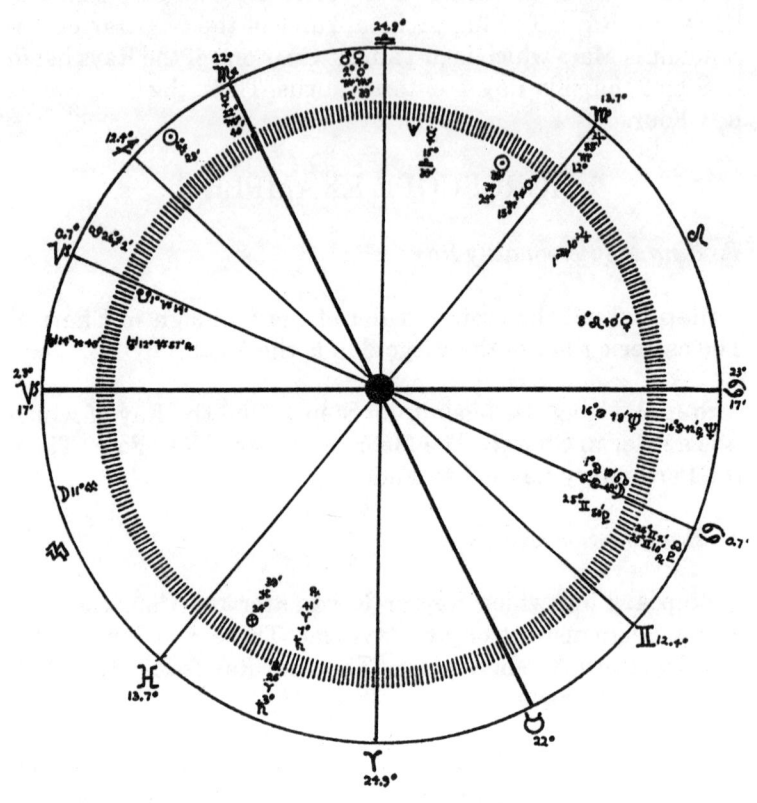

that both Ray One and Ray Seven enter. Therefore the Soul Ray is Ray One or Ray Seven.

Step 4. In Chart 4 find the hierarchical ruler of the Capricorn Ascendant sign. In the natal horoscope, find the sign the hierarchical ruler is in. If it is in a sign which only one of the Rays (found in Step 3) enters, that is the Soul Ray. The hierarchical ruler of the Capricorn Ascendant sign is Venus which is in Leo in the natal chart. Ray Seven does not enter Leo but Ray One does. The Soul Ray is Ray One.

HOROSCOPE EXAMPLE 7

To Find the Personality Ray

Step 1. Find the esoteric ruler of the Sun sign in Chart 4. The esoteric ruler of the Aries Sun is Mercury.

Step 2. Using Mercury from Step 1, find the Ray of which it is a ruler in Chart 5. Mercury is a ruler of Ray Four. Thus, the Personality Ray is Ray Four.

To Find the Soul Ray

Step 1. Find which Ray or Rays enter the Pisces Ascendant sign, using Chart 6. Rays Two and Six enter the Pisces Ascendant sign. The Soul Ray is Ray Two or Ray Six.

Step 2. Using Rays Two and Six from Step 1, find, in Chart 7, the three signs each of them enters. Ray Two enters Pisces, Virgo, and Gemini. Ray Six enters Pisces, Virgo, and Sagittarius.

Step 3. Find the esoteric ruler of the Pisces Ascendant in Chart 4. In the natal horoscope find the sign the esoteric ruler is in. If it is in a sign which only one of the Rays (found in Step 2) enters, that is the Soul Ray. The esoteric ruler of the Pisces Ascendant is Pluto which is in Leo in the natal horoscope. From Step 2 we see that Leo is not a sign that Ray Two or Ray Six enters. The Soul Ray is not yet found.

HOROSCOPE EXAMPLE 7

RAY 2 SOUL, RAY 4 PERSONALITY

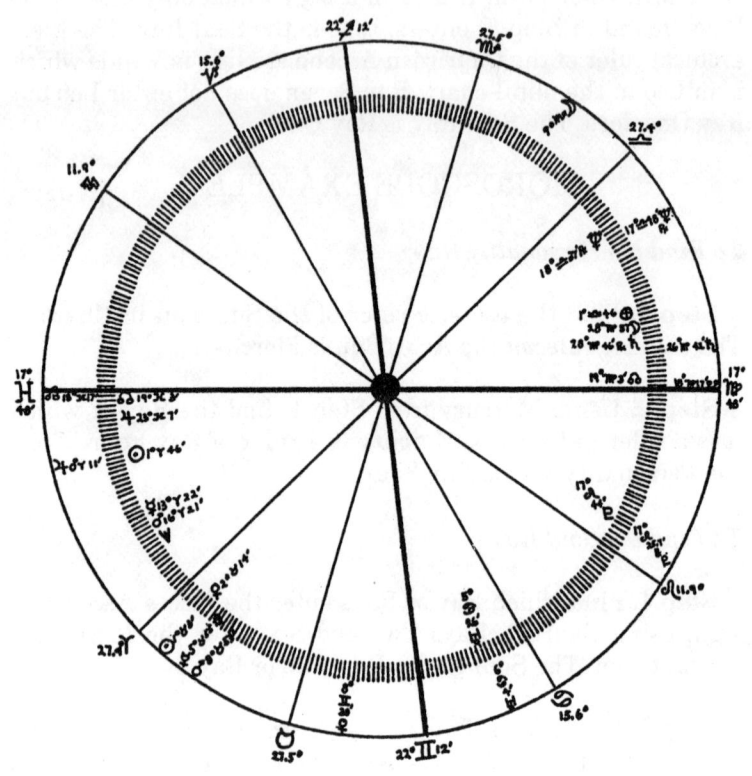

Step 4. In Chart 4 find the hierarchical ruler of the Pisces Ascendant sign. In the natal horoscope find the sign the hierarchical ruler is in. If it is in a sign which only one of the Rays found in Step 2 enters, that is the Soul Ray. The hierarchical ruler of the Pisces Ascendant sign is also Pluto which is in Leo. Since Leo is not a sign that Ray Two or Ray Six enters, the Soul Ray is not yet found.

Step 5. Find in the natal horoscope all planets found in any signs which Ray Two or Six enter. If more planets are found in signs that Ray Two enters than in signs that Ray Six enters, Ray Two is the Soul Ray. If more planets are found in signs that Ray Six enters than in signs that Ray Two enters, Ray Six is the Soul Ray. Ray Two—Jupiter in Pisces, Saturn and Moon in Virgo, none in Gemini. Ray Six—Jupiter in Pisces, Saturn and Moon in Virgo, none in Sagittarius. Since there are three planets in signs that Ray Two enters, and the same number of planets in the signs that Ray Six enters, the Soul Ray is not yet found.

Step 6. Find in Chart 4 the esoteric rulers of all signs, except the Pisces Ascendant, which Ray Two and Six enter. If more of these esoteric rulers are found in signs that Ray Two enters than in signs that Ray Six enters, Ray Two is the Soul Ray. If more of these esoteric rulers are found in signs that Ray Six enters than in signs that Ray Two enters, Ray Six is the Soul Ray. Ray Two—The esoteric ruler of Virgo is the Moon found in Virgo. The esoteric ruler of Gemini is Venus found in Taurus. Ray Six—the esoteric ruler of Virgo is the Moon found in Virgo. The esoteric ruler of Sagittarius is the Earth found in Libra. Only one of these esoteric rulers is found in signs that Ray Two or Ray Six enters, and that is the Moon in Virgo which is a sign that both Ray Two and Six enter. Therefore, the Soul Ray is not yet found.

Step 7. Use the hierarchical rulers found in Chart 4 in the same manner as the esoteric rulers were used in Step 6. Ray Two—The hierarchical ruler of Virgo is Jupiter found in Pisces. The hierarchical ruler of Gemini is the Earth found in Libra. Ray Six—The hierarchical ruler of Virgo is Jupiter found in

Pisces. The hierarchical ruler of Sagittarius is Mars found in Aries. Only one of these hierarchical rulers is found in signs that Ray Two or Six enters and that is Jupiter in Pisces which is a sign that both Rays Two and Six enter. Therefore, the Soul Ray is not yet found.

Step 8. Find all progressed planets except the Moon in the natal horoscope and use them in the same manner as the esoteric rulers were used in Step 6. Ray Two—None in Pisces, Saturn in Virgo, Venus in Gemini. Ray Six—None in Pisces, Saturn in Virgo, none in Sagittarius. Since there is only one progressed planet in signs that Ray Six enters, but two planets in signs that Ray Two enters, the Soul Ray is Ray Two.

The next chapter gives an in-depth interpretation of each of the Seven Rays. A thorough study of the Soul Ray which is the determining factor for one's purpose in this life, together with a thorough study of one's Personality Ray as a vehicle of expression of the Soul's purpose, is essential. This dual Ray study will enable the reader to develop an understanding of the characteristics, influences, and functions which, through a proper use, will lead to Soul evolvement by transmuting one's weaknesses into strengths and by the self-realization of the Soul's purpose (life plan).

In studying your Rays to determine your life's purpose, you must first clarify your motivation, which is the determining factor in success or failure. To assure success, your motivation must be unselfish service to others because of your love and concern for them. As a result, you will attract entities and conditions of a vibration similar to your own, both from the earth plane and the higher planes, giving help and protection so that part of God's Plan for earth can be realized through you. You must also become aware of your weaknesses and make a concerted effort to transmute them into strengths.

Chapter Three

INTERPRETING THE RAYS

RAY ONE—WILL AND POWER

Enters Aries, Leo, and Capricorn
Rulers—Vulcan and Pluto
Color—white

Ray One Souls and Personalities are strong-willed and have great power at their command. There is an independence and a one-pointedness in their thoughts, words, and actions. These persons can make strong impressions on the minds of others. They are consciously aware of the power within themselves and usually manifest it through their strong wills. They dramatically grasp what they want through the power of their wills.

The all-important question is what do they want? If they force their strong wills or ideas on others in a dominating or dictatorial way, this leads to personal ambitions of power, honor, fame, or wealth. Pride in attainment, then cruelty, impatience, and anger toward those who get in their way usually follow. They have the ability to harm others drastically. But by the same token, others then display power that is antagonistic and drastically harm *them*. Through this suffering they usually come in contact with their Souls. Their wants then change from self-centered desires to spiritual aspirations of helping others. They then try to rebuild what they have destroyed, and often find that they have rebuilt to an even higher level.

They are now beginning to acquire love and wisdom, the outpourings of Ray Two energy of the Sun. It must be remembered that these Seven Rays are but sub-Rays of Ray Two energy of the Sun, and unless they contact their Soul, they do not receive the love and wisdom that Ray Two energy disperses. Until love and the wise use of knowledge have found a natural place in their dealings with others, life will be difficult as a result of their intense thoughts, penetrating words, and controlling actions.

The colors correlating with Ray One are white and red. It is true that if you have about you clothes or surroundings that correlate with your Soul and Personality Ray colors, this helps you become attuned advantageously to your Ray energies. I would make only one exception among all Ray colors—red. Red is a powerful color but it is too forceful for humanity at this stage of its evolution. Unless your total thoughts, words, and actions are for the good of others, red clothes, linens, and furnishings will only increase your tendency toward aggression, irritability, and argumentativeness. This does not negate the advisability of using red for stop lights or any mechanical or computerized instruments as a warning or a precaution to change thoughts and behavior. The forceful impact of the sudden appearance of a red light is needed in certain circumstances.

Because an extremely high percentage of humanity is in the adolescent stage of Soul evolvement, white should be used for Ray One Souls and Personalities. Since white is a combination of all colors, it helps a Ray One Soul or Personality to raise his consciousness along the lines of all other Rays so that he can use his powerful Ray One energy with more intelligence, love, wisdom, harmony, and rhythm—the characteristics of the remaining Rays. The reason Ray One is in attunement with white, which is inclusive of all colors and hence all other six Rays, is because Ray One is the most divine of all Rays. The more divine a Ray, a star, a planet, or a person is, the more it includes other Rays, other stars, other planets, or other persons in its essence.

The zodiacal signs through which Ray One energy enters the earth are Aries, Leo, and Capricorn, all of which are more powerful than any of the remaining signs. Of these three, the most powerful is Aries, which is the controlling sign. It gives divine ideas, capacity for cooperation with God's Plan for earth, and pioneering leadership ability. It is the source of new beginnings at the present dawning of the Aquarian Age. Leo is the sign of personality integration in which the physical body, mental body, and emotional body are dedicated to a single purpose, leading to self-realization. It is the sign of a leader and a ruler, not so much a pioneer, but a leader who builds on the pioneering which preceded him. Capricorn is the sign of the organizing and working out of God's Plan in a very practical and down-to-earth way. It is the sign that gives persistence in self-discipline, resulting in enhanced spiritual evolvement.

The rulers of Ray One are Vulcan and Pluto. Just as Ray One is the most powerful of all Seven Ray energies, and the three signs it enters are the most powerful of all signs, so are its rulers, Vulcan, and Pluto, the most powerful of all the planets. For this reason, these two planets, as well as Ray One energy, can create havoc if not used with love and wisdom.

Pluto gives the power to destroy self-centered personality desires in order to achieve liberation. Because each planet seems to have been discovered at a time humanity was ready to benefit from what the planet offers, and since Pluto is the most recently discovered planet (1930), we know that humanity is beginning to attain a certain degree of love and wisdom. Pluto also gives the power to destroy the physcial body if it no longer will be used for Soul evolvement. Contrary to widespread belief, physical death is a blessing when the physical body can no longer serve the Soul's purpose.

The entity controlling Vulcan is more highly evolved than the entity controlling Pluto. Vulcan gives the power to crystallize and then bring weaknesses up from the depths of one's being and expose them to the light, deal with them, and release them. Even though Vulcan at the present time is hidden, its presence is being sensed. Therefore, we are beginning to benefit from the specific energy Vulcan sends us.

Humanity is slowly changing from selfish desires to spiritual aspirations. God's Plan of revealing Pluto to us and enabling us to sense Vulcan at this time is synchronized with our evolutionary development. Nothing occurs haphazardly in the Universe. Even though there are many things we do not yet understand at our stage of evolvement, metaphysicians are convinced that the minds of those highly evolved entities who control the heavens, do so for the good of All. "Isolated Unity" is the key phrase of the first Ray; this quality gives the possessor the ability to see all of the Universe (minerals, plants, animals, humanity, planets, and stars) as One and to realize that he is part of that Whole.

The divine principle of Ray One is Spirit; the sense it correlates with is touch; the element is Akasha which is the storehouse of Universal Mind; the stone is the diamond; the symbol most commonly used is the Eye of Shiva, the All-Seeing Eye, the Universal Eye which directs the will of God; the most ancient symbol is the Angel with the Flaming Sword who lovingly turns away those seeking admittance to the higher planes who are undeserving, thus protecting them from dangers they would encounter because of the big differences in their vibrations and those of the higher planes. Ray One has affinity with the Great Bear Constellation (Ursa Major); it also has affinity with Shambala which is composed of those extremely highly evolved entities in the spirit world who form God's Plan.

The chakra, the psychic center that corresponds to Ray One energy, is the head center, the thousand-petalled lotus, which energizes the pineal gland for those in contact with their Souls. For the undeveloped person, the base of the spine is the chakra that corresponds to Ray One energy. Unless one is a very advanced Soul, I would suggest that he pay no attention to the chakra or chakras correlating with his Rays. Because energy follows thought, centering one's mind on the individual psychic centers could easily be instrumental in opening them prematurely, causing nervousness and even more serious harmful consequences. These centers should be allowed to open naturally, like the flowers in the field. Then, when one has evolved spiritually enough so that the extra power will be used in the right way, they will open of their own accord. The safest chakra on which to center one's thoughts is the heart chakra, yet even here if one does not feel love toward others, there may be overstimulation which causes irresponsibility.

Sheer force of will is the method of following the Spiritual Path for this Ray. The Master of Ray One is Morya.

First Ray Souls are always leaders in something—either leaders with cold, hard, cruel natures with selfish purposes, or leaders who with courage and fearlessness put an end to oppressions. Those who use their energy wisely can be successful leaders in government, religion, or education. They can destroy outworn concepts and ideas which act as stumbling blocks to humanity's evolvement, and they are capable of substituting the presently needed concepts and ideas that are attuned to the New Age.

A Ray One leader in government work who is in contact with his Soul has the power to implement ideas of universality rather than nationalism, and cooperation rather than isolation, working toward the ultimate good of all nations rather than the selfish interests of his own nation. Once he understands the Law of Karma, he becomes aware that it works for nations just as it does for individuals; to fill the true needs of other nations means karmic rewards for his nation. His conscience urges him toward the good of all his constituents rather than certain partisan groups. Special interests in the United States have for years been highly organized, heavily financed, and operate with expertly trained staffs on both the national and state level. These groups, because of their power and self-centered interests, are influential in passing laws which favor their particular groups to the detriment of the people at large. The Ray One Soul or Personality in government work has a great challenge and the capacity to change laws which cater to special interest groups to laws for the common good.

If a Ray One Soul or Personality chooses to use his power and abilities in the religious field, there is much he can accomplish at this stage of evolutionary development. He can be instrumental in getting rid of outworn religious concepts which are now hindrances to Soul evolvement. Even though a baby is making progress in his physical development when he begins to creep, when he learns to walk it is best that he cease to creep. By the same token, certain religious concepts brought progress in the past to the spiritual evolution of humanity, but it is best that they no longer be used. All lasting progress is achieved in steps, and as we climb to the next higher step, we leave the lower one behind.

We are in the dawning of a New Age in which we must release those concepts that were helpful in the past Age, but which act as obstacles in the present. The past Piscean Age was a period of 2,160 years in which the great majority of the human race, with little or no education, looked to spiritual leaders for guidance. Just as a parent insists, according to his standards, that his children not do wrong, these spiritual leaders also wished to deter their followers from wrongdoing, and used fear-producing concepts to accomplish their purposes.

There are many religious concepts of the Piscean Age that must be destroyed and replaced with Aquarian Age concepts.

54

One is the fear-inducing fire and brimstone concept of ever-lasting damnation for sinning which must be replaced with the loving New Age concept that there is a spark of the divine within each of us, and that it is our heritage to become wholly One with God.

Another ingrained religious concept of the Piscean Age which must be lovingly and wisely destroyed, as must all out-worn concepts, is that one must belong to a certain religious sect or at least believe in God in order to be saved. This Old Age concept must be replaced by the idea that there are many roads to God and that neither belief or nonbelief in a diety is necessary to spiritual evolvement, but what *is* necessary is to become a more understanding and loving person. There must be respect for the spiritual beliefs or nonbeliefs of others. Jesus said when speaking to the Christians, "Other sheep have I which are not of this fold."

In the field of education, Ray One Souls and Personalities have the capacity to destroy outworn educational concepts and substitute new ones of the Aquarian Age. One example is to abolish the idea that if children do not fit what is considered the "normal class teaching procedure," they should be relegated to "retarded classes," thus branding them with a stigma that is difficult to remove. This should be replaced by the new con-cept of understanding, not only the problem child's, but every child's abilities, Soul purpose, character weaknesses, and strengths—through Ray-Centered Astrology. This should be followed by the necessary teaching and guidance to help the child change his weaknesses into strengths and attain self-realization of his dharma (destined life work).

Another educational concept that should be destroyed and replaced by one of a higher level is the concept that rote learn-ing and memorization are the all-important criteria for success. In its place, in tune with the New Age, is the concept that all knowledge is found within the self through the development of reasoning, contemplation, and meditative capacities and that books and the teacher's words are but the necessary priming to bring the innate knowledge to the surface.

Ray One energy manifests through sleeping and breathing. The following is a helpful exercise for all Ray One Souls and Personalities:*

* Bailey, Alice A., *Discipleship in the New Age,* Volume I, p. 246.

1. As you inhale deeply, say to yourself mentally, "with self-forgetfulness I gather what I need for the helping of my fellow-men."
2. Holding your breath, "ponder on the strength, wisdom, and love that must be shown to others."
3. Exhaling say, "with self-forgetfulness I breathe out love upon all others."
4. "Then ponder upon love to all beings."

Then repeat the process, this time carrying on entirely in the heart instead of the mind.

It is not easy for a Ray One Soul or Personality to begin work on his life plan. Because of the power inherent in his nature, his life is very difficult until he develops understanding and love toward others. A working knowledge of such Universal Truths as Reincarnation and Karma, and the resultant concept that each person creates his own environments are extremely valuable. This concept can help him to allow others the freedom he finds so desirable. When he begins to truly understand others' needs, love follows naturally. When understanding and love have become a part of his nature, he can identify with the Souls of all beings, feel at one with them, become aware of God's Plan on earth, and help to carry it out.

There is a tendency for Ray One Souls and Personalities to be too dynamic, thus driving away those they could help. First Ray energy *should* force issues and determine results, but unless this is done with understanding and love, it usually does more harm than good. Because of the force and power given to Ray One Souls and Personalities, understanding and love are often lacking in their makeup. These two character strengths are the most important for them to develop so that the intense power at their command will raise the vibrations of others rather than lower them.

Ray One energy may lead to a desire for separateness and isolation, but this desire can be transmuted into an unattached love for all without isolation from them.

Because Ray One energy is will and power, it has the capacity to destroy. When used wisely, it destroys all that brings suffering to man through his thinking. Ray One Souls and Personalities can destroy concepts and ideas that are no longer needed and which hold us back in government, religion, and education. It can then substitute the new concepts and ideas in rapport with the Aquarian Age.

At the present stage of evolution, Ray One energy brings about the death of the physical body when it can no longer help the Soul to progress in a particular lifetime. This is a blessing in that physical death not only eliminates additional suffering, but enables the Soul to work in the spiritual plane, allowing the Soul to reincarnate in a future new body when the time and conditions are right. When we become more spiritually evolved, Ray One energy will give us the power to leave our physical bodies without pain and suffering. We must remember that all Seven Rays are sub-Rays of everyone's Soul or Personality Ray. There are on earth today a few extremely advanced Souls who have the ability to leave their physical bodies without pain or illness once they have accomplished their purposes. They have overcome illness, suffering, and so-called "death" by overcoming their weaknesses and by service to others. There will come a time and a life for every one of us when we, too, will have overcome "death" as we now know it.

Since Ray One Souls and Personalities may have as part of their lifes' work the abolishing of destructive thought forms, the use of sandalwood incense which hastens this process is suggested. When a person is dying, sandalwood incense provides the Soul with more peaceful surroundings, and orange lights will give it more energy to make the transition.

The Ray One Personality can cause the Soul much difficulty when it is not subordinated in humility to the Soul Ray and its purpose. By cultivating loving kindness, and learning to stay in the background rather than in the center, these people can be a hidden force for encouraging others to work toward their Souls' purposes. It is important that a Ray One Personality not take over others' responsibilities, but with detached love and divine indifference to people's weaknesses, show them their inherent strengths.

With love and wisdom, these Ray One Souls and Personalities are capable of sacrifice and dedication to great causes through persistence, truthfulness, courage, enthusiasm, and leadership. Their Ray One energy can then be used to destroy feelings of isolation, superiority, hatred, religious and racial antagonisms among individuals and nations, and create in their place feelings of universal love and global consciousness in which there can be mutual understanding and helpfulness.

If they draw on the love and wisdom that Ray Two showers on all, Ray One Souls and Personalities are capable of bringing about great changes through their ability to see things as a whole and to identify with the Oneness, their integrity and capacity to take a stand on principle, their ability to recognize and destroy that which is no longer useful and develop valid replacements, their leadership characteristics which are dedicated to the good of all, their willingness to help others achieve independence and freedom, and their capacity for unattached love.

Following is a list of character traits which have been divided into two columns. On the left are the traits manifested when one has used Ray One energy unwisely. On the right are the traits manifested when one uses Ray One energy wisely. Deep concern for others helps us use this energy wisely, resulting in better health, better relationships, and joy and success in our work. Strong, self-centered desires indicate unwise use of this energy, resulting in many kinds of problems in career, relationships, and health.

Because awareness of our weaknesses and strengths which comes about through facing the self in all honesty is the first step to Soul evolvement, this list can be useful, not only in helping us identify our weaknesses and strengths, but in aiding us to know into which particular strengths our weaknesses can be transmuted.

Self-discipline in overcoming weaknesses is necessary, but the energy that was used in the manifestation of a specific weakness can create havoc if it is repressed. To be of benefit it must be used in other ways. This list provides the substitute strengths to be cultivated for the listed weaknesses; in the cultivation of the chosen strengths, the energy formerly manifested as a weakness is used to develop the strengths. Because energy follows thought, visualizing the strengths one wishes to develop makes the self-discipline that must follow easier.

A Ray One Soul will find this list of traits directed toward his Life Plan of service to others, while a Ray One Personality will find it of great help in carrying out his Soul Ray's Life Plan, whatever his Soul Ray may be.

CHART 8

UNWISE AND WISE USE
OF RAY ONE ENERGY

WEAKNESSES

1. Pride and arrogance
2. Failure to love resulting from feelings of isolation, separateness, and uncooperativeness
3. The self-centered desire for power and authority
4. Domination of others
5. Destructiveness
6. Stubbornness
7. Anger and cruelty
8. Self-pity
9. Impatience
10. Misuse of achievements

STRENGTHS

1. The strength to be humbly aware of God, and the awareness that one who is truly humble is greatly strong
2. The awareness of the Oneness of All in which each entity is vital for the evolvement of all others, leading to unattached love
3. Development of unselfish leadership in order to realize that contribution should be to the Whole through formulation, initiation, and synthesis of programs
4. Willingness to share independence with others, respecting their need for the freedom one defends
5. Ability to recognize and destroy that which is no longer useful, and to develop valid replacements
6. Integrity and capacity to take a stand on principle
7. Capacity for unattached love because of awareness of the Law of Karma which attracts those who have the same weaknesses, and the understanding of the lessons to be learned from karmic difficulties
8. Awareness that each person creates his own environment by thoughts, words, and actions, enabling him to assume responsibility for what happens to him through proper attitudes
9. Enthusiasm and action-orientation
10. Consideration and concern for others when striving and attaining
11. Dynamic single-pointedness with persistence and endurance while at the same time being able to identify with the rhythm of the universe so that one's attainment can be for the good of All.

RAY TWO—LOVE AND WISDOM

Enters Gemini, Virgo, and Pisces
Rulers—Jupiter and Sun
Color—blue

Ray Two is the Ray of love and wisdom. Its energy can instill in the mind and heart an awareness of the wise use of knowledge with love. Putting this awareness to use is wisdom. The Christ Consciousness, which is synonomous with Ray Two energy, is the urge in the Soul to develop an understanding nature so that each of use can feel impersonal love toward All.

Stars have Soul Rays just as do individuals, and because our Sun, a star which is the center of this solar system, has a Ray Two Soul, it sends this energy to all of us. No matter which Rays each of us possess, they are but sub-Rays of the Ray Two of our Sun.

At this stage of our evolution, Ray Two is the most important Ray for Soul evolvement. We are better able now, in the Aquarian Age, than in any period of time, to develop an understanding of spirituality; thus the concepts of Reincarnation and Karma are being accepted by ever-increasing numbers of searching Souls.

Because this Ray is our primary one, prompting us to contact our Soul and to develop the love and wisdom that is inherent in Ray Two, those who have it as their Soul or Personality Rays are fortunate in that they find it much easier to contact their Souls. After attaining wisdom and the capacity for unattached love through study and meditation, they are able to help others who are also searching.

When Ray Two Souls and Personalities use this energy correctly, they do not go out looking for people to serve. Those who are in need are drawn to them by their magnetism, the love they feel for humanity, and the wise use of the metaphysical knowledge they have acquired.

Light blue, the color of the sky, is attuned to Ray Two energy and is its specific color. Light blue is often associated with peace and the Christ Consciousness. Ray-Centered Astrology corroborates the rightness of that association. Looking up into the blue sky often brings thoughts of the gentleness, the magnetism, the love, and the wisdom of Jesus, who was the Christ. The pastel blue color, when entering our aura, helps us become more loving and understanding.

Because Ray Two, being the Soul Ray of the Sun, is the primary Ray of all humanity, it would be wise for us to use its color in clothes, furnishings, and linens. It is wiser still for Ray Two Souls or Personalities to use pastel blue frequently because the vibration of this color not only helps them to contact their Souls, but is instrumental in helping them to successfully serve others.

The zodiacal signs that Ray Two energy enters are Gemini, Virgo, and Pisces. Gemini is the controlling sign. The love inherent in Ray Two is coupled with the fluidity of Gemini, giving this sign the power to bring opposites together to work as a unit. Gemini is capable of combining the energies of all opposite signs in a loving, working fashion. It does this by forming triangles of energy with five sets of opposing signs. The sixth set of opposing signs, which is itself and Sagittarius, forms a triangle of energy with Pisces because it is the Piscean need to help the suffering that enables the love of Ray Two and the concrete fluid mind of Gemini to combine with the abstract mind of Sagittarius toward higher truths. Gemini can foster the enthusiastic self-expression of Aries toward Libra relationships and the public; it can combine the Taurus characteristics of carrying things through to completion with the Scorpio urge for spiritual regeneration; it can use the Cancer sensitivity and nurturing capacity along with the Capricorn disciplining function toward Soul evolvement; it can unite the Leo self-realization capacity with the Aquarian humanitarian service; it can use the Virgo analytical process of working toward perfection by helping the suffering with the Pisces compassionate characteristic.

Ray Two energy in Pisces gives the power and compassion to help others in their spiritual evolvement. The only oppostion in which Gemini is not the instigating energy in bringing energies of the signs together in a loving, working fashion is the opposition between it and Sagittarius. Pisces is the sign which completes this triangle of energy because the compassion for those in need helps to combine the Sagittarius Universal Truths with the Gemini communicative mind.

Perfecting oneself and service to others are the urges of Ray
Two energy in Virgo. These are the two basic requirements for
Soul evolvement. For this reason Virgo is considered the sign
of the Christ Consciousness. In Virgo there are urges and capacities to use the physical body and the mind for Soul purposes
in a practical way.

The rulers of Ray Two energy are Jupiter and the Sun. The
Sun gives love and wisdom, leading to self-realization. Jupiter
fuses love and wisdom, leading to humanitarian service.

The divine principle for Ray Two is the Soul which acts as
the bridge between the Personality and the Spirit. Ray Two is
associated with the Hierarchy, an order of extremely highly
evolved Souls who act as intermediaries in bringing God's
Plans to humanity. Ray Two energy of love and wisdom is
intensified in these entities, whether they are in or out of incarnation.

Of the five senses, Ray Two correlates with vision. It has an
affinity with the right eye which stands for wisdom. The element that is symbolic of Ray Two is the ether; the stone is the
sapphire; the star is Sirius.

The psychic center that receives Ray Two energy is the heart
chakra. Unless one is a very advanced Soul, I would suggest
that he pay no attention to the chakra or chakras correlating
with his Rays. Because energy follows thought, centering one's
mind on the individual psychic centers could easily be instrumental in opening them prematurely, causing nervousness and
even more serious harmful consequences. These centers should
be allowed to open naturally, like the flowers in the field. Then,
when one has evolved spiritually enough so that the extra
power will be used in the right manner, they will open of their
own accord. The safest chakra on which to center one's thoughts
is the heart chakra, yet even here if one does not feel love
toward others, there may be overstimulation causing irresponsibility.

Ray Two energy manifests in the physical body through the
heart, circulatory system, and nervous system.

The method of approaching the Spiritual Path for Ray Two
Souls or Personalities is by intense and earnest study of spiritual teachings until they become so much a part of consciousness that they are a part of daily living. These individuals

attract what they need through love and wisdom.

The Hierarchy has affinity with Ray Two. Just as the Soul symbolizing Ray Two energy is the bridge between the Spirit and the Personality, so is the Hierarchy which is associated with Ray Two the intermediary between Shambala, which forms God's Plan, and humanity.

When Ray Two Souls and Personalities put the energy they receive to proper use, they attract to themselves those they can help. Others are drawn to them by the magnetism created by the love and wisdom they reveal in their lives.

Their life service should be the healing of the spirit, mind, or body, involving many disciplines in the fields of religion, education, or health.

They can become excellent spiritual leaders. With proper motivation, the intuition this Ray gives can make them aware of what humanity needs for spiritual growth at this stage of its evolution. They can easily be in rapport with the Aquarian Age concepts of Reincarnation, Karma, humanitarian love for All, and the freedom of the individual to follow his own conscience. They may be ministers of a congregation, leaders in schools of the Ancient Wisdoms, or lecturers and writers promoting New Age concepts. Spiritually oriented astrological and psychological counseling would also be in this category.

Ray Two Souls and Personalities can also excel in the healing of the mind—as teachers, psychiatrists, psychologists, astrologers, and in any other discipline requiring wise counseling.

As doctors and nurses they can be successful healers of the physical body.

Working with plants, the green things of the earth, the trees, flowers, herbs, and vegetables, is another Ray Two career possibility. One who works with plants can contribute to healing the spirit, the mind, or the body of multitudes of people. Artistically planting and caring for trees, flowers, and grasses, because of the beauty of their arrangements of colors, and aromas, can uplift the hearts and minds of many. More appetizing and nutritious vegetables, fruits, seeds, grains, nuts, herbs, and medicinal plants can benefit the physical body of mankind if Ray Two workers learn to grow these without poisonous chemicals. They can contribute to the healing of mankind enormously, though indirectly, by preventing the wholesale cutting of trees which supply oxygen, and prevention of soil erosion and water runoff in order to maintain havens for the wild life that are so necessary to the equilibrium of nature. Crosspollination coupled with the loving care of plants by a Ray Two worker can produce new varieties of fruit, trees, vegetables, and flowers, not only increasing visual and olfactory satisfaction, but the nutritional value of our food.

In one particular life a Ray Two Soul will find that he is no longer interested in material desires. This changeover to spiritual aspirations may produce a temporary crisis—a major problem of advanced aspirants, leading many of them to seek help from psychiatrists and psychologists. Instead of helping them understand that the crisis is a result of their reaching out for contact with their Souls, most of these therapists try to eliminate the crisis by working with the personality, which relieves the problem only temporarily and may lead to a greater crisis. Whether the reaching out for Soul contact is on a conscious or unconscious level, it represents a strong need that must be fulfilled in order for the individual to feel at peace with himself. An analogy to this is a child who is proficient at creeping but desires and is ready to walk. As he tries to learn to walk he falls many times, but it is folly to encourage him to go back to creeping just because he is more secure in that infantile manner of locomotion. It would deny him the next step in the natural maturation process at a time when he is ready for it. Likewise, it is folly for therapists to lead these clients back to personality desires, thus arresting Soul development. Instead of recognizing and treating this difficulty as a sign of spiritual progress which indicates a highly evolved level, thus giving the patient the encouragement he deserves, the therapist usually treats the condition as a malfunction of the mind and personality. Although this is a time of pain and distress, as it is for the infant who keeps falling as he tries to walk, it is also a time of great opportunity. The patient can be brought through this crisis by recognizing that the personality and its selfish concerns must be negated in order for the Soul to come into its own. To be of real help to their clients, counselors must be aware of the proper technique for handling this type of crisis and use it along with the Universal concepts of Reincarnation and Karma. Although this crisis can and does appear in all of the Seven Ray Souls, it occurs more frequently and usually more severely in Ray Two Souls.

The following exercise can help one use Ray Two energy beneficially. It is helpful for everyone because we all receive Ray Two energy from the Sun as our primary Ray, as all Seven Rays are sub-rays of Ray Two. This exercise is especially helpful for all Ray Two Souls who are experiencing this crisis and for those Ray Two Souls who wish to receive more extensively and manifest more deeply the love and wisdom this Ray brings. Visualize the heart chakra, a rotating energy field in the etheric body directly outside the physical body between the shoulder blades. Next, visualize a deep blue light in this chakra; then let the blue light fade and visualize a rainbow in its place. Then contemplate the meaning of "understanding" through such concepts as Reincarnation, Karma, the responsibility of the individual for his own status, and the Oneness of All. The next word to contemplate is "love." If contemplation of understanding is successful, a feeling of love for All will follow. By contemplating the following words in the order given, you will find that each leads to the next: "stability," "serenity," "strength," and "service to others." Be aware of the occult fact that energy follows thought, therefore as you think of these things they become a part of you.

When Ray Two Souls and Personalities are manifesting on a Soul level, they have no fear—only love and the knowledge that everything happens for ultimate good. Yet if they experience fear, saying and feeling deeply the following mantra as they breathe out after deep inhalation is very useful, "I will learn that which I presently do not know; therefore there will be no fear within my being. I now know that everything happens for my ultimate good."

Ray Two Souls and Personalities have a tendency to become too attached to certain individuals, often resulting in an unhealthy dependence. If they allow this attachment to continue, they will be easily hurt by the weaknesses of the subject of their attachments, causing a loss of self-confidence. To overcome this tendency, a goal should be set in which love is given to All with no strings attached and no expectation of love in return. This unattached love can be given freely when one recognizes a "Oneness" with all of humanity. When this stage is reached, a self-confidence will return, and a divine indifference to the wrongdoings of others will develop.

The energy of love and wisdom that Ray Two Souls and Personalities receive often creates a conflict between selfish desires and the newly burgeoning Soul aspirations. Once the Soul reaches upward toward higher levels, the conflict is lessened and in time disappears.

Even though Ray Two people enjoy studying and acquiring knowledge which can be conducive to Soul evolvement, there may be a tendency to use the knowledge gained for selfish reasons, with none flowing out to those who need it. If this occurs, it acts as a blockage; much input and no output stunts Soul growth, causes frustration, and has a bad effect on the physical health. This does not mean that all knowledge gained should be immediately given to others. Sometimes it takes many years of study before one can successfully disseminate the subject matter. In these instances, the motivation for later use is the determining factor which aids Soul growth.

Ray Two Souls and Personalities are capable of developing and manifesting many strengths, the chief one being love for all people regardless of race, color, sex, or religion. It is a love that asks nothing for itself but gives joyously.

Ray Two energy urges them to acquire metaphysical knowledge which includes Universal Truths and Laws, such as Reincarnation and Karma. By using Ray Two energy properly one acquires understanding and develops intuition—thus providing the love and wisdom that Ray Two energy promises. At this time, one feels a responsibility toward humanity and manifests an ability to think positively, which leads to achievement of some illumination of God's Plan on Earth and the will to serve humbly in its implementation.

When most of the energy that formerly powered their weaknesses is channeled into these strengths, they magnetically attract those whom they are able to help. Their tactfulness and the love they feel exudes a radiance which draws others to them. They are then able to sense and understand more and more of God's Universal Laws which leads them to an awareness of the weaknesses of others and a divine indifference to those weaknesses. This leads them even further to an unattached love of personalities and identification with the Souls of All. They acquire an awareness of unseen energy such as thoughts and motivations. This awareness enables them to see more clearly the spiritual status of others, who are then given real help.

In summary, Ray Two Souls and Personalities are capable of showering love and wisdom on others because of their feeling of responsibility toward humanity, their desire for and love of learning Universal Truths, their intuitive and understanding capacities, their ability to achieve illumination, their capacity to understand and carry out part of God's Plan, their awareness of others' thoughts and emotions, their positive thinking, and their ability to magnetically attract others in order to help them.

Following is a list of character traits divided into two columns. On the left are the traits manifested when Ray Two energy is used unwisely as a result of strong self-centered desires, which cause problems in such areas as personal relationships, career, and health. On the right are the traits manifested when Ray Two energy is used wisely out of deep concern and love for others, resulting in better relationships, improved good health, and joyful success in work.

Because awareness of one's weaknesses and strengths through determination to face the self in all honesty is the first step toward Soul evolvement, this list can serve a useful purpose not only in helping identify one's weaknesses and strengths but in aiding one to know into which particular strengths the weaknesses can be transmuted.

Using self-discipline to overcome weaknesses is necessary, but the energy that was used in the manifestation of a specific weakness can create havoc if it is repressed. To be of benefit it must consciously be used to advantage in other ways. The list includes those strengths which are to be cultivated to replace the weaknesses. In the process the energy formerly manifested in weaknesses is used to develop the strengths. Because energy follows thought, by visualizing the strengths one desires to develop, the self-discipline that is required will become easier.

A Ray Two Soul will find this list of strengths directed toward his life plan of service to others, while a Ray Two Personality will find it of great help in carrying out his Soul Ray's life plan, whatever his Soul Ray may be.

CHART 9

UNWISE AND WISE USE
OF RAY TWO ENERGY

WEAKNESSES	STRENGTHS
1. Fears	1. Love, knowledge, and understanding
2. Conflict between selfish desires and Soul aspirations	2. Foresight and the realization that the benefits of Soul aspirations far outweigh the benefits of selfish personality desires
3. Lack of willpower	3. Positive thinking
4. Strong attachment to certain personalities	4. Ability to magnetically attract others, and unattached loved for All (giving without expecting anything in return)
5. Acquisition and use of knowledge for self only	5. Realization through intuition and illumination that the individual is a part of the Whole and if that part lives only for itself, it does not long survive
6. Contempt for the mental limitation of others, and indifference to them	6. Awareness of the Oneness of All, yet the diversity and uniqueness of each, leading to tactfulness, love, patience, and endurance, which leads to illumination of part of God's Plan and the capacity to carry it out
7. Impracticality	7. Realization that one must be practical as well as spiritual to fulfill life's purpose
8. Lack of trust	8. A cautious acceptance of all people at their present level of Soul development with the understanding that if one wrongs another, karmic lessons have to be learned by both

RAY THREE—INTELLIGENT ACTIVITY

Enters Cancer, Libra, and Capricorn
Rulers—Saturn and Earth
Color—yellow

Stimulation of the higher mind, which is the abstract mind, is the result of Ray Three energy coming to us. Physical energy is also a product of Ray Three because it is through the physical body, which includes the brain and all other organs and structures, that intellectual activity is carried out. This Ray coexists with incarnation in a physical body and with the intellectual activity that the physical body exhibits. The highest expressions of Ray Three energy are education and experience which lead to evolution of the consciousness and of the physical body.

As stated earlier, all Seven Rays are sub-Rays primarily of Ray Two of the Sun, giving all of us the energy, if used properly, for love and wisdom. Because the predominant Ray of planet Earth is Ray Three, we all receive the energy of this Ray in large amounts, also. Those who have Ray Two or Three as their Soul or Personality Rays will find that particular Ray doubly strong in their natures.

Rays One, Two, and Three are vibrationally the highest Rays that mankind receives and are symbolic of the Holy Trinity or the Three Persons in God. God, the Father (Spirit) is symbolic of Ray One energy which is power and will; God, the Son (the Soul) is symbolic of Ray Two energy which is love and wisdom; God, the Holy Spirit (the personality and physical body) is symbolic of Ray Three energy which is intelligent acitivity. These first Three Rays are the Rays of Aspect because they are the three aspects of the God within each of us and are thus the Divine Rays.

It is a Universal Law that humans in general progress from a lower state to a higher state, whether in physical or spiritual evolution. Rays Four through Seven are the Rays of Attribute because they are the necessary stepping stones to the first Three Rays. In the distant future, when the human race has reached a higher level of evolvement, there will be no need for Rays Four through Seven; thus, we will receive only Rays One through Three. If we look even further into the future, we will find that Rays Two and Three will not be necessary and the only Ray we will need and receive will be Ray One. To reach this goal requires the proper use of Ray Two energy of love and wisdom. Ray Three energy of intelligent activity functioning through the mind and physical body is prerequisite to the development of love and wisdom. Thus, Ray Three is of extreme importance at this stage of our evolvement. We need the understanding of Universal Laws, such as the Law of Reincarnation and the Law of Karma, which Ray Three energy can elicit. We also need physical bodies that Ray Three energy supplies so that we can have karmic experiences for Soul evolvement. Both the understanding and the physical bodies are necessary to use Ray Two energy of love and wisdom for earthlings.

The color associated with Ray Three is yellow. In order to enhance the effectiveness of Ray Three energy, it is advisable to use yellow in some of the following—clothing, bed linen, towels, and home furnishings including walls. Since we receive an ample supply of Ray Three energy as the major Ray of our planet, it is wise for all of us to use yellow. Yellow will help one to be ruled by intellect rather than emotions. Of the multitude of situations that might be cited, two are pertinent—when taking tests, and when the emotions are difficult to control.

Two of the primary colors, red and blue, are associated with Rays One and Two. Therefore, the other primary color, yellow, must be the color of Ray Three because the first three Rays are the divine or all-inclusive Rays, just as the primary colors are the all-inclusive colors. Those whose Soul or Personality Ray is Three are advised to use yellow frequently in order that they become more attuned to the specific energy needed for their Souls' purposes.

Ray Three energy enters Cancer, Libra, and Capricorn. The controlling sign is Cancer, which is responsible for the physical manifestation of entities so necessary to freedom and release through Earth experiences for learning the needed karmic lessons. In Libra, Ray Three energy can balance the life of the Spirit with the necessities of matter through the intellectual capacities. Ray Three energy in Capricorn gives discipline and the capacity for sustained work, aiding in the attainment of success in the life plan or Soul's purpose, and in raising the level of consciousness.

The planetary rulers of Ray Three of intellectual activity are Saturn and Earth. The Earth provides physical bodies and materials for the relationships and experiences necessary for Soul growth. Saturn provides restrictions resulting from wrong thoughts, words, and actions, and rewards for right ones. Both restrictions and rewards are requisites for Soul growth—restrictions to change that which impedes Soul growth, and rewards to make conditions easier for hastening Soul growth. Together, Earth and Saturn provide events for certain people in certain circumstances. If the intellect is properly used in understanding the Laws of Karma, these events provide a climate in which we can swiftly discharge karmic responsibilities from many lifetimes. We thus learn some lessons needed for helping ourselves and others to progress on the Path.

For many years a doctrine in the field of occultism has conferred upon certain planets a sacred status and upon others a nonsacred status. Saturn is considered a sacred planet, and at the present time the Earth is considered nonsacred. It is surmised that within the next hundred years the transition to a sacred status may be accomplished by the Earth and its dwellers.

In the past few years an increasing number of writers have predicted Earth changes of varying natures and degrees of severity. Their time schedules cluster around the end of the present century. If they do take place, it would be unwise for any of us to be deeply concerned about where to go to escape the changes because it is not *where* you are but *what* you are that will determine your survival. The current predictions have their origin in powerful negative thought forms in many areas of the Earth. Because energy follows thought, these strong forms can produce drastic undesirable Earth changes which will act as a purifying process by destroying the negative thought forms. These changes do not have to happen or at least their severity can be lessened if enough people raise their consciousness to a higher level by working on overcoming weaknesses and helping others do the same. Powerful positive thought forms are thus created which can destroy the negative forms, and prevent earth changes. As a result, the earth will be a more peaceful, loving, and beautiful place and then become a sacred planet.

Earth's outstanding Ray at this time is Ray Three, its Personality Ray. Therefore, Ray Three strongly influences humanity, giving to all, but especially to Ray Three Souls and Personalities, the energy to become integrated personalities whose mental bodies are the masters of their emotional and physical bodies, leading them toward a one-pointed purpose—their life plan in attunement with the Soul Ray.

The divine principle for this Ray is the Universal Mind from which all knowledge comes. The sense associated with Ray Three is sight; the symbol is the left eye which stands for the personality and common sense; the element is fire by friction; the stone is the emerald; the heavenly affinity is the Pleiades consisting of seven sister stars; the physical bodily processes associated with Ray Three energy are assimilation and elimination.

Ray Three energy expresses itself through the sacral center (gonads) for the average person, through the throat center for the advanced person, and the ajna center near the middle of the forehead for the very advanced person. Unless one is a very advanced Soul, I would suggest that he pay no attention to the chakra or chakras correlating with his Rays. Because energy follows thought, centering one's mind on the individual psychic centers could easily be instrumental in opening them prematurely, thus causing nervousness and even more serious consequences. These centers should be allowed to open naturally like the flowers in the field. Then when one has evolved spiritually enough so that the extra power will be used properly, they will open of their own accord. The safest chakra on which to center one's thought is the heart chakra, yet even here if one does not feel love toward others, there may be overstimulation which leads to irresponsibility.

The way to approach the Spiritual Path for Ray Three Souls and Personalities is to think deeply on philosophical or metaphysical subjects until you are led to the recognition that Spirit exists and is within you. This recognition impels you to further thinking and study from which to select that which satisfies the growing need for understanding and Soul evolvement through intelligent activity. The leaders of Ray Three are the Masters R. and Hilarion.

Abstract thought and an active imagination can be products

of this Ray energy. A Ray Three Soul is a dreamer and a theorist who has ideas in all walks of life, but is often too impractical to carry them out unless his Personality Ray gives him what is needed. If both his Soul Ray and Personality Ray are Ray Three, his life plan should be concerned with theories and ideas, the practical use of those ideas and the validation of the theories formulated by others.

A person with a Ray Three Soul and a Ray Five Personality may have the following potentialities: he could be a good historian who sees the broad picture and yet notices specific details; he could be a great mathematician, using highly abstract thought on practical purposes; he could be a scientist whose theories could be useful in daily life; and he could be an excellent writer. One with a Ray Three Soul and a One, Four, or Seven Personality Ray could also be an excellent writer.

A Ray Three Soul's life service should be directed toward one or more of the following: metaphysics, philosophy, astrology, history, writing, psychology, higher mathematics, science, business, finance, law, education, working with animals, and understanding of sex.

The higher abstract mind of Ray Three energy can be used successfully in business or finance for Soul evolvement. The right and fair use of money are practices which a dedicated Ray Three person could well perform in order to serve humanity. Machiavellian, shrewd, and selfish tactics work for a limited time only, and then the walls fall down and others see that the foundation is only a mound of sand. The Law of Karma, "As ye sow, so shall ye reap," operates in the business world as well as any other area of life.

Metaphysics, philosophy, astrology, psychology, law, and education lend themselves to the successful utilization of Ray Three energy because all these disciplines require an abstract mind which is capable of highly creative and theoretical work.

A Ray Three Soul may be instrumental in giving to humanity a better understanding of sex—its use and its misuse—and in arriving at and enhancing his understanding by drawing from the wisdoms derivable from metaphysics, philosophy, astrology, psychology, law, and education.

Ray Three as well as all odd-numbered Rays give their possessor, because of the feeling of being in command and because of the absence of fear, the capacity for working successfully with animals.

As with all other Ray Souls and Personalities, Ray Three persons have specific weaknesses they tend to manifest when using the energy unwisely. One of these is intellectual pride. Because of their refined abstract thinking and their comtemplative capacity, they are capable of originating excellent ideas and theories. However with further contemplation and meditation, they are apt to become aware that their knowledge comes from many minds, most more advanced than their own.

Ray Three people must be very careful not to impose their views on others. They must realize that though their views may be valid, they are only part of the whole. They should remember that conclusions which are valid and helpful at this point will be replaced by higher and better answers as progress and evolution continue. This thought should help all of us maintain a certain degree of humility.

Ray Three persons have the capacity to use force to reach a goal, either selfishly or for the common good, and to use energy wastefully or efficiently.

Some Ray Three Souls and Personalities exhibit various degrees of coldness, stubbornness, and isolation. When they feel the need to relate to others, remembering that we all receive the energy of Ray Two of love and wisdom will aid them in thawing the cold, easing the stubbornness, and emerging from the isolation.

There is a tendency for some Ray Three persons to manipulate others due to overconcern for self. The result could be an unhappy entanglement in the webs they weave. The best way to use their Ray Three energy is to create their opportunities through right thoughts, words, and actions which will bring them true and lasting success.

Criticism of others is another weakness of Ray Three Souls and Personalities. If they were to focus their attention on the strengths and abilities of others, with the help of their acute awareness and intellectual capacity, they would stimulate and inspire those whose contemplative ability is not yet awakened.

They are capable of clear thinking because of their developed, abstract minds. They are able to concentrate deeply on a subject with patience and caution, yet with single-mindedness. There is an absence of fear and worry in their attitudes, and this positiveness gives them enormous physical energy. Their minds can easily master their physical desires and their emotions, thus giving them the ability to achieve personality integration and self-realization.

Although Ray Three energy in itself does not provide the ability to do detailed work, it provides the capacity to see the whole picture in abstract concepts. It is the Ray of concepts, theories, and inventions in many fields. Its energy gives a desire for deep understanding which leads to beauty and truth. Thus, good will toward others becomes almost second nature.

There is much force in this Ray and when this force is used for God's Plan, there is right motivation, sincerity of purpose, and rhythmic activity, resulting in peace, joy, and self-realization.

The Third Ray is related to mental unfolding and to the nature of time and space in the third dimension. Mental unfolding can turn either inward into the world of Spirit or outward into the physical. When it is turned inward it brings a better sense of values; when it is turned outward these values can be used in the world at large.

In summary, if used wisely, Ray Three energy bestows on its recipients clear thinking, good concentration, contemplation, patience, caution, a desire for understanding, and a positive attitude. All these strengths enable them to cultivate wide, abstract concepts, to see the whole picture, to use their great energy rhythmically with sincerity of purpose and with goodwill in order to reveal beauty and truth in cooperation with God's Plan. By using knowledge with love, they also are able to raise the consciousness of others in many ways, one of which is the stimulation of those whose contemplative ability has not yet awakened.

Following is a list of character traits divided into two columns. On the left are the traits manifested when Ray Three energy is used unwisely because of strong self-centered desires, resulting in various problems in relationship, careers, and health. On the right are the traits manifested when Ray Three energy is used wisely out of deep concern for others, resulting in better relationships, better health, and joy and success in work.

Because awareness of one's weaknesses and strengths through determination to face the self in all honesty is the first step to Soul evolvement, this list can serve a useful purpose not only in helping to identify one's weaknesses and strengths but in learning into which strengths the weaknesses can be transmuted.

Using self-discipline to overcome a weakness is necessary, but the energy that was formerly used in the manifestation of a specific weakness can create havoc if it is repressed. To be of benefit, it must be used in other ways. This list provides the substitute strengths to be cultivated for the weaknesses specified, and in the cultivation of the chosen strengths, the energy formerly manifested as weaknesses is used to develop the strengths.

Because energy follows thought, by visualizing the strengths one wishes to develop, achieving the self-discipline that must follow becomes easier.

A Ray Three Soul will find this list of traits directed toward his life plan of service to others, while a Ray Three Personality will find it of great help in carrying out his Soul Ray's life plan, whatever his Soul Ray may be.

CHART 10

UNWISE AND WISE USE OF RAY THREE ENERGY

WEAKNESSES

1. Pride of intellect
2. Imposing opinions and conclusions on others
3. Manipulation of persons or events to satisfy selfish desires
4. Criticism of others
5. Inaccuracy in details
6. Absent-mindedness
7. Separativeness and isolation
8. Desire for fame and possessions
9. Coldness and stubbornness

STRENGTHS

1. The humble awareness that knowledge comes from many minds
2. Realization that one's conclusions may be valid but not the only answer, and that as time goes on better answers will be reached
3. Clear thinking and deep concentration leading to the realization that what is best for the general good is ultimately best for every

10. Wasting energy on tasks that do not help Soul evolvement

individual

4. Wise use of the concept, "energy follows thought" so that the energy formerly used in criticism and pulling others down can be used in sending thoughts of understanding and love

5. Patience and caution leading to the importance of detailed parts of the whole

6. Contemplation and ability to see the whole picture with wide views on abstract concepts

7. Capacity to practice good will and raise the consciousness of others by using knowledge with love and stimulating the intellect of those whose contemplative ability has not yet awakened

8. Revealing beauty and truth leading to rhythmic activity in cooperation with God's Plan of serving others

9. Positive attitudes, giving increased energy toward one-pointed attainment

10. Right motivation and sincerity of purpose

RAY FOUR—HARMONY THROUGH CONFLICT

Enters Scorpio, Taurus, and Sagittarius
Rulers—Mercury, Moon
Color—green

Harmony and peace which Ray Four energy promises can be attained only as one experiences conflicts and learns from them—which is why the Law of Karma and its understanding is tied so closely with this Ray. Pertinent to Soul progress is the awareness that each person creates his own environment through past thoughts, words, and actions, and that his future environment is determined by his present thoughts, words, and actions. The karmic implications of this statement are that when we experience difficulties and conflicts, it is because we have lessons to learn. It is only through conflicts with others and with ourselves, the awareness of these conflicts, and learning lessons from them that we can attain harmony. One has learned from karmic experiences when his consciousness tells him he would never again hurt anyone the way he has been hurt by others. When he understands this concept and makes it a part of his everyday living, he is able to take the responsibility for where he is without wasting energy on self-pity, but using it to transmute weaknesses into strengths so that he will become happier and more fulfilled.

All of us receive a great supply of Ray Four energy because it is the Ray of the Human Kingdom. There are seven kingdoms associated with the Seven Rays. Ray Seven is the Ray of the Mineral Kingdom; Ray Six is the Ray of the Plant Kingdom; Ray Five is the Ray of the Animal Kingdom; Rays Three, Two and One are the Rays of higher Kingdoms. The lower the Ray number, the higher the level in the evolutionary development of the kingdoms.

Rays are not only associated with kingdoms but with stars and planets. Ray Three is the Ray of planet Earth and Ray Two is the Ray of our Sun. All of us receive not only enormous amounts of Ray Two energy from the Sun and Ray Three energy from the Earth, but also Ray Four energy as members of the human race. No matter what the Soul or Personality Rays of an individual are, he receives primarily Rays Two, Three, and Four in large quantities.

Because Ray Four is the Ray of humanity, it is inevitable that each member of the human race will experience conflicts and have to resolve them to attain harmony and peace. Even though Ray Four is basically the Ray of all humanity, Ray Four Souls and Personalities receive an extra supply of its energy, finding it dominant in their lives.

Ray Four energy helps to produce harmony, beauty, and unity among ourselves as members of a family or any group, and within ourselves as individuals through learning from existing or potential conflicts. To avoid a potential conflict by changing to better attitudes is wisdom, but to think and act in such a way that we believe we can evade a conflict is folly. If we run away from an individual with whom we have a conflict, we will then experience greater conflict within ourselves, either on a conscious or unconscious level until we once more, either in this life or a future life, relate to that person and resolve the conflict. There are times when we can remove ourselves temporarily from the presence of those with whom we have conflict, but we cannot remove ourselves permanently until the conflict is resolved. Yet there are situations when it is best for one to separate from another, and that is when neither party desires to resolve the conflict. In such cases, separation will prevent deeper conflict. If there is no chance to resolve this conflict later in life, a meeting will take place in a future life. At times we meet people we seem to dislike instinctively for no apparent reason. This is an age-old experience as illustrated by the rhyme: "I do not like thee, Doctor Fell. The reason why I cannot tell. But this I know and know full well. I do not like thee, Doctor Fell." If we are wise, we will relate to the "Doctor Fells" we meet because with understanding and love we can resolve that past life conflict and thus attain the peace and harmony we all seek. To attain this harmony we must spend time—working and learning from the conflicts we have with others and within ourselves on a more or less simultaneous basis. We must realize that our personalities may often want to avoid those with whom we experience difficulties, but our Souls always attract people who can teach us something. This is why many people who divorce their mates often find that they attract a second and a third mate with the same and even more pronounced weakness than the first. Our personalities are often selfish and want everything to be easy and pleasant, but our Souls know that we can only attain the harmony we desire by working for it. Conflicts within ourselves and with others co-exist. We cannot evade contact with our inner selves in order to avoid conflicts. Gregariousness cannot serve as a cushion between our inner beings and our inner conflicts because the inner conflicts will lead to outer conflicts with those around us. Neither evasion of relationships nor evasion of looking within is the answer. We must meet ourselves at every level, within and without, whichever way we turn.

Ray Four energy helps us work through our lesson-teaching karma in order to attain harmony. The lessons taught by karma are those difficult yet necessary experiences for Soul evolvement. An example: if we deserted our children in a past life, we may in this life be deprived of parental love. Thus, knowing how it feels to be the recipient of a wrong we have done to others, we will never do harm in that way again. I have heard a number of young adults, in mentioning how their parents mistreated them, say emphatically that they would never treat their children the way they were treated. They have learned from their lesson-teaching karma which was precipitated by past life wrongs.

We all have taken on karma in this life, which is the reason we came back on earth—to have the needed experiences for evolvement. Yet those with a Ray Four Soul or Personality have taken on a great deal more karma than the average person because they want to evolve quickly in this life. The career purpose of those with a Ray Four Soul is to help others benefit from their karmic experiences. Ray Four Personalities also will express their Soul Ray Life Plans by helping others work through their conflicts.

The goal of every entity is to evolve from the self-centered personality upward toward manifestation as a Soul with a life plan of serving others. Ray Four, as the pivotal or middle Ray of the ascending series of Ray Seven to Ray One, is a source of energy for aiding the entity in making this usually slow and difficult transition. Because of its nature as the Ray of harmony through conflict, Ray Four causes the most suffering of any of

the Rays, yet it is the one from which the most spiritual progress can be made. Rapid evolution is attained through karmic
suffering with which Ray Four is concerned. Karmic suffering
followed by changed attitudes helps people achieve harmony,
beauty, and unity within and amongst themselves.

The color harmonizing with this Ray is green. This is the
color of harmony, relaxation, equilibrium, and healing. It is
the basic color of nature, of trees, grass, leaves, vegetables, and
most plants. The earth offers its inhabitants renewal if they
but seek it. Since Ray Four is the Ray which confers harmony
through the experiencing of conflicts, and is the Ray of the
human race, it would be wise for all to use green in order to
benefit from its influence, especially in times of conflict, anxiety, and tension. It is wiser still for Ray Four Souls or Personalities to use green frequently because of the added conflicts
and karmic lessons they experience. Walking in the woods amid
the greenery eases tension. Desirable effects can also be ob-
tained by wearing green clothes and using green bed linens,
towels, and room furnishings.

The signs Ray Four enters are Scorpio, Taurus, and Sagittarius. The controlling sign is Scorpio which is the most powerful and intense of these three signs. Because of its innate
power it provides many tests and trials necessary to starting
on the Spiritual path. Through Scorpio one has the capacity to
delve to the depths of materialistic selfish desires and also to
reach great Spiritual heights. Taurus can give Spiritual illumination, an awareness of God's Plan on earth, and the determination to step on the Path and stay on it. Sagittarius gives
enthusiasm to search for Spiritual truths, single-mindedness
in goal attainment, and the desire to reach one goal after another.

The planetary rulers of Ray Four are Mercury and the Moon,
the two planets most likely to produce conflicts. The Moon is
associated with the emotions, the personality, and habits of
past lives. It sometimes influences one's moods—towards ela-
tion or depression, but the moods change rapidly. Mercury is
associated with the mind and the thoughts. The clue to alle-
viating Ray Four pain and suffering is found through Mercury
and the mind. The unwise use of both the mind and the emotions brings problems, but it is through the wise use of Mercury,

the mind, that we can master our emotions and change our thoughts.

The divine principle associated with Ray Four is intuition, which is a grasp of the truth; the sense is smell; the element is air; the stone is jasper. Two symbols represent this Ray. One is the rainbow which stands for the bridge between the personality and the Soul, and also the bridge between material and spiritual concerns. The other symbol is a golden bird on a rosy cross which stands for the sacrificing of selfish desire for the joy of Soul contact and harmony.

Ray Four energy produces crises in all who are in a high stage of evolutionary development—those possessing good character and integrated personalities. These crises result from the clashing of the Soul and personality and bring "a sense of isolation, a sense of futility, a determination to refuse to admit defeat, and then a sudden recognition of the clashing of the Soul and personality and the will to victory."*

The chakra, the psychic center in the etheric body surrounding the physical body, that corresponds to Ray Four is the center at the base of the spine whose energy enters the physical body through the adrenals. Unless one is a very advanced Soul, the chakra correlating with his Rays should not be mentioned to him. Because energy follows thought, it is unwise to center one's thoughts on the psychic center because this center could be opened prematurely and cause nervousness and other more serious consequences. The center should and will open naturally when one has evolved spiritually enough so that the extra power will be used in the right way. The only exception is the heart chakra, and yet when thoughts are placed in that area, if one does not feel love toward others, overstimulation might result leading to irresponsibility.

The method of approaching the Spiritual Path by one whose Personality or Soul Ray is Four is by self-control and discipline through which tranquility among the warring forces of one's nature is achieved. Ray Four people have a strong need for harmony which they can attain by overcoming weaknesses.

The life work of Ray Four Souls and the areas in which Ray Four Personalities can contribute to their Soul Rays' life plans

* Bailey, Alice A., *Esoteric Psychology,* Vol. II, pp. 365, 366.

are those which can act as bridges or contact points between the personality and the Soul, between Piscean ideas and Aquarian ideas, or between the lower kingdoms of minerals, plants, and animals and the higher kingdoms of the Soul and Spirit. Often there is a combination of two or all of these areas in the life plan of the Ray Four worker.

The first career possibility which acts as a bridge between the personality and the Soul is creative art and beauty as an expression of truth through good color sense, articulateness, harmonious sounds, and beautiful music, all of which can help others uplift their consciousness which in turn makes it easier for them to contact their Souls. Gazing at a beautiful picture, reading a Soul-inspiring book, or listening to music by a master composer can change one's selfish personality desires to spiritual aspirations.

The second career possibility which acts as a bridge between the personality and the Soul is esoteric psychological or astrological counseling. The esoteric knowledge of the concepts of Reincarnation and Karma is basic to such counselling. With a depth of understanding of these concepts, counsellors can help their clients become aware that they have created their own environments through thoughts, words, and actions of past lives and the past of this life, and that the clients' Souls attract to them certain people and experiences to teach them lessons for Soul growth. When the clients have fully realized the meaning of these concepts, the counsellors will have achieved the basic task of dispelling self-pity and blaming others for their difficulties. The counsellors then are able to help their clients use their energy to change weaknesses into strengths through taking responsibility for where they are and making concerted efforts toward where they want to be.

The third career possibility which acts as a bridge between the personality and the Soul is in religion and metaphysics which are based on teachings of the Hierarchy (sometimes referred to as the White Brotherhood). This career could manifest itself as ministering, lecturing, or writing, or any combination of these. The concepts of Reincarnation, Karma, and responsibility for one's environment are the basics for these career possibilities.

Contemplation of mathematical exactitudes, as found in

beautiful architecture, is the fourth career possibility which acts as a bridge between the personality and the Soul. Those who study and appreciate the beauty of the design and construction can become aware of the importance of intellect in this type of creativity. This insight can easily affect the use of the mind and understanding so that their personalities can contact their Souls and enjoy the beauty of that contact.

The second general career area which acts as a bridge or contact point is that between the Piscean Age beliefs and the New Age Aquarian ideas. In order to avoid a dangerous gap or break during the present period of transition between the Piscean Age and the Aquarian Age, the Ray Four person can harmonize the older beliefs of the Piscean Age with the newer ideas of the Aquarian Age. Even though it is necessary to discard some of the old concepts of the Piscean Age (which Ray One workers are very apt at doing) to make way for the newer and more evolved concepts of the Aquarian Age, there are still a few Piscean ideas that can be of help to us and which must be kept in harmony with the new Aquarian ideas. The Piscean idea of faith in the God without us (the Hierarchy whose main purpose, through love and wisdom, is to help us evolve) combined with the Aquarian teachings of the God within us, gives us a better perspective of spiritual reality—the ability to contact our Soul with the help of higher entities. It is through the combination of the Piscean inspirational contacts and the Aquarian understanding of these contacts that we are able to evolve. The Piscean faith, inspiration, and contact with higher entities of the Spirit plane must go hand-in-hand with the Aquarian understanding of the inspiration received. The Piscean urge for compassion can easily be combined with the Aquarian belief in the freedom of the individual to act as his own conscience dictates, not what others dictate. If he is in contact with his Soul, his conscience will urge him to act, not only with Aquarian understanding and brotherly love, but with Piscean compassion and kindness.

The third general category of careers of Ray Four workers involves those which act as bridges or contact points between humanity and the three lower kingdoms of minerals, plants, and animals. Some scientists recently have accepted the fact there is a consciousness in the atom which occultists have known for ages. Since there is Spirit or a consciousness in each member of all the kingdoms, the Ray Four worker can help them to become the best they are capable of becoming. Although Ray Four persons can help the evolvement of all three lower kingdoms, they have more affinity with plants than with minerals or animals. In the plant kingdoms they can help the vegetables, fruits, nuts, and grains to become more nutritious, palatable, and abundant, and the flowers to become more beautiful and aromatic through love, cross-pollination, use of natural fertilizers, and prevention of soil erosion. All these processes when carried out by the Ray Four worker are services not only to humanity but to the lower kingdom. In serving the human kingdom better, the lower kingdoms evolve, just as a human being evolves only by serving a higher kingdom, that of his Soul. It is an occult fact that to evolve, each kingdom must serve one higher than itself.

In summary, the Fourth Ray career possibilities can be found as: ministers, lecturers, and writers on religion and metaphysics based on teachings of the Hierarchy, creative artists, architects, esoteric psychological and astrological counsellors, and workers with plants, minerals, and animals.

Even though the energies of all Rays when used wisely produce perfection, the energy of Ray Four tends to produce perfection faster. Ray Four stands for unification—the integrated personality becoming at one with the Soul. This Ray energy is conducive to unity, harmony, and beauty through conflict and struggle which results in Soul contact and the death of selfish personality desires. A crisis often occurs when there is a strong conflict between a lower and a higher mode. A crisis can be a great opportunity if it is handled well (see Ray Two section).

The major weakness that is manifested when Ray Four energy is used unwisely is self-centeredness with very little or no concern for the welfare of others. Self-centeredness reveals itself in a multitude of ways, including lack of moral courage, strong passions, extravagance, worry, and laziness.

Many conflicts with self and with others through confusion, misinformation, and lack of intuition may result from the wrong use of Ray Four energy. A feeling of not being in tune with the "whole" can permeate one's being. The failure of karmic tests brings constant crises. Hypersensitivity to the personality of self and others is a weakness often associated with the crises experienced.

When one uses any of the Seven Ray energies unwisely, certain health problems may occur. Ray Four Souls and Personalities can receive benefit from massage.

Awareness of one's weaknesses and concerted efforts to transmute them into strengths result in long-term benefits of good health, Soul evolvement, and success and joy in relationships and work.

Ray Four energy precipitates conflicts so that karmic lesson-teaching experiences will result in harmony, which leads to the elimination of a weakness and the possibility of attaining illumination. When Ray Four persons face tests and crises, they can benefit greatly by using the innate Ray Four strengths of good judgment, logical reasoning, quickness of perception, skill in action, and physical courage. When a crisis is dealt with successfully, Ray Four energy can bestow a feeling of peace, harmony, and Oneness with All. This often leads to mysticism.

Because of their generous natures and the love and sympathy Ray Four Souls and Personalities are capable of feeling for others when they use this energy wisely, they become magnetic, drawing many others to them. They are then able to relate well, and through these relationships can perfect their own personalities and that of the others. When their consciousness is at a high level, they are able to heal others through their voices.

Another Ray Four strength is in understanding the New Age concepts of Reincarnation, Karma, and other spiritual truths which are Ancient Wisdoms but being accepted into the consciousness of more and more people. Their increased understanding, perceptive potentialities, feelings of harmony and unity, ability to act as a bridge between any two unrelated groups, ideas, or concepts give Ray Four persons who are in contact with their Souls the capacity to harmonize the New Aquarian Age with the older Piscean Age so there is no gap, but only a continuous flow of better and better understanding as time progresses.

In summary, Ray Four energy recipients are able to attain

harmony for themselves and others because of their ability to contact the Soul's wisdom through crisis experiences resulting in illumination, because of their love and sympathy which is followed by magnetism and the ability to relate well with others and to perfect the personality through relationships, because of their quickness of perception and good judgment, because of their generosity and physical courage, because of their ability to heal through voice and their mystical capacity when consciousness is at a high level, and because of their skill in action and their ability to harmonize the New Aquarian Age ideas with some of the older Piscean beliefs that are still useful.

Following is a list of character traits divided into two columns. On the left are the traits manifested when Ray Four energy is used unwisely because of strong self-centered desires, which result in problems such as in relationships, career, and health. On the right are the traits manifested when Ray Four energy is used wisely because of deep concern for others, which results in better relationships, better health, and joy and success in work.

Because awareness of one's weaknesses and strengths through the determination to face the self in all honesty is the first step to Soul evolvement, this list can serve a useful purpose not only in helping to identify one's weaknesses and strengths but in aiding one to know the strengths into which the weaknesses can be transmuted.

Using self-discipline to overcome weaknesses is necessary, but the energy that was formerly used in the manifestation of specific weaknesses can create havoc if it is repressed. To be of benefit it must be used advantageously in other ways. The list provides the substitute strengths, and in the cultivation of these strengths, the energy formerly manifested as weaknesses is used to develop them. Because energy follows thought, by visualizing the strengths one wishes to develop, the self-discipline that must follow will be easier.

A Ray Four Soul will find this list of traits directed toward his life plan of service to others, while a Ray Four Personality will find it of great help in carrying out his Soul Ray's life plan, whatever his Soul Ray may be.

CHART 11

UNWISE AND WISE USE
OF RAY FOUR ENERGY

WEAKNESSES

1. Self-centeredness
2. Extravagance
3. Strong passions and lack of moral courage
4. Conflicts with self and others through confused thinking
5. Failure of karmic tests producing constant crises
6. Hypersensitivity to the personality of self and others causing guilt feelings and critical thought
7. Laziness and inaccuracy
8. Worry and not being in tune with the "Whole"

STRENGTHS

1. Love and sympathy toward others resulting in magnetism
2. Generosity to those who are in need
3. Ability to contact the wisdom of the Soul through crisis experiences
4. Illumination resulting from facing conflicts and understanding them
5. Ability to learn the necessary karmic lessons, thus ending the crises
6. Divine indifference to the weaknesses of others, resulting in better relationships, and an absence of guilt feelings for weaknesses of self
7. Quickness of perception which gives understanding and good judgment, leading to physical courage in skillfully helping others
8. Harmony and universality which can give healing capacity through the voice and the ability to harmonize Aquarian Age ideas with certain Piscean beliefs

RAY FIVE—CONCRETE KNOWLEDGE

Enters Leo, Aquarius, and Sagittarius
Ruler—Venus
Color—indigo

Concrete knowledge, especially knowledge that is scientifically proved through research, is the hallmark of Ray Five energy. The essence of this Ray is its capacity to weigh and sift common knowledge through discriminative procedures so that what is proved to be accurate will be accepted.

Ray Five Souls and Personalities should not find it difficult to achieve integrated personalities leading to self-realization because their one-pointed minds can easily control their emotions and physical appetites.

It is through Ray Five energy of the lower mind and the knowledge it attains that contact can be made with the abstract contemplative mind and eventually with the Soul. With Ray Five energy, a person can more easily unite his lower mind, his higher mind, and the universal mind. In its ultimate capacity, Ray Five energy is the bestower of the knowledge of God. Its energy can bring about the realization and expression of Divine Knowledge by mankind.

"Knowledge expressing itself eventually through wisdom, is attained only through the agony of successfully presented choices. These, submitted to the discriminating intelligence during the process of the life experience, produce at last the sense of true values, the vision of the ideal, the capacity to distinguish reality behind the intervening glamour."* It is through knowledge discriminatively gained in life experiences that Soul growth is accomplished.

Because we are now in the Aquarian Age of understanding, humanity is beginning to live more in the mind than in the emotions. For this reason Ray Five energy is very much in tune with Aquarian Age energy, each enhancing the power of the other. Knowledge, logic, and understanding are the key words of Ray Five energy and Aquarian Age energy. Together these energies, as they become increasingly potent, will enable mankind to become more aware of certain Universal Laws,

* Bailey, Alice A., *Esoteric Psychology*, Vol. I. p. 343.

especially Reincarnation and Karma, and to understand their logic.

The color consonant with this Ray is indigo. It would be advisable for Ray Five Souls or Personalities to use this color frequently on their persons or in their surroundings in order to utilize more easily this particular energy that is so necessary for their purpose in life. In addition to the colors of one's Soul and Personality Rays, blue, yellow, and green should be used frequently, not only for Ray Five persons, but for everyone because they are associated respectively with Rays Two, Three, and Four, the basic Rays we receive from the Sun, the Earth, and the Human Kingdom.

The signs through which Ray Five energy comes to us are Leo, Aquarius, and Sagittarius. The controlling sign is Leo which leads to self-realization by helping one become aware of one's capabilities and by achieving integration of the personality through using the mental body for a specific purpose in which the emotional and physical bodies are servants to it. It is fortunate that so many people are trying to feel good about themselves and "doing their own thing" as long as they meet their responsibilities and hurt no one. The Leo part of our beings tells us to be aware of our Divine potential so that we have something to give others later. Through Aquarius, Ray Five urges the self-realized person to achieve universal consciousness, a consciousness which is concerned with the needs of all humanity rather than with the one self, the one group, or the one nation. As we progress in the Aquarian Age, the controlling sign will be Aquarius, under which many will be merging their Leo consciousness of self with the Aquarian universal consciousness. Sagittarius gives a one-pointed goal direction in which the mind efficiently uses the emotions and the physical body for achievement. When a goal is reached, there is an urge to reach for another goal, then another goal, and on and on.

Rays Five and Seven are the only two which have only one planetary ruler each. The ruler of Ray Five is Venus. Exoterically, Venus, the ruler of Taurus and Libra, signifies personality desires in a traditional delineation. In Ray-Centered Astrology, Venus, as the ruler of Ray Five, signifies the mind and is the esoteric ruler of Gemini, an intellectual air sign.

Venus is the hierarchical ruler of Capricorn, contributing to the raising of the consciousness level of the mind through persistent discipline.

The element consonant with Ray Five is the flame of fire; the Divine principle is higher knowledge; the stone is the topaz. This Ray has an affinity with the thyroid gland and the throat chakra. Unless a person is a very advanced Soul, the chakras correlating with his Rays should not be mentioned. Because energy follows thought, centering one's mind on the individual psychic centers could easily be instrumental in opening them prematurely, causing nervousness and even more serious consequences. These centers should be allowed to open naturally, like the flowers in the field. Then when one has evolved spiritually enough so that the extra power will be used in the right manner, they will open of their own accord. The safest chakra to center one's thoughts on is the heart chakra, yet when the consciousness is placed in that area, if one does not feel love toward others, there might be overstimulation which causes irresponsibility.

The method of approaching the Spiritual Path on this Ray is by scientific research, leading to acceptable findings by differentiating and discriminating procedures.

The leader of Ray Five is Master Hilarion. There are many phrases by which the Lord of Ray Five is known. The one I prefer is "The Door into the Mind of God."

The Ray Five Soul should have as his life work (Soul's purpose) one of the following and the Ray Five Personality should express his life work (according to his Soul Ray) through one of the following: science, psychology, philosophy, Christian Science, social science, surgery, education, economics, scientific writing, and working scientifically with animals.

Ray Five is very strong in scientists. Because they work on mental levels and because the mind is the bridge to the Soul, they often reach their Souls through their work. True scientists are nonseparative and noncompetitive with other scientists—they enjoy sharing their knowledge with each other. There seems to be a Oneness with good scientists all over the world. Many leaders of organized religions are ruled by their emotions and can easily become fanatic and competitive. In some cases, they are not as close to their Souls as the dedicated scientists who are ruled by their minds, not their emotions.

Science means working with ideas, proving them true or false through investigation. There are many scientific disciplines, with new ones appearing as mankind advances. At present, science is predominately concerned with matter. When it enters into nonphysical realities, its methods and measurements will be changed and it will discover the creativity from which the material world emerges.

The scientific discipline to which much attention has been given over the last decade is the study of energy. The finding has been that everything in the universe is energy, differentiated by rates of vibration. Much is still to be discovered in this area.

Another of the new disciplines is the Science of the Soul. In the not too distant future, it is possible that the existence of the Soul will be proven scientifically. It is also possible that a machine will be invented which will picture the Soul leaving the physical body at the time of death. This breakthrough will help those who are not aware of life after death to relate to those Souls who have discarded their physical bodies, and more importantly to know that after their death, their Souls will still live.

Fifth Ray workers have as their task the expanding of the consciousness of humanity. "The energies of the aspirants and disciples on the Third and Fifth Rays are turned to the work of expanding the human consciousness, of bringing to light the hidden wonders of the universe, and of hastening the unfoldment of the latent powers of mankind. These powers, when awakened, will be extensions of many of the present senses and will admit man into that world which lies behind the veil of ignorance and matter."*

It is possible that in time Ray Five workers will prove scientifically that love is the purpose behind all knowledge, and that love and knowledge, both so necessary for Soul evolvement, will eventually reveal each other. Both love and wisdom, which is knowledge used wisely, are necessary for reaching a high level of Soul evolvement. When scientists can prove that

* Bailey, Alice, A., *Esoteric Psychology,* Vol. I. p. 178

there is no wisdom without love, and no real love without wisdom, they may then be in a position to prove that knowledge reveals love and love reveals knowledge. At the start they many try to prove that knowledge is the only criterion needed to attain peace. As they probe deeper, they may come to prove that both love and knowledge are the prerequisites, and that the basic reason people acquire more and more knowledge is to use it out of their love for humanity.

All disciplines which lend themselves to scientific investigation such as psychology, esoteric psychology, chemistry, philosophy, education, Christian Science, and economics are Ray Five career possibilities. There has been research in all these fields, yet much more is needed in each.

Surgery is considered a Ray Five career because much detailed medical knowledge resulting from scientific research is necessary for success.

Ray Five writers must not only be very precise and accurate, but must offer their readers the detailed results of scientific investigations.

Ray Five persons are not only capable of helping others transcend the animal nature of humanity, consisting of the lower physical and emotional desires, but can also help the animal kingdom to evolve, thus helping animals become closer to the human kingdom through the domestication, care, and love shown them.

The weakness Ray Five Souls and Personalities most often exhibit when using their energy unwisely is a lack of love. This can manifest itself in many ways. They may tend to harbor prejudices which are narrow, separative, and antisocial. Having worked hard to raise their intellectual capacities, they may believe that the intellect is all that matters. They may be arrogant and lack sympathy for others. They may be easily angered toward those who do not think as they do. They may have distorted views of the truth. There is a tendency for Ray Five persons to lack radiation of Soul life toward others. This is most likely to be true if one also has an odd-numbered remaining Ray; his mind will be keen and his will strong, and though he has much to give, he may lack the willingness to give with love. Giving with love and concern for others should be his major goal, and as he strives toward it, he will experience peace and joy.

Another weakness often manifested by those who use Ray Five energy unwisely is to blame their weaknesses on circumstances or other people instead of facing and overcoming them. This is called rationalization—a defense mechanism which may be appropriate as a short-time crutch for a Ray Five person who is finding it extremely difficult to discharge his responsibilities. Because of his keen mind and his perfectionistic attitudes, this is usually the first response to his failure to cope. Though this provides momentary relief from anxiety, when his mental health improves he must give up this crutch in order to make permanent progress. Even though he is proficient in discriminating imperfections in himself and others, he must realize that imperfections are the lot of all, and that accepting and loving himself and others irrespective of faults is the only way to progress. Awareness of his specific imperfections comes easily to him if he does not cloud it with rationalization.

He must be careful that in the awareness of his and others' weaknesses, he does not express them harshly or harbor critical thoughts. Because energy follows thought, dwelling for any length of time on weaknesses will only intensify this unwanted condition. If he is wise, he will visualize the perfected characteristics or perfected results because Ray Five energy gives power to actualize visualization.

Another weakness occasionally found in Ray Five persons is preoccupation with time-consuming and useless pursuits.

The weaknesses mentioned prevail only when Ray Five energy is used unwisely. These weaknesses may be transmuted into several strengths.

One of these strengths is of major importance—having a keen and powerful mind with the power to establish mastery of the emotions. Because Ray Five persons can do this easily they can readily attain integrated personalities which lead to realization of their life plans.

Common sense, truthfulness, the capacity to be unaffected by flattery and favors, fairness in making decisions, and independence are additional Ray Five strengths.

Ray Five Souls and Personalities can excel in analytical and detail work with unusual perseverance. They have the ability to gather and interpret information, make accurate observations, and verify their findings.

Because detachment from people and events is comparatively

easy for them, they do not find it difficult to maintain a stability, an equilibrium, and a divine indifference to the weaknesses of others. Fortunately, they are able to easily become aware of their own weaknesses and the difficulties which result, giving them a strong impetus to visualize the strengths into which they can be transmuted and to attain them.

The day may come when it is conclusively established that intelligence and knowledge exist primarily to prove the importance of love and its expression over any other function of the human consciousness. This day will in all probability be reached by the minds of Ray Five Souls or Personalities. It will be reached when the concept that everything in this universe is energy (which scientists have already proved) is carried to a deeper level. Perhaps this deeper level might concern the measurement of the rates of vibration of love and intelligence with the finding that love has the higher vibration. This in itself could be the impetus for the development in Ray Five persons of unattached love, a love free from emotion and sentiment and personal emphasis, a love that sacrifices and understands and that acts with strength and decision—not in the interest of any one group or individual, but on behalf of all of humanity. They would then realize that the intellect, important as it is, is not all that matters, but is important for enabling them to become aware of and express a higher function, that of unattached love. Their innate capacity to be detached from people and events will then make them capable of unattached love.

The ability for one-pointed concentration of Ray Five persons makes it easy for them to cultivate telepathy and increase their capacities for contemplation and meditation. This will increase their inspiration and creative capacities. Even if they were not aware of the existence of the Soul before they attained this proficiency, they could easily become aware and contact it. Soul memory of past lives might then become a reality for them. The spiritual devotion they achieve as a result of contact with the Soul, together with their mental acuity, could enable them to know reality and become receptive to wisdom. When they have made contact with their Souls, they will become aware that all knowledge comes from those whose intellect is at an even higher level than theirs, and that the knowledge they have acquired, however extensive, is only part of all knowledge. This knowledge of reality combined with a sensitivity to wisdom can enable them to understand the Universal Law of Karma—that wrong thoughts, words, and actions bring karmic suffering, while right ones bring karmic rewards. They are then able to understand why wealth, power, fame, and self-indulgence does not bring lasting happiness; that only in serving others with love can joy be experienced. Their mental powers are great not only to understand this concept, but to make the better choice.

In summary, if Ray Five Souls and Personalities use their energy wisely, then through their keen minds, one-pointed concentration, common sense, truthfulness, fairness, independence, perseverance, capacity to gather, observe, and interpret facts accurately, detachment from people and events, and mental control of emotions, they will be able to become creative, inspirational and telepathic, to combine mental and spiritual devotion and thus know reality, to become aware of the Soul and be able to contact it, to become receptive to wisdom, and to experience unattached love. These are the marks of the Masters.

The following is a list of character traits divided into two columns. On the left are the traits manifested when Ray Five energy is used unwisely out of strong self-centered desires, resulting in various problems such as in relationships, career, and health. On the right are the traits manifested when Ray Five energy is used wisely out of deep concern for others, resulting in better relationships, improved health, and joyful success in work.

Because awareness of one's weaknesses and strengths through the determination to face the self honestly is the first step to Soul evolvement, this list can be useful not only in helping one identify one's weaknesses and strengths, but in aiding one to know the particular strengths into which one's weaknesses can be transmuted.

Using self-discipline to overcome weaknesses is necessary, but the energy that was formerly used in the manifestation of a specific weakness can create havoc if it is repressed. To be of benefit, this energy must be directed consciously in other ways. The list provides the substitute strengths to be cultivated for Ray Five weaknesses. In the cultivation of the chosen strengths, the energy formerly manifested as weaknesses is used to develop the strengths.

Because energy follows thought, by visualizing the strengths one wishes to develop, the self-discipline that must follow will be easier.

A Ray Five Soul will find this list of traits directed toward his life plan of service to others, while a Ray Five Personality will find it of great help in carrying out his Life Plan which his Soul Ray indicates.

CHART 12

UNWISE AND WISE USE
OF RAY FIVE ENERGY

WEAKNESSES	STRENGTHS
1. Lack of love	1. Powerful keen mind
2. Harsh criticism	2. Mental control of emotions
3. Arrogance	3. Ability to excel in analytical and scientific work
4. Prejudice	4. Stability and perseverance
5. Opinionated	5. Truthfulness and fairness
6. Separative and anti-social	6. Independence
7. Strongly materialistic	7. Common sense unaffected by flattery and favors
8. Harboring harmful thoughts	8. Ability to attain self-realization easily
9. Blaming others for one's weaknesses	9. Proficiency of one-pointed concentration
10. Unforgiving temper	10. Unattached love and Soul contact
11. Detailed interest in areas which are of no help to self and others	

RAY SIX—IDEALISM AND DEVOTION

Enters Sagittarius, Pisces, and Virgo
Rulers—Neptune and Mars
Color—Silvery rose

Ray Six energy intensifies idealism and devotion. It is an energy which is basically emotional yet one-pointed. Ray Six Souls or Personalities are very devoted to one person, one cause, one desire, one concept, or one religion. They express their energy either in intense devotion to materialistic concerns or intense devotion to religious matters.

Before the Ray Six person contacts his Soul, he is apt to be separative and fanatical, believing intensely that his religion, his cause, or his idea is the only right one. Ray Six individuals should master the study of cycles because of their tendencies to be fanatical and to experience highs and lows in a cyclic fashion; they can then be aware of periods of possible difficulties and learn to forestall them through raising their level of consciousness by prayer and meditation.

While these persons are basically gentle, they can become intensely angry. Their strongly emotional focus makes it difficult for them to relate to others who do not believe as they do. Everything is either black or white. They tend to feel that what they believe is "perfect" and all else "imperfect." They will give generously to the subjects or objects of their devotion, but will give nothing to those who do not believe as they do.

Ray Six energy is expressed in churches, organized religions, and groups embodying laws and creeds which originated from Avatars, but as time progressed, departed grossly from their sources. There is a misplaced idealism, devotion, and often a fanaticism in many of the leaders and followers of various religions and religious groups; they not only believe that what they think is the only right way, but many of them try to impose their beliefs on others. It is sad because they will suffer difficult karmic experiences until they understand that there are many ways to God and that each person must be allowed to choose his own, and what is right for one person is not necessarily right for another.

Ray Six energy was very strong on Planet Earth during the

98

Piscean Age. "This energy produced the great idealistic religions with their visions and their necessary narrowness—a narrowness that is needed to safeguard infant souls."* The Great Ones in charge of the universe see with their wisdom, their love, and their power that certain Ray energies become more potent when we are more in need of them, and wane when we are less in need of them. The Piscean Age, in which we have had many lives and learned much, has passed. We have grown from the "spiritual children" we then were to the "spiritual adolescents" we have become. Ray Six energy, with its devotion and idealism so necessary in the past, is no longer needed and is waning in manifestation. The Great Ones never permit an abrupt start or ending to any Ray energy or to any Age. They make these changes gradually so that humanity can more easily adjust. There are therefore some Ray Six Souls and Personalities because they have not yet acquired the understanding or made the effort to rise above the Ray Six energy. When they begin to contact their Souls, they can transmute their Ray Six energy to either Ray Two or Ray Three energy. Those who are born with Ray Six Souls or Personalities can, through understanding and disciplined effort, transmute their Ray Six to Ray Two or Ray Three.

Every New Age brings with it in accelerating amounts a certain Ray energy for all humanity. In this, the Aquarian Age, it is Ray Seven of ordered rhythmic living through the use of the mind. The sixth Ray of emotionalism was potent during the Piscean Age. When one Age is finished and another begins, as is now the case, the Ray associated with the Old Age wanes in manifestation, and the Ray associated with the New Age waxes. Ray Six is slowly being replaced by Ray Seven until a period will come in which, through Soul evolvement of the human race, there will be no more Ray Six Souls and Personalities on Earth. When that time comes, humanity will have learned to be guided by the mind and the heart instead of the emotions; the energy from the chakras below the diaphragm will have entered those chakras above the diaphragm.

The color in harmony with Ray Six is silvery rose, a shade of pink. This color, when worn or used in one's surroundings, helps one feel real love for others. Since Ray Six is the most

* Bailey, Alice A., *Esoteric Astrology*, p. 239.

emotional of all Ray energies, by using pink frequently, Ray Six Souls or Personalities can help themselves to transmute whatever undesirable emotions they may be experiencing into love. Love is considered by many to be the highest of all emotions. When the love one experiences is above possessiveness, is above giving of self in order to get something in return, and has grown to be an unattached love for all of humanity out of a sense of Oneness, that love is no longer an emotion but an expression of one's true essence.

Ray Six enters our solar system through Sagittarius, Pisces, and Virgo. Sagittarius is the controlling sign which gives focused one-pointed goal direction. There are three symbols for Sagittarius that are representative of successively higher states of consciousness. The first is the centaur (half human and half horse) which signifies fused duality in which one's selfish animalistic nature is intermingled with his thinking nature. The second is the archer in which there is still duality in one's being, but the animalistic and thinking nature are not attached to each other; each are separate but in conflict with the other. The third is the bow and arrow, signifying a one-pointed mind that is used to change animalistic desires to spiritual goals. His intuition and idealism lead to spiritual aspirations which enable him to see God's Plan and direct his path toward it.

In Pisces, Ray Six persons are intensely emotional and devoted to a concept or a religion. If one has a Pisces Ascendant and a Ray Six Soul, and is expressing his energy in this fashion, he can elevate his consciousness by transmuting emotionalism into love and his devotion into spiritual aspiration. He then accepts or rejects concepts or religions as they aid or fail to aid him in his spiritual growth. He no longer idolizes a leader but learns from him to become independent and fulfilled.

In Virgo, Ray Six people tend to express fear and worry, and give too much attention to nonessentials. Awareness of these weaknesses, coupled with a sincere desire to overcome them, allows for their transmutation into a sense of proportion, breadth of vision, and the ability to give more time to larger important issues.

The ruling planets of Ray Six are Neptune and Mars. In their lower vibratory states, Neptune confuses them in that they do not see the broad view clearly, steeping them in emotionalism and materialistic desires, while Mars gives impulsiveness and one-pointedness to fight for one's religion, concept, or leader, hurting others on the way. Together in their lower use, Neptune and Mars spell emotionalism and fanaticism. In their higher vibratory states, Neptune gives inspiration for spiritual truths and creative projects, and a feeling of Oneness and love for All, while Mars gives the courage and energy to change one's selfish desires into spiritual aspirations.

The sense correlated with Ray Six is taste; the gemstone is the ruby; the element is water indicative of the emotions; the divine principle is the desire for physical sensation expressed as indulgence. Contrary to the thoughts of many, physical desires are a divine principle. It is through these indulgences and the lessons learned from them that one is given the impetus to transmute the energy formerly so used into spiritual aspiration so that one can enjoy the life that follows.

This Ray has affinity with the pancreas gland in the physical body and with the solar plexus chakra in that position of the etheric body surrounding this area of the physical body. Ray Six also has an affinity with the astral body, the source of emotional energy. Because spiritual evolvement requires that the mind control the emotions, one should not send thoughts to these areas of the body which will tend to strengthen the emotions.

Unless one is a very advanced Soul, the chakras correlating with his Rays should not be mentioned. Because energy follows thought, centering one's mind on the individual psychic centers can easily be instrumental in opening them prematurely, producing nervousness and even more serious consequences. These centers should be allowed to open naturally like the flowers in the field. Then, when one has evolved spiritually enough for the extra power to be used in the right manner, they will open of their own accord. The safest chakra to center one's thoughts on is the heart chakra, yet when the consciousness is placed in that area, if one does not feel love toward others, there may be overstimulation which causes irresponsibility.

When a Ray Six Soul or Personality has learned to use his mind to master his emotions, he becomes deserving of either Third or Second Ray energy. Ray Three energy becomes his when he uses the mind to control the emotions. Ray Two energy is his when he can transmit solar plexus energy to the heart chakra by changing self-centeredness into understanding and love.

The following exercise is helpful to develop mental control of the emotions for all, especially Ray Six persons: Visualize a budding flower opening in the heart chakra in the etheric energy field outside the physical body on the back between the shoulder blades; then visualize the color of indigo there; then visualize a rainbow there; then think about the following words, meditating deeply on each in successive order, at the same time realizing that one follows the other as night follows day: understanding, love, stability, serenity, strength, and service.

For Ray Six Souls or Personalities, "The way of approaching the Path would be by prayer and meditation, aiming at union with God. The method of healing for this Ray would be by faith and prayer."* Ray Six Souls select what they want by responding to idealism in an emotional fashion.

The Master of Ray Six energy is Jesus upon whose teachings of love and wisdom the Christian churches were founded almost two thousand years ago. With the aid of the Piscean Ray Six energy of devotion and idealism, His followers were able to raise their level of consciousness when they followed His principles. His divine principles are becoming less and less a part of the present Christian churches which is the reason for their disintegration. Jesus is giving less and less of His time and energy to Ray Six because the need for devotion and idealism has decreased rapidly since the close of the Piscean Age. As Ray Six energy is waning, Ray Two energy of love and wisdom is waxing and Jesus is giving more and more of His time and energy to the latter Ray. The Lord of Ray Six has many names, one of which is, "Negator of Desire."

Career potentials for Ray Six individuals derive from the ease with which they can help others recognize ideals and aspire toward what is good and true. Among these careers are psychology, religion, humanitarian activities such as nursing or volunteer work, writing poetry and other inspirational works, including sacred music, lecturing, and working with the plant kingdom. If they have Ray Four or Seven as their other

* Bailey, Alice, A., *Esoteric Psychology*, Vol. I. p. 210.

Ray, their chances for success in artistic pursuits are appreciably increased.

Lack of success or dissatisfaction in a career is often the result of unwise use of Ray energy. Ray Six energy when used unwisely is usually manifested in extreme emotionality. Until this weakness is faced and dealt with through the guidance of the mind and the understanding it offers, a number of other weaknesses often result, some of which are: argumentativeness, anger, violence, unhealthy dependence on others, possessive love, inability to understand the viewpoints of others, superstition, confused thinking, sectarianism, fanaticism, oversexuality, suspiciousness, bewildered idealism, and strong desires for wealth, fame, and power.

Of these weaknesses, argumentativeness, anger, and violence are recognized first. This leads to a feeling of alienation because of the difficulty in establishing friendly or loving relationships. For the person on whom he does not vent his anger, he may develop a selfish possessive love. This, together with the alienation produced by argumentativeness, anger, and violence will lead to an unhealthy dependence on those who will tolerate him. He becomes suspicious of others' motives and has difficulty understanding their viewpoints, which prevents the formation of harmonious relationships. Because he is so unhappy in his search for fulfillment of his needs, he may develop strong desires for wealth, power, fame, or sexual relations, believing that these will help him find happiness. When one of these strong desires is fulfilled, he finds no real happiness because he still has the weaknesses that led to the desire. Finding that he still suffers as a result of his weaknesses, the selfish desires will change into spiritual aspirations. Even though it may seem to some that Ray Six energy is not conducive to Soul evolvement, the contrary is the case—expressing intense, undesirable emotions and suffering the karmic consequences provides an impetus for change.

Two more weaknesses Ray Six persons may manifest are confused thinking and bewildered idealism which may lead to idolizing others. Instead of idealizing the truths that certain persons transmit through their teachings, Ray Six persons often make the mistake of idolizing the teachers, and instead of using their minds to differentiate between the truths and untruths of leaders, they often accept untruths with intense emotion.

Ray Six persons have a tendency to worship, adore, and idolize a deity or a personal God, believing if they accept this deity as their Savior, they will enter heaven at the time of their death. They are often not aware that heaven is a high state of consciousness that can be realized no matter whether or not one has a physical body, and that the higher state of consciousness does not automatically come by accepting a deity as one's personal Savior but must be earned through the upliftment of consciousness.

Sectarianism and fanaticism are two more weaknesses that Ray Six people may develop if the energy is not used wisely. They then believe that their particular religious sect is the only true one. They do not understand that there are many roads to God, and that each person should choose his own according to where he is and what will be of help to him at his present stage of evolvement. Because of this lack of understanding, they often become fanatical and try to force their beliefs on others.

When this energy is used wisely, the strengths of Ray Six persons can be expressed through true Christianity, that which Christ stands for—love and wisdom, a humanitarian, unattached love which encompasses all mankind irrespective of religion, sex, or race, and a wisdom which understands Universal Laws and attempts to adhere to them.

If Ray Six people use their energy wisely, they can, with their intense emotion, sincerity, intuition, and innate one-pointedness pierce through their wrong concepts, which will lead them to universal truths. They can then become aware of the Oneness of All, and with that awareness can develop a feeling of love and reverence for every human being, regardless of the stage of evolvement of each one.

Additional Ray Six strengths are loyalty and tenderness, which can be expressed in loyalty to their new-found universal concepts and in tenderness to those who do not think as they do. A sympathy for others' viewpoints can then be a part of their nature. A true idealism and a sensitivity toward All can be cultivated, through which Ray Six Souls and Personalities can discover where each person is in his evolvement and what his next step can be.

Another Ray Six strength is the capacity to substitute spiritual aspirations for materialistic desires. Still another is the ability to learn breadth of vision and the attainment of a universal consciousness rather than a separative one. Peace can be attained by honoring and respecting the good in all people. Visualization and imagination which Ray Six individuals have in abundance are very desirable strengths when used to reinforce the understanding and practice of universal truths and to radiate love to all people.

To summarize, the following strengths of Ray Six energy of idealism and devotion: sincerity, intuition, and one-pointedness can lead to the awareness of universal truths. Loyalty can be established to the new found truths, followed by a sincere desire to adhere to them and the ability to substitute these spiritual aspirations for materialistic desires. Imagination and visualization will help change wrong concepts, thoughts, and feelings to right ones; then there can be a devotion to these truths, manifested as sympathy for others' viewpoints, a true idealism, and a sensitivity toward all, which comes with the realization of where each person is and what his next step can be, and a tenderness, a reverence, and a love for each person, and an acquired peace by honoring and respecting the good in all people.

Following is a list of character traits divided into two columns. On the left are the traits manifested when Ray Six energy is used unwisely because of strong self-centered desires, resulting in various problems such as in relationship, career, and health. On the right are the traits manifested when Ray Six energy is used wisely because of deep concern for others, resulting in better relationships, increased health, and joyful success in work.

Because awareness of one's weaknesses and strengths through the determination to face the self in all honesty is the first step to Soul evolvement, this list can serve a useful purpose, not only in helping to identify one's weaknesses and strengths, but in aiding him to know the strengths into which the weaknesses can be transmuted.

Using self-discipline to overcome weaknesses is necessary, but the energy that was formerly used in the manifestation of specific weaknesses can create havoc if it is repressed. To be of benefit this energy must be consciously directed in other ways. This list provides the substitute strengths to be cultivated for Ray Six weaknesses; in the cultivation of the chosen strengths, the energy formerly manifested in weaknesses is used to develop the strengths.

Because energy follows thought, by visualizing the strengths one wishes to develop, the self-discipline that must follow will be easier.

A Ray Six Soul will find this list of traits directed toward his life plan of service to others, while a Ray Six Personality will find it of great help in carrying out his Soul Ray's life plan, whatever that Soul Ray may be.

CHART 13

UNWISE AND WISE USE
OF RAY SIX ENERGY

WEAKNESSES

1. Intense emotionality
2. Argumentativeness, anger, and violence
3. Unhealthy dependence on others
4. Selfish possessive love
5. Lack of understanding the viewpoints of others
6. Suspicion of others' motives
7. Confusion and bewildered idealism—idealizing personalities instead of Universal Truths
8. Sectarianism—belief that your religion, your concepts, and your nation are the only good ones
9. Fanaticism—trying to force one's beliefs on others
10. Strong desires for power, fame, wealth, and oversexuality

STRENGTHS

1. A strong feeling of love
2. Imagination and visualization
3. Sincerity and loyalty
4. Tenderness
5. Respect for the identity and independence of each person
6. Sensitivity to others' viewpoints
7. Idealism of Universal Laws
8. Intuition leading to Universal Truths
9. One-pointed concentration
10. Breadth of vision and sense of proportion

RAY SEVEN—CEREMONIAL ORDER OR MAGIC

Enters Capricorn, Aries, and Cancer
Ruler—Uranus
Color—violet

Ray Seven energy is rhythmic energy manifested in an orderly fashion to attain that which is desired. Through the building and vitalizing of thought forms, it combines spirit with matter to produce beauty, order, and peaceful relationships. Because energy follows thought, there can be potent power in thought forms, depending on the intensity and the one-pointedness of the thoughts. Ray Seven Souls and Personalities are capable of very powerful thoughts which can be extremely influential. They can bring deep changes in the thoughts and attitudes of others, especially in the realm of freedom which is so important in the present Aquarian Age. This is accomplished through their thoughts which enter the ether as energy accumulations, known as thought forms. As those who are influenced receive these thoughts, they add to the potency of the original thought form, thus increasing the possibility of influencing still more people.

Organization is the key word for this Ray. It is easy for Ray Seven people to bring order out of chaos and rhythm out of disorder because of the power of their thoughts and because of the rhythmic and orderly way they think, speak, and act. Seventh Ray energy gives power to organize, integrate, and synthesize. Seventh Ray Souls and Personalities are adept at creating changes in organizations and in relationships.

The highest expression of Ray Seven energy is White Magic which is enormous power generated through thoughts, words, and actions directed toward helping others. The white magician is one whose motive is the good of others, one who fosters brotherly love and gentleness, and one who can control his mind. Those who use Ray Seven energy in its higher form can integrate the personality so that the mind is the master of the emotions, resulting in self-realization. They then have the ability to fuse the integrated personality with the Soul so that love and understanding become paramount in their life work.

We must be aware that the lowest expression of Ray Seven

energy is black magic which is enormous power generated through thoughts, words, and actions of a selfish nature directed at harming certain others. It is difficult for black magicians to harm those of a relatively high level of Soul evolvement. If these target persons feel at One and have love for All, no matter what the level of evolvement, the intended black magic cannot affect them, but will bounce off their auras and return to the senders, for whom this is called instant difficult karma. Black magic can, however, harm those who have not attained a high level of Soul evolvement, but the one who suffers most is the one who sends this energy out because of the Law of Karma. This Law in essence is that for every wrong thought, word, or action, we experience difficulties until we have learned our lessons, and that for every right thought, word, or action, we are rewarded. Because of this Universal Law and its lessons, all black magicians will in time become white magicians. Anyone interested in learning white magic on a deep level might benefit from *A Treatise on White Magic* by Alice A. Bailey.

Ray Seven energy brings opposites or dualities together, such as spirit-matter, positive-negative, man-woman, life-form, Soul-body, and conscious-unconscious.

Ray Seven energy helps produce a union between man and woman, not only on the physical plane, but on the emotional and mental planes. When an ideal union on all three planes is achieved, the children will be highly evolved souls, especially if the mother's thoughts are elevated, and if she takes good care of her body through proper nutrition, rest, and exercise, and avoids sexual intercourse during pregnancy.

It is important to remember that every Ray has sub-Rays of all the Rays. For this reason, no matter what the Soul and Personality Rays, we all have Ray Seven as one of our sub-Rays. Therefore, we all engage in ritual and ceremonial living, which is why we are concerned with clocks, calendars, and astrological cycles in our relationships. Ceremony and ritual are necessary in scientific healing so that the Soul and body can be brought together, and also in group work in order to attain uniformity of action and in sending forth energy and forces for the benefit of the human, the animal, the plant, and the mineral kingdoms.

There are periods in the evolutionary development of Earth inhabitants when certain of the Seven Rays are needed more than others. Presently, Ray Seven is one of these and therefore is waxing. Its increasing strength is helping us adjust to and be in rapport with the Aquarian Age.

Ray Seven energy urges us to use our conscious minds to reach the unconscious where repressions, guilt feelings, and undesirable attitudes may be stored, causing many problems. This energy enables us, through the bringing together of the dualities of the conscious and unconscious minds, to summon these conflicts to the light of day, examine them, and through understanding, resolve them.

Violet is the color that has affinity with Ray Seven. Just as Ray Seven is the intermediary between matter and spirit, so is its color the intermediary between the other six materialistic colors and the spiritual colors which cannot be seen by the physical eye. Because energy is matter at its lowest vibration and spirit at its highest vibration, and because violet is the color with the highest vibration of the spectrum, it is the bridge between matter and spirit. For this reason it is the optimum color to use when contacting spirit, and when raising one's level of consciousness. It would be wise for all to use violet occasionally, and for Ray Seven Souls and Personalities to use it frequently to help them in all phases of their lives.

Ray Seven energy comes to us through Capricorn, Aries, and Cancer. The controlling sign is Capricorn through which strong materialistic desires can be overcome and through which the raising of one's consciousness to a high enough level to merit initiation can be accomplished by spiritual aspiration and self-discipline. Through Aries, Ray Seven energy inspires spiritual ideas with fiery enthusiasm for new beginnings that can be used in practical ways. Through Cancer, Ray Seven energy gives psychic awareness of the present needs of people, making it possible to know which of the new spiritual ideas and to what degree they are ready to be assimilated at any particular time.

Each of five of the Rays has two ruling planets. Each of the other two Rays, Rays Five and Seven, has only one. Uranus rules Ray Seven. Ray Seven and Uranus are very active now, heralding in the New Aquarian Age. The power of Ray Seven and Uranus will be stronger still as we go further into this

Age. It is understandable that Uranus is the ruler of Ray Seven because it is through the instantaneous changes of the mind that spirit can unite with matter. Uranus, the exoteric ruler of Aquarius, is helping us make the necessary changes from self-centered personality desires to soul aspirations which the Aquarian Age urges. It is largely through Uranus that the reorganization and rebuilding of the world structure will take place in this Age of Aquarius. Uranus and Aquarius signify unattached universal love for all humanity regardless of religion, ethnic origin, sex, or level of Soul evolvement.

Through Uranus and Aquarius, humanity is related to the Pleiades, the constellation that affects intelligent activity. Uranus and Aquarius are related more closely to one specific Star of the Pleiades, Alcyone, which is called the "star of intelligence." The Aquarian Age is extremely important in evolutionary progress because it is in this period that we have the opportunity to serve others through knowledge, understanding, and enlightenment.

Uranus is related to the scientific mind and to divine knowledge. The mystic way of feeling which characterized the Piscean Age was tied in strongly with Ray Six and the emotions, and is now giving way to the understanding of Divine Law and Wisdom which characterizes the present Aquarian Age tied in with Ray Seven. Ray Six is slowly going out of manifestation while Ray Seven is accelerating. As a result, Divine Ancient Wisdoms, ruled by Uranus, which have been held undercover for long periods of time, are again beginning to see the light of day.

Uranus is the planet of spiritual awakening through trials and testing, with the result that the inner subjective life can be blended with the outer personality life. It produces spontaneous action which results in Soul evolvement, followed by a transference from intellectual to Soul focus. Because Uranus rules occult wisdom, when Astrology is studied in depth and applied to a chart, it manifests Uranian qualities and becomes a marvelous aid to spiritual awakening. When we begin the study of Astrology we must learn the basics in order to become competent, but if we probe below the surface level, we are bound to become aware of the spiritual aspects.

Because Uranus is the exoteric ruler of Aquarius, the esoteric ruler of Libra, and the hierarchical ruler of Aries, these three signs constitute a triangle of Uranian power. It would be wise to study the houses and the planets in these signs, especially Ray Seven Souls or Personalities.

The divine principle of Ray Seven is creative energy; the element is earth; the sense is hearing; the stone is amethyst. Ray Seven has affinity with the etheric body—the energy field which both penetrates and surrounds the physical body and is responsible for the vitality of the physical body.

Incarnation of the physical bodies of humans, animals, plants, or minerals is made possible by Ray Seven energy. The elemental Ray Seven energy combines in different ratios to make different forms. Even though each of the Rays gives a specific energy to the human kingdom and the lower kingdoms, each Ray is basically associated with one kingdom. With Ray Seven it is the mineral kingdom.

There are three psychic centers or chakras through which one receives Ray Seven energy—the one chiefly utilized depending upon the level of Soul evolvement. The ordinary person would receive this energy through the sacral center, releasing it chiefly into the gonads. The advanced person receives it at the base of the spine chakra, releasing it chiefly into the adrenals. The very advanced person receives Ray Seven energy from the Ajna center, which is in the etheric body (as are all the chakras) directly outside the middle of the forehead and releases this energy chiefly into the pituitary gland for creativity. As one evolves spiritually, Ray Seven energy changes its path into the body from below the diaphragm to above it, and its use changes from self-centered concerns to service toward others.

Unless one is a very advanced Soul, the chakras correlating with one's Rays should not be mentioned. Because energy follows thought, centering one's mind on the individual psychic centers could easily be instrumental in opening them prematurely, causing nervousness and even more serious harmful consequences. These centers should be allowed to open naturally like the flowers in the field. Then, when one has evolved spiritually enough so that the extra power will be used in the right manner, they will open of their own accord. The safest chakra on which to center one's thoughts is the heart chakra, yet when the consciousness is placed in that area, if one does not feel love toward others, there may be overstimulation leading to irresponsibility.

Ray Seven Souls and Personalities can approach the spiritual path through rites and rituals. The spiritual entity in charge of Ray Seven is Master Rakoczi. There are many names by which the Lord of Ray Seven is known, one of which is "The Creator of the Form."

A Ray Seven Soul has a number of careers from which to select a life plan. The Ray Seven Personality must similarly make a choice to help him express his Soul's purpose according to his Soul Ray. Among the choices are the following: careers which specifically develop order, organization, and rhythm, such as executive, organizer, and financier; science which relates the physical body or any matter to spirit; careers which establish right human relations in business between employers and employees, men and women, minorities and majorities; esoteric psychology, esoteric astrology, psychoanalysis, psychology; occultism, which is the wise use of energy; working toward a unified or world religion; politics, law enforcement, the military; working with animals; study of minerals; healing and nursing; study and use of cyclic phenomena. If the other Ray is Four—artistic work in sculpture, design, painting, music, and literature.

Any future science which relates spirit to matter will be a Ray Seven career. It is my hope that science will establish evidence of the etheric body as an energy field that is penetrating and surrounding physical bodies of humans, animals, plants, and minerals. There are seven chakras (vortices of energy) in the human etheric body which are channels for the functioning of the glands. The level of optimum functioning of the chakras is determined by emotional health, which in turn is determined by thoughts and attitudes which are determined by one's level of spiritual evolvement. This explains why Ray-Centered Astrology improves emotional and physical health by raising one's consciousness level. It is hoped that science will prove, through the knowledge of the etheric body, that healing of the physical body requires effort toward spiritual evolvement. When the scientific evidence of the etheric body is established, there will be a wonderful revolution in medicine, diet, and all areas of daily life.

Because Ray Seven is strongly associated with the Mineral Kingdom, it is possible for Ray Seven Souls and Personalities to work scientifically in this field, for example, working with the radiation of minerals. Another science which relates matter to spirit is one in which energy at its lowest vibration, which is matter, is changed to energy at a higher vibration, which is spirit. When minerals become radioactive, they manifest on a higher level. Just as the human body radiates when it reaches a certain level of spiritual evolvement (witness the halos on paintings of sainted persons by sensitive artists), so do minerals radiate when they undergo changes of refinement. Radiation of minerals is the result of condensation and transmutation which is actually the passage of one state of being to another. A number of minerals are radioactive, yet many other mineral radiations still remain to be discovered by science. As time goes by and Ray Seven becomes more potent, more minerals will become radioactive. There will also be an accelerating awareness of the cyclic appearances of these radiations. A challenge for Ray Seven Souls and Personalities is to scientifically direct radioactivity into constructive and helpful channels.

A third example of how Ray Seven persons can serve humanity is through the scientific study of electricity. The knowledge that the brain of man is an electrical organ is widely used, in fact, the bodies of all living things utilize electrical functions at times. The scientific study of electricity may expand our understanding of its functions beyond our wildest dreams, leading to universal peace and good will.

Ray Seven energy, along with Aquarian Age energy, will give the power to understand God's Plan on Earth, and will help to bring about unified religious thinking. A Ray Seven Soul or Personality may be instrumental in bringing about a fellowship of world religions, with each religion respecting the minor differences of the others while focusing on the major similarities which should lead to the knowledge that there are many Paths to God. For those who cannot accept organized religions, Ray Seven persons can promote awareness of the New Age concept of the "God spark within each person" and opportunities for its flowering. When they have attained a certain degree of this flowering, they are candidates for white magic, which through intensely focused thoughts, words, and actions, is of great help to others.

Some Ray Seven Souls and Personalities will have the restoring of the ancient sacred mysteries to humanity as their life work. One tool for accomplishing this is Masonry, whose symbols and allegories have deep spiritual meaning. The present Aquarian Age energies of enlightenment and universal brotherhood, coupled with the waxing Ray Seven energy, can help Ray Seven persons apply Masonry in utilizing the symbols and allegories, not in a materialistic and separative fashion, but spiritually to restore the ancient sacred mysteries for all.

Esoteric Psychology, another Ray Seven career possibility, is becoming better known and more widely accepted because the Aquarian Age energies which foster its growth are accelerating. Esoteric Psychology holds that the Soul controls the personality through ritual. "The new science of Psychology could well be described as the science of rituals and rhythms of the body, of the emotional nature, and of the mental processes, or of those ceremonials (inherent, innate or imposed by the self by circumstances and by environment) which affect the mechanism through the Soul functions."* A ritual is any discipline or rhythmic activity which is needed for the successful functioning of an entity, a home, business, organization, class, army, or church.

Esoteric Astrology, like Esoteric Psychology, is rising from its slow beginnings to a more rapid growth. Both complement each other and although each discipline in its own right can be enormously beneficial, together they work optimally to enable the Soul to reach the personality for more successful living. The most definitive and practical form of Esoteric Astrology today is Ray-Centered Astrology.

Another Ray Seven career is occultism which is the wise use of energy. This will become increasingly more widespread as time goes on. It includes those wisdoms which help to use energy wisely and more efficiently with potency and love. One is white magic which through thoughts, words, and actions, one is able to serve others by bringing about better attitudes and conditions for them. Another is spiritually oriented Astrology which can help us become aware of the energies we possess and how to change those that had been used destruc-

---

* Bailey, Alice A., *Esoteric Psychology*, Vol. I. p. 366.

tively to those that are used constructively and wisely. In both examples, rewarding karmic experiences are a product.

Healing and nursing are Ray Seven careers when they are used to uplift the consciousness, which unites the spirit with the physical body more closely, resulting in better physical health and a higher level of spiritual evolvement. The end product is a refinement of the physical body.

Certain weaknesses are manifested with each Ray when the energy is used unwisely. Awareness of our weaknesses is the first step to transmutation. Unwise use of Ray Seven energy may result in one or more of the following weaknesses:

Pride and lack of love and gentleness. Because they are often acutely aware of the power they possess, Ray Seven people may feel they are special and a little above others, a superficial judgment which often leads to bigotry, narrowness, and superstition.

When there is a strong, selfish misuse of Ray Seven energy, it may be manifested as black magic or sex magic. Because Ray Seven is psychically powerful, its energy, if used for selfish purposes through wrong thoughts, words, or actions, can harm others severely. Whether one is harmed by this potent energy depends on his level of consciousness. If it is on a high level, the negative energy will ricochet off his aura, back to the sender. This is often referred to as instant lesson-teaching karma and can be very unpleasant to the Ray Seven sender but helpful for the future wiser use of his energy. If the one to whom the negative energy is directed is also on a low level of consciousness, the energy can reach him. In this case, the lesson-teaching karma will come to the sender at a later time, unless he raises himself to a high Soul level and thereby suffer no lesson-teaching karma.

The Law of Karma is not "an eye for an eye or a tooth for a tooth" or a means of punishment, but a Universal Law which exists as a deterrent to more wrongdoing.

Ray Seven Souls and Personalities are strong and powerful, both in their weaknesses and in their potentialities. Once they are determined to transmute their weaknesses, they have great power to do so. They can develop the following strengths if they do not already possess them:

The primary strength is the understanding of God's Plan and the power to cooperate with it. They are able to organize and attain rhythmic, balanced living for themselves and others in the home, in business, education, government, and religious work.

Ray Seven Souls and Personalities can become telepathic, that is, they can learn to send and receive thoughts.

They can utilize white magic which is spiritual in its nature. Their motivation is then directed toward the common good, and they acquire the power to destroy what is no longer useful, and to attract and rebuild what is needed.

Building strong useful thought forms and vitalizing them through the etheric body, thus energizing the physical body, is another strength Ray Seven Souls and Personalities can develop. They then have great vitality and can also energize other people, animals, and plants.

The wise use of Ray Seven energy bestows upon its users courage, self-reliance, perseverance, courtesy, and extreme care in details.

In summarizing the strengths Ray Seven Souls and Personalities can develop, we find that they fall into three categories. The first category contains the characteristics of courage, self-reliance, perseverance, and courtesy. In the second category are the abilities to understand cycles, organize details, build vital thought forms, use white magic, and stimulate and refine the physical bodies of people, animals, and plants. The third category embraces a faculty for rhythm and order, for the wise use of strong, innate psychic power, for telepathy used for spiritual purposes, for understanding and cooperating with God's Plan for Earth.

Following is a list of character traits divided into two columns. On the left are the traits manifested when Ray Seven energy is used unwisely because of strong self-centered desires, resulting in various problems such as in relationships, career progress, and health. On the right are the traits manifested when Ray Seven energy is used wisely because of deep concern for others, resulting in better relationships, increased health, and joyful success in work.

Because awareness of one's weaknesses and strengths through the determination to face the self in all honesty is the first step

116

to Soul evolvement, this list can serve a useful purpose, not only in helping identify one's weaknesses and strengths but in aiding one to know particular strengths into which the weaknesses can be transmuted.

Using self-discipline to overcome weaknesses is necessary, but the energy that was formerly used in the manifestation of specific weaknesses can create havoc if it is repressed. To be of benefit, this energy must be directed consciously in other ways. This list gives the substitute strengths to be cultivated for the weaknesses specified and in the cultivation of the chosen strengths, the energy formerly manifested as weaknesses is used to develop the strengths.

Because energy follows thought, by visualizing the strengths one wishes to develop, the self-discipline that must follow will be easier.

A Ray Seven Soul will find this list of traits directed toward his life plan of service to others, while a Ray Seven Personality will find it of great help in carrying out his Soul Ray's life plan, whatever his Soul Ray may be.

CHART 14

UNWISE AND WISE USE
OF RAY SEVEN ENERGY

WEAKNESSES

1. Pride
2. Lack of love and gentleness
3. Hurting others through powerful wrong thoughts
4. Use of psychic power for selfish purposes
5. Narrowness and bigotry
6. Superficial judgment
7. Disorder and chaos because of misunderstanding

STRENGTHS

1. Use of strong psychic power to help others
2. Courage and self-reliance
3. Perseverance
4. Courtesy
5. Building and vitalizing good thought forms
6. Telepathy for spiritual purposes
7. Ability to use white magic
8. Ability to vitalize and refine physical bodies
9. Faculty for rhythm and order
10. Ability to understand cycles
11. Ability to organize details
12. Understanding and cooperating with God's Plan

Suggested additional reading on the proper use of Ray energies can be found in Chapter Three of *Esoteric Healing* by Alice A. Bailey.

Even though the knowledge of one's Soul and Personality Rays and their interpretation are basic to Ray-Centered Astrology, the signs of his Ascendant and Sun and their meanings found in the next chapter provide illuminating esoteric nuances, while succeeding chapters broaden and deepen the entire delineation.

Chapter Four

INTERPRETATION OF ZODIACAL SIGNS
FOR SOUL AND PERSONALITY

For an in-depth study of one's Rays, a thorough study of the signs of the Ascendant and Sun is essential. The Ascendant sign information as an adjunct to that of the Soul Ray can aid in determining the Soul's purpose, and the Sun sign information as an adjunct to that of the Personality Ray can more clearly show how one's personality can be of service to the Soul's life plan. This chapter not only provides details about the important characteristics of each sign, but makes it possible to determine whether a person is manifesting on a Soul level, and if so, to what extent. A guide is given for each sign to reveal whether the person is average, advanced, or very advanced. If he is average or advanced and wishes to evolve to the next level, he may take advantage of the suggested specific goals to be reached.

In clarifying the Soul's purpose, it is imperative that we add the interpretation of the Ascendant sign to the delineation of the Soul Ray. Recalling that each Ray enters three signs, the Soul Ray of one person can also be the Soul Ray of those with two other Ascendant signs. Adding the Ascendant sign's interpretation to the Soul Ray's delineation, helps to differentiate among three individuals with different Ascendant signs but the same Soul Ray.

In helping to clarify how the Personality can serve the Soul's purpose, it is important to add to the interpretation of one's Personality Ray, the interpretation of the Sun sign itself. The esoteric planetary ruler of the Sun sign indicates the Personality Ray, and because five of the Seven Rays have two ruling planets, the Sun sign information helps to differentiate persons with the same Personality Ray but different Sun signs.

From the esoteric point of view, people are divided into three groups. The largest number are average people who are interested only in themselves and what the world can provide them. In a smaller group are those advanced persons who are trying to overcome their weaknesses and at the same time serve others

118

119

consonant with their Soul Rays. In the smallest group are the very advanced who are not only working diligently on overcoming their weaknesses and serving others consonant with their Soul Rays, but are beginning to feel through unattached love a Oneness with all.

The energies of planets function at different levels depending on the level of consciousness of the individual. Each sign has an exoteric, esoteric, and hierarchical planetary ruler, and each planet (except the Sun, Saturn, and Pluto) is an exoteric, esoteric, and hierarchical ruler of three different signs. Although the esoteric ruler of a sign operates at a higher level than the exoteric ruler of that sign, and the hierarchical ruler operates at a higher level than the esoteric ruler, the use of the three different rulers depends on the level of consciousness of the user.

Every sign has an exoteric ruler which Astrologers have been using for centuries and which functions as the only zodiacal sign ruler for the average person.

For each sign there is also an esoteric ruler which, in addition to the higher level functioning of the exoteric ruler, functions for the advanced person.

The hierarchical ruler of a sign functions for the very advanced person who also receives the energies of both the exoteric and esoteric rulers, but on a higher level than even the advanced person.

The energy of each sign can range in manifestation from the very lowest level (on which the person wastes his energy, thinks and lives solely materialistically, blocking his own potentiality and Soul growth), to successively higher levels, at each of which he frees himself more and more from personality desires and begins to build the highly evolved being that he is destined to become.

ARIES

Exoteric ruler—Mars   Esoteric ruler—Mercury
Hierarchical ruler—Uranus

A certain type of Light is found in every sign. In Aries it is the Light of Life, referred to as Spirit, which seeks whatever can be used for divine expression. Whether it is another rein- carnation (life on earth) to learn lessons needed for spiritual growth, or the instigating of new ways for reaching a higher spiritual plateau, Aries persons have so much energy, enthu- siasm, and optimism at their command that nothing can hold them back. It does not take them long to overcome obstacles.

"Let form again be sought"* applies to an Aries person man- ifesting on a personality level. Someone with an Aries As- cendant or Sun at this stage is desirous of another earth life in which to fulfill materialistic desires and express emotions.

"I come forth and from the plane of mind I rule"* applies to an Aries person manifesting on a Soul level. In the past, he was ruled by his desires and emotions, and as a result, suffered difficult karmic experiences. He has now decided to be ruled by his mind instead of his physical desires and emotions. Be- cause it takes hard work to break a bad habit such as anger, he begins by using his mind to develop understanding, realizing that we all have certain weaknesses and that becoming angry when one is the target of a certain weakness of another is folly. Instead, when he has been wronged by someone, he waits for a time when he can talk quietly, gently, and lovingly to the person, helping him to change; or in his own quiet moments, send out thoughts of love and help to the wrongdoer; or he does both. In any case, he accepts with love the wrongdoer where he is, knowing that some people have had fewer earth lives than others in which to learn needed lessons. Where once he would have become angry, letting his emotions rule him, he is now ruled by his mind.

Aries is the most powerful sign in the zodiac. Its element is fire, signifying spirit; its mode is cardinal, signifying activity;

*Bailey, Alice A., *Esoteric Astrology*, p. 653.

and its gender is masculine, signifying intellect and assertiveness. Every fire and water sign purifies the spirit in a special way. In Aries it is the power to burn and destroy everything that hinders divine expression. Because the Sun is exalted in Aries, it is easy for the life of the spirit to come to full expression. Its activity principle along with its assertiveness and high level of intelligence gives it the energy, the impetus, and the understanding to express itself strongly in its element, fire, which can purify the spirit of one, who has an Aries Ascendant or Sun, with cosmic fire to help him become aware of the Oneness of All.

Because Aries is the sign of the birthplace of divine ideas and is the most powerful sign of all, it gives to those with an Aries Ascendant or Sun the capacity to pioneer new beginnings in the instigation and promotion of necessary concepts during the present dawning of the Aquarian Age. Perhaps the cosmos was telling us just this, and that the time is now, because on April 4, 1981 there was a very unusual conjunction of four planets, Sun, Moon, Mars, and Venus at fourteen degrees Aries, just one degree from the center of the sign.

Enthusiasm and power for spiritual evolvement is showered on the Aries person, first, through Martian activity of idealism and struggle, then through Mercurian vision by the awareness of God's Plan and by the harmony achieved in solving the conflict of personality and Soul, and finally through Uranian creative capacity. The combined energies of all three planetary rulers of Aries give him physical energy, mental acuity, and courage to put his creative ideas, consonant with God's Plan, into action.

CHART 15

LEVELS OF EVOLVEMENT FOR ARIES ASCENDANT OR SUN SIGN PERSON

1. The *average* person is subject to the exoteric ruler, Mars. He manifests on a wholly materialistic level, expending his energy on self-centered personality desires such as aggres-

siveness, competitiveness, impulsiveness, greed, and short-temperedness.

2. The *advanced* person is subject mainly to the esoteric ruler, Mercury. He is controlled by his mind rather than his emotions. He also receives the energy of Mars but on a higher level than the average person. Mars together with Mercury gives him the energy, the optimism, and the courage to use his mind, not only to understand and control his emotions but to serve others with logic and reason.

3. The *very advanced* person, being highly intuitive and creative, is subject mainly to the hierarchical ruler, Uranus. He also receives the energies of Mars and Mercury but on a higher level than even the advanced person. He receives optimally the energy, courage, and self-confidence of Mars, the keen reasoning capacity of Mercury, and the intuitive flashes from Uranus—original ideas that come to him when he is concentrating. He is a true pioneer and can open up new paths of learning in the field of his life plan that is consonant with his Soul Ray.

To advance from one level to a higher one, it is necessary for a person to be aware of his weaknesses, to work on transmuting them into certain strengths, and serve others according to the Soul Ray's purpose.

TAURUS

Exoteric ruler—Venus   Esoteric ruler—Vulcan
Hierarchical ruler—Vulcan

A specific type of Light is found in every sign. In Taurus it is a beam of Light received from the divine ideas emanating from Aries, bringing illumination which results in needed changes in attitudes and values, and an uplifting of consciousness.

"And the Word said: Let struggle be undismayed"* applies to one with a Taurus Ascendant or Sun who is manifesting on a personality level. Because of strong materialistic desires for money, possessions, and oversexuality, he has many conflicts resulting from unlearned karmic lessons. He does not lose courage when struggling with his conflicts, but in time is led to the musings of his Soul.

"I see, and when the eye is opened, all is illumined"** applies to a Taurus person who is beginning to manifest on a Soul level. He begins to understand that his conflicts, struggles, and suffering—whether physical, emotional, or financial—are the karmic results of his selfish desires. He now begins to change his selfish desires into concern and help for others, and as a result, finds his needs being met. In addition, he begins to feel that peace and joy for which he has been searching many lifetimes.

Taurus is the most stable sign in the zodiac. A person with a Taurus Ascendant or Sun is not easily swayed by others. Because of his fixed nature, his energy is directed toward having his own way or to overcoming his weaknesses, depending on the vibration level of his energy source. Because it is a sign of strong willpower, serious problems and conflicts arise when Taurus energy is used in self-centered desires for fame, wealth, and oversexuality.

Oversexuality is caused by a strong desire for unity. Within each person there is a longing for continuous unity, but sexual behavior brings only momentary unity. Expecting more from

*Bailey, Alice A., *Esoteric Astrology,* p. 653.
**Bailey, Alice A., *Esoteric Astrology,* p. 654.

something than it can supply causes frustration. A continuous feeling of unity can be achieved by the uplifting of one's consciousness to a very high level, which results in a balance of one's masculine and feminine characteristics. The resulting finely balanced nature then enables him to feel at One with All others.

Great rewarding karmic experiences will be his lot when his energy is used for overcoming weaknesses and helping others. Spiritual illumination can be attained when his determined behavior coincides with his Soul urges. Vulcan, the esoteric and hierarchical ruler of Taurus, can crystallize Universal Truths for him so that they can be used in practical ways. Although Vulcan's presence in our solar system is questioned by astronomy, metaphysicians and Masters of Wisdom are aware of it and its location. However, in the nineteenth century, some astronomers believed there was another planet near Mercury. This belief came about when it was determined that Mercury's rate of perihelion advanced thirty eight seconds of arc per century, faster than theory would indicate. In 1849, in a note to the French Academy of Science, the astronomer Leverrier, urged astronomers to search for transits of an intramercurial planet during eclipses of the Sun. An amateur astronomer, Lescarbuilt, saw the transit of a small object across the Sun. After checking Lescarbuilt's instruments and observations, Leverrier was convinced that Vulcan had been sighted.

CHART 16

LEVELS OF EVOLVEMENT FOR TAURUS ASCENDANT OR SUN SIGN PERSON

1. The *average* person is subject to the exoteric ruler, Venus. He has strong desires for materialistic things such as money and possessions, and physical overindulgences (overeating and oversexuality).

2. The *advanced* person is subject mainly to the esoteric ruler, Vulcan, which gives him intense power to crystallize his guilt feelings, repressions, and other buried undesirables from the

past, bring these to the conscious mind, and through under-standing, destroy them. He also receives the energy of Venus but on a higher level than the average person. Venus helps him feel love toward others. Together Vulcan and Venus help him to lovingly rid himself of unconscious negative attitudes.

3. The *very advanced* person is subject mainly to the hier-archical ruler, Vulcan, which is also the esoteric ruler of Tau-rus. As a hierarchical ruler, Vulcan's energy is used for higher spiritual purposes than with the advanced person. It gives him persistence and the endurance to destroy all his deepest weak-nesses, and also endows him with true lasting unity by tran-scending his sexual energy into creativity. This intense, powerful energy enables him to change his individual will to the Divine Will, which leads to illumination of the highest order and cooperation with God's Plan. He also receives Venus energy but on a higher level than even the advanced person, giving him the capacity to feel unattached love for All.

To advance to a higher level, it is necessary to be aware of one's weaknesses, to work on transmuting them into strengths, and to serve others according to the Soul Ray's purpose.

GEMINI

Exoteric ruler—Mercury   Esoteric ruler—Venus
Hierarchical ruler—Earth

A specific type of Light is found in every sign. In Gemini it is the Light of the interplay of spirit and personality. This Light brings an intellectual reckoning of the results that come from manifesting on a personality level when concern is only for self, as compared to the results of manifesting on a spiritual level when major concern is for others. The Light of the interplay of personality and spirit creates certain karmic effects, either lesson-teaching or rewarding, giving a person with a Gemini Ascendant or Sun an awareness which will in time induce him to lean more and more toward spiritual evolvement and less and less toward materialistic desires.

"And the Word said, let instability do its work"* applies to one who is manifesting on a personality level. Because there is a beginning awareness of two kinds of thought patterns, those of personality desires and those of Soul urges, conflict arises which results in nervous instability. The suffering resultant from the nervous instability coupled with lesson-teaching karma from self-centered choices is the impetus for contacting the Soul. The conflict is then resolved and the instability is eradicated by Soul-infused thought patterns.

"I recognize my other self and in the waning of that self I grow and glow "**applies to one who is beginning to manifest on a Soul level. Such a person is aware of his lower personality concerns but gives them less and less thought while at the same time giving more energy to his real self, his Soul. He grows spiritually and develops a glow, a radiance that can be easily observed by those with a sensitive disposition.

Gemini is the most fluid and adaptable of all signs. It can relate to all of them better than any other sign. It gives sensitivity, a good understanding of people, and a quick reaction to any stimulus.

*Bailey, Alice A., *Esoteric Astrology*, p. 653.
**Bailey, Alice A., *Esoteric Astrology*, p. 654.

A good supply of energy is a characteristic of a Gemini even though the amount is dependent on the level of Soul evolvement. The reason that Gemini has a great deal of energy is because it has affinity with the etheric body which is the energy field that interpenetrates and surrounds the physical body.

Sometimes those with Ascendant or Sun in Gemini seem unstable because of the duality of their nature. There is often a conflict within them, fired by their extreme physical and mental energies, as to whether they want to use their energies to further selfish desires or Soul aspirations. As they begin to work in their Soul evolvement, the conflict and instability lessens until it is completely under control. With their innate great mental and physical energy, they can now make relatively fast Soul progress.

The awareness of the relationship between personality and Soul is found in this sign. Geminis can easily understand the need of the personality to serve the Soul, and the problems that ensue if one lets his personality master his Soul. When a Gemini is manifesting on a Soul level, his radiance attracts many others who also desire to contact their Souls.

CHART 17

LEVELS OF EVOLVEMENT FOR GEMINI ASCENDANT OR SUN SIGN PERSON

1. The *average* person is subject to the exoteric ruler, Mercury. He tends toward irresponsible behavior and emotional instability, resulting in many lesson-teaching experiences and conflicts. Yet this same Mercury energy gives him the ability to relay messages between his mind and the Soul. Though the double-bodied character of the sign, Gemini, precipitates many conflicts, it is only in experiencing and resolving them that real growth can be accomplished; and it is through the exoteric ruler, Mercury, signifying the mind, that he can make contact with his Soul.

2. The *advanced* person is subject mainly to the esoteric ruler, Venus. He attains an integrated personality through the men-

tal energy from Venus, in which the mind becomes the master of the emotions and the physical body, leading to self-realization. He also receives the energy from Mercury, the exoteric ruler, but on a higher level than the average person, giving him greater mind contact between Soul and brain than he had before he advanced.

3. The *very advanced* person is subject mainly to the hierarchical ruler, Earth, giving him a great deal of energy for the experiences and actions needed for serving others. He also receives energies from the exoteric and esoteric rulers, Mercury and Venus, but on a higher level than even the advanced person. These planets give him an easy flow of energy between Soul, brain, and mind. Together, these three rulers help him to use his Soul knowledge in practical ways for serving others.

To advance to a higher level, it is necessary for a person to be aware of his weaknesses, to work on transmuting them into certain strengths, and to serve others according to the Soul Ray's purpose.

CANCER

Exoteric ruler—Moon   Esoteric ruler—Neptune
Hierarchical ruler—Neptune

A specific type of Light is found in every sign. In Cancer it is the Light within the personality. Cancer gives energy for sensitivity and psychic ability, helping one become aware of the reasons for his suffering when manifesting on a personality, self-centered level. This awareness gives impetus to the search for a better way of life and getting in touch with one's Soul.

"And the Word said: Let isolation be the rule and yet the crowd exists"* applies to a person who is manifesting on a personality, self-centered level. He has a tendency to withdraw and isolate himself from others when his hypersensitive nature causes him suffering. He has not yet learned that he cannot be hurt emotionally unless he allows it to happen, and that when he is wronged, it is a karmic lesson resulting from his own past wrongs. Once he accepts lesson-teaching karmic experiences without irritation, he will have no more need to withdraw. Until he makes these wisdoms a part of his being, because of his feelings of insecurity, he has a strong urge to isolate himself when the going gets rough. Yet he finds it impossible to exist separately from others, which brings him added suffering. It is often in suffering and in crises that a person begins to change thought patterns and to realize that only by raising his level of consciousness can he attain a higher degree of happiness.

"I build a lighted house and therein dwell,"**applies to a person who is manifesting on a Soul level. Through understanding and self-discipline he begins to realize that he will no longer allow himself to feel insecure because of what others do or fail to do to or for him. He can now accept the wrongdoings of others without irritation, knowing that these are lesson-teaching experiences that will help him to evolve. As he dwells more and more in the lighted house he is building for himself,

*Bailey, Alice A., *Esoteric Astrology,* p. 653.
**Bailey, Alice A., *Esoteric Astrology,* p. 654.

his suffering becomes less and less, and his joy of living becomes greater and greater. His psychic capacity, which in the past was used in feeling sorry for himself, is now used for inspiration and for awareness of the needs of others who become aware of his nurturing capacity and come to him for aid. Cancer bestows much psychic sensitivity which is used either for self-centered purposes which create difficult karmic experiences, or for humanitarian purposes which create rewarding karmic experiences.

As water purifies the physical body, so does every water sign purify the personality. In Cancer, water purifies through emotional experiences. When a Cancer person is concerned only for self, he goes through intense emotional suffering which is an effective lesson-teaching experience leading to concern for others. Cancer is the most nurturing of all signs, and when Cancer Ascendant and Sun sign people are in contact with their Souls, they often take into their homes and bring back to self-sufficiency those who could not at that particular time fend for themselves.

Cancer persons instinctively know what the majority of people are thinking and what their needs are. Counselling and business are among the many fields in which their talents can be used successfully.

CHART 18

LEVELS OF EVOLVEMENT FOR CANCER ASCENDANT OR SUN SIGN PERSON

1. The *average* person is subject to the exoteric ruler, Moon. He allows himself to be ruled by his emotions, and as a result of his hypersensitivity, his feelings are hurt very easily. He then has a tendency to withdraw. Having a psychic and sensitive nature, and more than likely not understanding the Law of Karma, he suffers greatly. He is very aware of others' weaknesses but has not learned that he is his own creator and that others wrong him because of his wrongs of the past, and that in experiencing difficult karma, he is learning to overcome his own weaknesses.

2. The *advanced* person is subject mainly to the esoteric ruler, Neptune. Neptune energy helps him make contact with his Soul in order to become aware of his weaknesses and to work toward overcoming them. He is also subject to the Moon, the exoteric ruler, but on a higher level than the average person. The Moon's energy in this category, when combined with that of Neptune, helps him to tune in to others' needs and to serve them to the best of his ability.

3. The *very advanced* person is subject mainly to the hierarchical ruler, Neptune. Even though Neptune is also the esoteric ruler of Cancer, as a hierarchical ruler in this category it gives higher vibrational energy than for level two. Neptune offers deeper Soul contact so that one with a Cancer Ascendant or Sun not only can become more aware of his weaknesses and the best ways to transmute them, but he can begin to feel at One with All. He no longer feels hurt when someone wrongs him, but is now aware that his Soul, in attracting that person to him, is teaching him a karmic lesson. His sensitivity now helps him to know that often those lowest on the evolutionary scale need the most love and nurturing, and that he can give it successfully by sensing just what each person needs and how to best fill that need.

To advance to a higher level, it is necessary to be aware of one's weaknesses, to work on transmuting them into strengths, and to serve others according to his Soul Ray's purpose.

LEO

Exoteric ruler—Sun   Esoteric ruler—Sun
Hierarchical ruler—Sun

A specific type of Light is found in every sign. In Leo it is
the Light of the Soul. In the Age of Leo, man first manifested
on the Earth plane as an entity with an individual Soul. Previously, many species of animals, each of which manifested as
a group Soul, were the closest to humanity. One with a Leo
Ascendant or Sun is very aware of the power and Light of his
individual Soul, which awareness leads him to self-realization.
He feels good about himself because of the special Light that
comes from his Soul. He knows who he is, a god in the making;
a divine spark glows brightly within him, waiting to burst out
in all its glory.

"And the Word said: Let other forms exist. I rule,"* applies
to one with a Leo Ascendant or Sun manifesting on a personality level. Like the proud lion, he tries to be the center of
attention and the one to whom, he believes, all others should
be subservient. Aware of the power within him, but not yet
aware of its optimal use, he alienates others, resulting in difficult karmic experiences.

"I am That and That am I,"** applies to one who is beginning
to manifest on a Soul level. Because of his past karmic suffering
while manifesting on a personality level, he is now aware that
he is not better or worse than others even though some may
have reached a higher level of evolvement and some may not
have reached his level. Yet he still feels that surge of power
within him, but it is now directed toward helping others because he knows that in helping them reach their destiny, he
will fulfill his own destiny. He knows his real essence is of his
Soul. He knows now who he really is—a god in the making.
With this knowledge he climbs to undreamed of heights, becoming a self-realized person who is in attunement with his
Soul and Personality Rays.

*Bailey, Alice A., *Esoteric Astrology,* p. 653.
**Bailey, Alice., *Esoteric Astrology,* p. 654.

Self-consciousness and self-awareness leading to personality integration and self-realization are the Leo trademarks. These are desirable traits because, unless one is aware of who he is and what he can become, he can be of little help to himself or to others in Soul evolvement. All zodiacal energies are used either destructively or constructively. When used destructively, a Leo with nothing of true worth to give others, may be domineering and try to be the center of attention. If the energy is used constructively, he will feel good about himself, will work with courage toward his own potential, and will inspire others to do the same. He will then have earned the leadership for which he is qualified.

Leo energy gives one the will and determination to acquire knowledge and to formulate a definite plan for his life's service. He has the courage to be what he can be.

All three fire signs are conducive to optimistic and spiritual aspirational dispositions, yet the fire in Leo (the Sun in this sign occurs during the hottest time of the year) is the most intense, fixed, and determined. In Leo, everything that hinders divine expression can be burned and destroyed.

CHART 19

LEVELS OF EVOLVEMENT FOR LEO ASCENDANT OR SUN SIGN PERSON

1. The *average* person is subject to the exoteric ruler, the Sun. Though he has good physical vitality, he uses it for self-centered desires, wanting praise and with the urge to dominate others, he strives to be the center of attention. As a result of his pride and because his motivation is not for the good of others, he suffers many difficult experiences.

2. The *advanced* person is subject mainly to the esoteric ruler, the Sun veiling Neptune. He has more physical vitality than the average Leo person. He has a need to be a magnanimous ruler, someone who is concerned less for himself than for those he leads or rules. His compassion for the suffering increases his inspirational capacity to come up with successful

ideas for leadership and to give love to those he leads.

3. The *very advanced* person is subject mainly to the hierarchical ruler, the Sun veiling Uranus. He receives the energy of both the exoteric and esoteric rulers also, but on a higher level than even the advanced person. His physical vitality is greater, his motivation is on a higher level, his capacity for inspiration and creativity is enhanced, and his love for others is deeper and more unattached. He is primarily subject to the hierarchical ruler, the Sun veiling Uranus. This gives him the ability to fuse his Leo energy with its polarity, Aquarius, making it possible for him to attain self-realization and serve humanity in rapport with Aquarian Age principles, the foremost of which is unattached love.

To advance to a higher level, it is necessary for a person to be aware of his weaknesses, to work on transmuting them into strengths, and to serve others according to his Soul Ray's purpose.

VIRGO

Exoteric ruler—Mercury   Esoteric ruler—Moon
Hierarchical rule—Jupiter

A specific type of Light is found in every sign. In Virgo it is the blended Light of matter and Soul. Virgo energy helps one become aware of the Soul housed in its personality and of how the personality comprising the physical body, the emotional body, and the concrete mind can be of service to the Soul in blending the Soul's urges with the personality expression.

"And the Word said: Let matter reign,"* applies to one with a Virgo Ascendant or Sun who is manifesting on a personality level. He is of the earth, and materialistic concerns such as money, possessions, and honor are uppermost in his thoughts. But his analytical mind tells him that the results of these desires do not bring him happiness. He searches for something better, and finding it in spiritual matters, begins to manifest on a Soul level.

"I am the Mother and the Child. I god, I matter am,"** applies to one who is beginning to manifest on a Soul level. He realizes that he is both matter and Soul and that his physical body is the temple of his Soul. It is through the physical body that karmic experiences for lesson-teaching reasons can occur and it is through the physical body that serving others takes place, both of which are necessary for Soul evolvement. The Mother (matter-physical body) gives birth to the Christ Child (Soul). For this reason Virgo is the sign of the Christ consciousness.

Virgo gives energy for gestation, awakening, shielding, nurturing, and revealing the Christ Consciousness. Although it is the sign of perfection, initially it manifests in the average person as criticism of others' weaknesses. Though fairly accurate in depicting the shortcomings of others because of his keen analytical ability, the Virgo person often is not aware of the harm he does whether in thought or words, but he soon receives his lesson-teaching karma from which he can learn easily. This

---

*Bailey, Alice A., *Esoteric Astrology*, p. 653.

**Bailey, Alice A., *Esoteric Astrology*, p. 654.

awakening precipitates the gestation of the Christ consciousness within him with the realization that his task is not to
dwell on the wrongs of others but to perfect himself. As he does,
he is able to see the good in others and be indifferent to the
wrongs, while at the same time probe his own mind with his
keen analytical faculty for becoming aware of and working
toward overcoming his own weaknesses. When he is well advanced on this road through nurturing the Christ Consciousness within, he then is able to put his discriminative abilities
to constructive use in successfully serving others, thus finally
revealing the Christ Consciousness.

CHART 20

LEVELS OF EVOLVEMENT FOR VIRGO ASCENDANT OR SUN SIGN PERSON

1. The *average* person is subject to the exoteric ruler, Mercury. The mind sorts out his experiences, and analyzes the
results of those experiences, and in time puts him in contact
with his Soul. The mind working as a mediator between Soul
and matter enables him to fit into the next category after he
has had enough self-centered experiences resulting in karmic
suffering.

2. The *advanced* person is subject mainly to the esoteric
ruler, the Moon veiling Vulcan and Neptune. This combination
gives him the sensitivity and inspiration of the Moon and Neptune to contact his Soul, and the energy to feel deeply the power
of Vulcan which can dredge weaknesses from his unconscious
and get rid of them. He also receives the energy of the exoteric
ruler, Mercury, but on a higher level than the average person.
Here Mercury along with Moon veiling Neptune and Vulcan
gives him all the types of energy necessary to subordinate his
personality desires to his Soul aspirations.

3. The *very advanced* person is subject mainly to the hierarchical ruler, Jupiter. This gives him the ability to understand
certain Universal Laws and spiritual wisdoms, and the capacity to feel real love for humanity. He also receives the energy

of the exoteric ruler, Mercury, and the esoteric ruler, Moon
veiling Vulcan and Neptune, but on a higher level than even
the advanced person. Here, the synthesis of all these energies
enables one with a Virgo Ascendant or Sun to benefit optimally,
because of unattached love, from the understanding of such
Universal Laws as Reincarnation and Karma by implementing
them to contact his Soul and eliminate weaknesses.

To advance from one level to a higher one, it is necessary to
be aware of one's weaknesses, to work on transmuting them
into certain strengths, and to serve others according to his Soul
Ray's purpose.

138

LIBRA

Exoteric ruler—Venus   Esoteric ruler—Uranus
Hierarchical ruler—Saturn

A specific type of Light is found in every sign. In Libra it is the Light that moves to center itself at a point of balance. Here there is the will, however subtle, to express harmony between spirit and matter. Libra energy helps balance the life of the spirit and the personality with neither dominating. The Libran has the capability of weighing values by seeing both sides of a problem, and the intuition for making good decisions, especially in matters of relationships, law, sex, and money.

"And the Word said: Let choice be made,"* applies to one who is manifesting on a personality level. Because Libra is the sign of the scales (weighing one decision against another), it is the sign in which one decides either to delve more deeply into matter through strong personality desires or to start climbing the spiritual ladder by getting rid of weaknesses and helping others according to his Soul Ray's urges.

"I choose the way that leads between the two great lines of force,"** applies to one who is starting to manifest on a Soul level. The two great lines of force are the materialistic desires (such as for money, possessions, and fame) and spiritual aspirations. A person with a Libra Ascendant or Sun may have a strong urge to continue his materialistic desires but at the same time to feel burgeoning spiritual urges. His reasoning mind, intuition, and balancing capacity (trademarks of the Libra potential) tell him to choose between these two lines of force—the Soul being both matter and spirit and the bridge between matter and spirit. Before a person can become one with spirit as have all avatars, he must manifest on a Soul level. As Christ said two thousand years ago, "None can go to the Father but through Me." God, the Father, is analogous to spirit, and God, the Son, is analogous to the Soul and the Christ Consciousness.

*Bailey, Alice A., *Esoteric Astrology,* p. 653.
**Bailey, Alice A., *Esoteric Astrology,* p. 654.

Libra is the most social of all signs. Relationships are essential to the Libran and help him immensely in his Soul evolvement because he has the ability to weigh cause and effect, therefore learning much from each relationship. He could be a successful counsellor or mediator because he can tune in to all sides of a conflict and offer just and fair solutions.

If he is manifesting on a low level of consciousness, he tries to be all things to all people, and ends up being indecisive. He would do well to acquire the integrity of Aries, Libra's polarity, which he instinctively will do as he begins to manifest on a higher level.

Balance, justice, cooperation, peace, and beauty are the essence of the character of the Libran, and it is through the utilization of these characteristics that he makes his contribution to humanity.

CHART 21

LEVELS OF EVOLVEMENT FOR LIBRA ASCENDANT OR SUN SIGN PERSON

1. The *average* person is subject to the exoteric ruler, Venus. He has a strong desire for close, peaceful relationships, for beauty in his surroundings, and for affection from others. His logical mind leads him to give affection to others solely in order to receive it. His concern is self-indulgent, and he therefore attracts only those who are of like mind and not able to give true love to others. In time he realizes that what he needs—real love, peace, and beauty—can be attained only as he gives of himself freely without expecting anything in return. He then becomes an advanced person.

2. The *advanced* person is subject mainly to the esoteric ruler, Uranus. This gives him the capacity to feel unattached love for others and the intuition to know that his basic needs for peace and beauty will be met as he gives love with no strings attached. He also receives the energy of the exoteric ruler, Venus, but on a higher level than the average person. His

logical mind tells him that all good comes to him to the extent that he is deserving. He eliminates his strong desires and uses that energy to serve others with love, thus finding more than he desired previously. The energy of Venus coupled with Uranus puts him very much in tune with the Aquarian Age, and gives him a charisma which attracts others to him. He begins to feel a freedom to do what his conscience tells him to do, no longer being bound by man-made dogmas and the creeds of certain religions.

3. The *very advanced* person is subject primarily to the hierarchical ruler, Saturn. The Saturn energy gives him persistence to identify his weaknesses, to transmute them into strengths, and to serve others. He also receives the energies of the exoteric and esoteric rulers, Venus and Uranus, but on a higher level than even the advanced person. Saturn, together with Venus and Uranus, give him the joy, the intuition, and an urge to work persistently in using Aquarian Age principles in a practical, useful manner for himself and others. One of the most important of these principles is that each person is responsible for his emotional, physical, and spiritual health, and through the understanding of certain Universal Laws such as Reincarnation and Karma, he can benefit greatly.

To advance to a higher level, it is necessary to be aware of one's weaknesses, to work on transmuting them into certain strengths, and to serve others according to his Soul Ray's purpose.

SCORPIO

Exoteric ruler—Pluto   Esoteric ruler—Mars
Hierarchical ruler—Mercury

A specific type of Light is found in every sign. In Scorpio it is the Light of Day in which three Lights meet and blend—the Light of the personality, the Light of the Soul, and the Light of the Spirit. The symbols for these three Lights are the scorpion, the eagle, and the phoenix.

The Light of the personality is symbolized by the scorpion. The scorpion uses its tail to sting enemies to death, or when unable to escape, stings itself to death. For a person with a Scorpion Ascendant or Sun this signifies a deep involvement with materialistic, self-centered desires such as vengeance and the misuse of sèx. These characteristics start out creating problems for others, but ultimately lead to the Scorpio's own downfall if no changes are made in these powerful desires.

The Light of the Soul is the bridge between the personality and the Spirit. As a blend of both, it is symbolized by the eagle, which represents the ability to rise to a higher level, to fly above materialistic concerns, to leave behind difficult karma and the suffering it entails as a result of the lessons learned.

The Light of the Spirit is symbolized by the phoenix. Just as in the legend of the phoenix which gives up its life and from its ashes is born a better and more noble being, the Light of the Spirit enables a Scorpio to give up his life of personality-centered desires for one of service to others, and in giving up the old, finds a more satisfying, successful, and joyful life.

"And the Word said: Let Maya flourish and let deception rule,"* applies to one who is manifesting on a personality level. Scorpio is the sign of intense power, and in this case the power is used for delving deeply and intensely into areas that are not of the Soul, but are personality desires for revenge, for accumulating wealth for selfish reasons, for fame, and for the misuse of sex. A person operating on this level is deceived into thinking that his real being is the self-centered, indulgent per-

*Bailey, Alice A., *Esoteric Astrology,* p. 653.

142

sonality. In time, such a person has difficult lesson-teaching karmic experiences, suffers greatly, and then becomes aware of his real Self and listens to the stirrings of his Soul.

"Warrior I am and from the battle I emerge triumphant,"* applies to a person who is beginning to manifest on a Soul level. It is not easy to live through the sign of Scorpio because of its intense power. Because it offers many choices, it is a sign of severe testing and yet one in which great spiritual progress can be made. Scorpio energy is used courageously to fight the tendency toward selfish personality desires in order to transmute this energy into spiritual aspirations.

Scorpio is probably the most difficult sign to experience as one's Ascendant or Sun because it is the sign of the greatest temptations and testing. Every fire and water sign has the potential for purification, but in Scorpio it often takes place as a result of the many experiences and lessons learned from the testing. It is also the most intensely energized of all signs; a Scorpio can either fall to the very depths of his being or raise himself to great spiritual heights. If he chooses to indulge in selfish concerns without considering the welfare of others, through the intensity innate in his sign, he suffers very difficult karmic experiences. The results of this suffering impel him to change his personality desires to spiritual aspirations. For this reason many Scorpios dwell on the heights of their spirits and are a source of inspiration to others.

CHART 22

LEVELS OF EVOLVEMENT FOR SCORPIO ASCENDANT OR SUN SIGN PERSON

1. The *average* person is subject to the exoteric ruler, Pluto, which gives him intense power that is used mostly in the satisfaction of self-centered, materialistic desires. He suffers greatly from lesson-teaching induced karma.

*Bailey, Alice A., *Esoteric Astrology*, p. 654.

2. The *advanced* person is subject primarily to the esoteric ruler, Mars, which gives him the courage and energy to fight selfish desires of his personality. He also receives the energy of Pluto, but on a higher level than the average person. The energy of Pluto coupled with that of Mars gives him the drive and the power to destroy unwholesome desires, to survive crises, and to bring hidden weaknesses from the unconscious and destroy them.

3. The *very advanced* person is subject mainly to the hierarchical ruler, Mercury, which gives him a keen awareness of the difference between lesson-teaching karma resulting from the selfish use of energy, and rewarding karma resulting from the proper use of energy for the good of All. He is also subject to the energies of the exoteric and esoteric rulers, Pluto and Mars, but on a higher level even than the advanced person. The combined energies of these three ruling planets in this category enable him, through mastering his emotions, to use his intense power courageously not only in bringing himself to spiritual heights but in uplifting others.

To advance to a higher level, it is necessary for a person to be aware of his weaknesses, to work on transmuting them into strengths, and to serve others according to his Soul Ray's purpose.

SAGITTARIUS

Exoteric ruler—Jupiter   Esoteric ruler—Earth
Hierarchical ruler—Mars

The Light in Sagittarius is a beam of focused Light that reveals greater Light. The energy of Sagittarius is the most goal-directed and one-pointed sign of the zodiac. One goal is reached after another, each at a higher level than the one that precedes it. All fire and water signs purify so that there may be divine expression, but each in a different way. In Sagittarius the physical body is purified by fire, and the one-pointed consciousness burns brightly toward successive goals.

"And the Word said: Let food be sought,"* applies to one who is manifesting on a personality level. His ambitions center in materialistic matters and he one-pointedly devotes most of his time and energy to such concerns as career advancement, increased income, prestige, and fame.

"I see the goal. I reach the goal and see another,"** applies to one who is beginning to manifest on a Soul level. He is aware of something beyond and better than mundane desires. The realization that if he uses his time and energy to reach a spiritual goal, his mundane needs will be satisfied—the real meaning of "Seek ye first the Kingdom of God, and all else will come unto you" is sinking deep within his consciousness. As his seeking continues, the goals appear before him, each successively higher as far as his spiritual vision reaches.

Sagittarius is the optimal sign for the teaching of Universal Laws and spiritual concepts. It is not only a fire sign denoting honesty, love, confidence, and the search for truth, but is also a mutable sign which provides the urge to teach and the flexibility to change concepts and values when warranted.

Because of its one-pointedness and ability to get to the heart of a matter quickly along with its frankness, honesty, and outspokeness, it is the least tactful of all signs. As one with a Sagittarius Ascendant or Sun evolves spiritually, he learns the

*Bailey, Alice A., *Esoteric Astrology*, p. 653.

**Bailey, Alice A., *Esoteric Astrology*, p. 654.

wisdom of weighing his words and using only those which convey truth without hurt.

He can look far into the future and often see, beyond many of his brothers, that peace and joy are the rewards of those who set spiritual goals and work toward them.

CHART 23

LEVELS OF EVOLVEMENT FOR SAGITTARIUS ASCENDANT OR SUN SIGN PERSON

1. The *average* person is subject to the exoteric ruler, Jupiter. He has confidence, enthusiasm, and is goal-directed, but he thinks erroneously that the materialistic goals are the only ones worth working toward.

2. The *advanced* person is subject primarily to the esoteric ruler, Earth, giving him the physical energy and opportunities for many materialistic experiences, and the intellectual perception of the nuances and ramifications of the resulting karmic lessons. He also receives the energy of the exoteric ruler, Jupiter, but on a higher level than the average person. The energy of Jupiter coupled with that of Earth gives him the enthusiasm, confidence, and optimism to change from self-centered desires to spiritual aspirations and the knowledge to become aware of the benefits he will receive from the change.

3. The *very advanced* person is subject mainly to the hierarchical ruler, Mars, giving him immense energy and courage to reach successive spiritual goals in a relatively short time. The combined energies of Jupiter, Earth, and Mars enable him to see each new vision clearly, direct his course toward it, and by his accomplishments benefit not only himself but many others in day-to-day living.

To advance to a higher level, it is necessary for a person to be aware of his weaknesses, to work on transmuting them into strengths, and to serve others according to his Soul Ray's purpose.

146

CAPRICORN

Exoteric ruler—Saturn   Esoteric ruler—Saturn
Hierarchical ruler—Venus

In Capricorn the Light is the Light of Initiation which helps one with a Capricorn Ascendant or Sun to raise his consciousness to a much higher level. The self-discipline and persistence characteristic of the Capricorn person make him a candidate for initiation. When one starts to change self-centered desires into spiritual aspirations in order to overcome weaknesses and serve others consonant with his Soul Ray, he has attained the First Initiation. After he has attained the First Initiation, whether in a past life or the present one, he is capable of attaining the Second Initiation. When he has learned to use his mind, through understanding, to control his emotions, he has attained the Second Initiation. There are a number of initiations beyond the second, but most of us are working toward the first two. Capricorn strength and humility are essential for attaining an initiation on a higher level. This sign has affinity with the bony structure of the body, particularly the knees (symbolical of kneeling in humility).

"And the Word said: Let ambition rule and the door stands wide,"* applies to one who is manifesting on a personality level. His driving ambition will assure wealth and an outstanding position. His choices are many because he is a hard, consistent worker, is self-disciplined, disciplines his employees, and is well organized. He puts so much time and effort into achievement that he has little left to enjoy the flowers on the way. Therefore, he very often reaches an impressive position and accumulates great wealth, but he has little left of himself to give to people. A greedy and cold disposition creates many difficult lesson-teaching experiences for him.

"Lost am I in light supernal, yet on that light I turn my back,"** applies to one who is manifesting on a Soul level. When he becomes aware that the capacity for discipline and

*Bailey, Alice A., *Esoteric Astrology,* p. 653.
**Bailey, Alice A., *Esoteric Astrology,* p. 654.

hard work that was used to attain prestige and wealth did not bring him happiness, but only loneliness, he uses his attributes to overcome his weaknesses. In so doing he is bathed in light and joy, and symbolically he comes back down from the mountain top to serve others in the valley below. Because he has made progress in his Soul growth, he wishes to give of himself to others. In helping others attain his level of evolvement, he himself attains a still higher level.

Those with a Capricorn Ascendant or Sun, though considered by many to be slow and plodding, do accomplish much over time. They are steady, cautious, cool, and well organized and do not take long rest or recreational periods. Their self-discipline and reliability are usually very high, enabling them to accomplish much more over a long period than many of other signs who work in enthusiastic spurts, and thus need more time for recuperation.

When manifesting on a low consciousness level, they are self-centered and greedy, showing no love or concern for others. When manifesting on a higher level, they provide a sense of stability to those who need it; they can work long hours during emergencies without collapsing; they can be an inspiration to those who are not self-directed; and they can move to a much higher level of Soul evolvement through overcoming weaknesses and serving others.

CHART 24

LEVELS OF EVOLVEMENT FOR CAPRICORN ASCENDANT OR SUN SIGN PERSON

1. The *average* person is subject to the exoteric ruler, Saturn. He works hard, is ambitous, selfish, and desirous of the prestige of advancement. His symbol is the goat—the greedy seeker for satisfaction of desires. Because the energy of Saturn gives lesson-teaching karma almost instantly, he suffers many restrictions and problems. The most prevalent being the lack of love

from others because of his coldness and unconcern for them. "Scrooge" must have been a Capricorn in this category.

2. The *advanced* person is subject to the esoteric ruler, which is also Saturn, but the energy is used on a higher than average level. Having experienced the difficult karmic lessons resulting from selfish materialistic concerns before he advanced to this level, he devotes more time to Soul evolvement. He begins to feel concern for others and his coldness slowly turns to warmth and care for them. His symbol is the crocodile—which lives both in the water and on land. The water symbolizes Capricorn's desire for high position and wealth without concern for others. The land symbolizes discipline used in changing materialistic desires into spiritual aspirations. Like the crocodile, he goes back and forth from the water of self-concern to the land of concern for others. Eventually, having tasted both, he realizes he must make a choice, not only for his benefit but for that of others.

3. The *very advanced* person is subject to the hierarchical ruler, Venus. He uses his mind logically toward Soul evolvement and as he begins to understand Universal Truths, he implements them in his life. He also receives the energy of Saturn, but on a higher level than even the advanced person. Together, Venus and Saturn give him the understanding of Universal Laws, such as Reincarnation and Karma, and the self-control and discipline to benefit from them. His symbol is the unicorn, its one horn like a spear upon its brow, symbolizing one-pointedness toward Soul evolvement.

AQUARIUS

Exoteric ruler—Uranus   Esoteric ruler—Jupiter
Hierarchical ruler—Moon

In Aquarius the light is the Light that shines on earth, cleansing it. This Light is becoming brighter as we progress into the Aquarian Age from its starting point in 1945. Although we are now only in the dawning of the New Age, we are beginning to benefit from the cleansing effect of its Light. Even though the Age of Pisces was heralded by Christ's Ministry of love and service to humanity, it soon became altered by the growing power of the church through the imposition of dogmas, creeds, and laws. The concepts of the Age of Pisces with its organizèd religions and authoritarian laws have served their purpose and, no longer needed, are being cleansed from the consciousness of humanity by the Light of Aquarius. These concepts are being replaced by those needed at the present evolutionary level of the race. Such concepts include the freedom of the individual to think, speak, and act according to his conscience—not according to the man-made rules of certain churches. Another Aquarian Age concept that is being more widely accepted is Reincarnation. We all have had different past lives with different experiences, and are at different levels of evolvement. The belief is growing that we cannot, in all fairness, judge what is right for another. The Aquarian Cleansing Light is developing our intuition so that we can more easily contact the God within to receive needed answers and to perceive a Oneness of All, leading to unattached love.

"And the Word said: Let desire in form be ruler,"* applies to one who is manifesting on a personality level. Independence and freedom from responsibility are uppermost in his thoughts so that self-centered desires can be satisfied. Rebellious and erratic, he is ruled by his desires; he insists that he will do what he wants when he wants, regardless of the concerns and needs of others.

*Bailey, Alice A., *Esoteric Astrology*, p. 653.

"Water of life am I, poured forth for thirsty men,"** applies to one who is manifesting on a Soul level. He believes in the freedom of the individual to be guided by his own conscience; he feels unattached love for all, regardless of race, color, age, sex, or religion. Sensing this, others reach out to him and are served by him.

Aquarius, more than any other sign, is synonymous with world service. True brotherhood and Oneness are the products of the Aquarian energy that is acceleratingly reaching the Earth in this, the Aquarian Age.

All disciplines that are directed toward humanitarian service are linked with Aquarius. Esoteric Astrology and Esoteric Psychology when practiced by New Age leaders, who themselves are progressing spiritually, will become the most useful tools for helping mankind reach the optimal level of joyful living that the Aquarian Age promises. It is in these two disciplines that people can be helped to become aware of their weaknesses, strengths, and abilities, and to eradicate their weaknesses and use their strengths and abilities for their life plan consonant with their Soul and Personality Rays.

The present Aquarian Age is the Age of consciousness raising, the Age in which all mankind will again become aware of Ancient Wisdoms and Universal Laws, the Age in which the understanding of these Wisdoms and Laws will become paramount. An understanding of Reincarnation, Karma, Esoteric Psychology, and Ray-Centered Astrology will be basic to the education of all.

Many New Age concepts which are now being introduced slowly into the consciousness of humanity, and which are necessary aids for spiritual evolvement at this time, will become commonplace as this Age advances. Some of these concepts are: the presence of God within each of us, and the freedom to think, speak, and act according to one's conscience which will replace the manipulative authoritative pronouncements of certain religious leaders; the realization of the joy that is attainable once we can progress to a certain Soul level, no matter how many lives it takes, is replacing the hell-and-damnation thought forms expressed in many present religions; the universal un-

**Bailey, Alice A., *Esoteric Astrology*, p. 654.

attached love evolving from increased awareness of the Oneness of All is replacing the concept of giving, by both individuals and nations, only to receive.

The world needs leaders to bring these and other consciousness-raising concepts to the minds and hearts of all people. It
is those with the Ascendant, Sun, or even planets or important
points in Aquarius who can become these leaders.

The energy from the sign Aquarius is increasing in potency
as this Age progresses. This energy may be used by some who
are operating on a low consciousness level, especially those
with an Aquarius Ascendant or Sun, with a desire for freedom
yet a lack of determination to work responsibly to bring the
desire to fruition. In its growing pains, the earth can become
either a place of chaos or a place where brotherly love prevails;
it depends on how we use this Aquarian energy.

CHART 25

LEVELS OF EVOLVEMENT FOR AQUARIUS ASCENDANT OR SUN SIGN PERSON

1. The *average* person is subject to the exoteric ruler, Uranus.
He desires freedom without responsibility. He is apt to rebel
against authority when he believes, often rightly, that conditions should be changed. Being unpredictable and erratic in
his behavior, he is liable to revolt against what he believes is
wrong without offering something better, sometimes causing
damage.

2. The *advanced* person is subject to the esoteric ruler, Jupiter, which helps him understand certain Universal Laws and
Ancient Wisdoms. He also receives the energy of Uranus, but
on a higher level than the average person. Jupiter, together
with Uranus, gives him the intuition to perceive what needs
to be changed, and to make the change at a time and in a way
that is conducive to the betterment of others. Uranus, the exoteric ruler of Aquarius, is the ruler of Ray Seven in which
spirit and matter meet, indicating that these energies are conducive to the acceleration of contact with one's Soul in this

New Age. When contact is made, the esoteric ruler of Aquarius, Jupiter, which is the ruler of Ray Two, confers love and wisdom.

3. The *very advanced* person is subject to the hierarchical ruler, the Moon veiling Vulcan, providing the power to crystallize wrong thought patterns in the unconscious, to bring them into the conscious mind, and to release them. He also is influenced by the exoteric and esoteric rulers, Uranus and Jupiter, but on a higher level than the advanced person. He is more intuitive and more aware of the Universal Laws and Ancient Wisdoms, understands them better, and uses them more beneficially in making changes consonant with God's Plan. Because he is very advanced, he is able to help others make the progress he has made.

To advance to a higher level, it is necessary to be aware of one's weaknesses, to work on transmuting them into strengths, and to serve others according to the Soul Ray's purpose.

PISCES

Exoteric ruler—Neptune   Esoteric ruler—Pluto
Hierarchical ruler—Pluto

In Pisces the light is the Light of the World that ends the darkness of matter. The energy of Pisces helps one become aware of the Light that leads to joy and spiritual concerns which end the darkness and suffering resulting from undue emphasis on materialism. The realization of the Oneness of All and the recognition of the suffering of those residing in the darkness of materialism impels the Pisces person to bring them into the Light through compassion and kindness. One kind deed for a sufferer in the darkness, motivated by compassion and love, is often enough to bring him to the spiritual Path.

"And the Word said: Go forth into matter,"* applies to one who is manifesting on a personality level. He needs experiences on the earth plane to learn his karmic lessons. All fire and water signs purify the entity, but each in a different way. In Pisces it is accomplished through repeated incarnations on earth.

"I leave the Father's Home and turning back, I save,"** applies to one who is manifesting on a Soul level. Because he has made much progress in overcoming his weaknesses and in serving others, he is entitled to a great deal of help from those more evolved than he, but he chooses instead to turn back to where he once was and again help those who have not attained his level. Since his motivation was compassion, and not merely to do good to uplift himself, he finds he has been raised to a still higher level and receives help, either knowingly or unknowingly, from more advanced entities because of his higher auric emanations.

Pisces is the most empathetic sign of the zodiac. It can also be the most compassionate and kindest of all signs. The energies of this sign, more than any other, help one dissolve egotistic, separative feelings in order to become at One with all

*Bailey, Alice A., *Esoteric Astrology*, p. 653.
**Bailey, Alice A., *Esoteric Astrology*, p. 654.

people. If he is manifesting on a low level of consciousness, he may attract to himself similar thoughts of others, both incarnate and discarnate, which can be very difficult. This suffering will in time impel him to lift his thoughts and thus not only be able to feel peace within himself and transmit it to others, but help him receive inspiration in applying his talents. Persons with problems, especially those of a sensitive nature, can receive much help from the gentleness of those with a Pisces Ascendant or Sun.

CHART 26

LEVELS OF EVOLVEMENT FOR PISCES ASCENDANT OR SUN SIGN PERSON

1. The *average* person is subject to the exoteric ruler, Neptune. Being of a sensitive nature, he is easily influenced by the thoughts and feelings of those around him and by the thought forms floating in the ether. He attracts to himself the thoughts or thought forms of the same nature and intensity as his own. When his thoughts are of a low vibration, lacking understanding and love toward others, the added similar thoughts he receives can be very difficult to cope with. For this reason those with a Pisces ascendant or Sun who habitually harbor wrong thoughts have a tendency to escape reality through drugs, alcohol, overeating, illness, or withdrawal, with the result that any of these in any combination makes his problem more difficult. The only solution lies in his determination to raise his level of consciousness by teaching himself to think good thoughts. Because like attracts like, and energy follows thought, it is impossible to absorb the negative thoughts of others at a time one's own thoughts are constructive, kind, and loving. By understanding the Law of Karma, he will know that people with certain weaknesses will come into his life to teach him needed lessons. Through this understanding he can give compassion, kindness, and love to those who wrong him, and in

this giving he attracts to himself the loving thoughts of those on a higher level, and finally the peace he so strongly desires becomes his.

2. The *advanced* person is subject to the esoteric ruler, Pluto, which gives him enormous will power to raise his consciousness to a higher level. He has the ability to delve into his unconscious to see what is hidden and impeding his Soul progress, and to bring this material into his conscious mind in order to deal with and dissolve it. He also receives the energy of Neptune, but on a higher level than the average person. Together, the energies of Pluto and Neptune help him change his feelings of self-pity into compassion for and kindness to those who wrong him, and to change his negative thinking into positive thinking. He now is able to receive positive, loving, inspirational thoughts from others.

3. The *very advanced* person is subject to the hierarchical ruler, Pluto, which is also the esoteric ruler. However, in this category, he receives the energy of Pluto on a higher level than the advanced person in that his will power for overcoming his weaknesses is stronger, and that he has the aspiration and ability to change his individual will to Divine Will by helping others who have not yet attained his Soul level. He also receives the energy of the exoteric ruler, Neptune, but on a higher level than even the advanced person in that his psychic sensitivity is more enhanced and his inspirational, creative capacity is greater.

To advance to a higher level, it is necessary to be aware of one's weaknesses, to work on transmuting them into strengths, and to serve others according to the Soul Ray's purpose.

Before a Ray-Centered delineation is attempted, it is important to have the information found in the next chapter. Because Ray-Centered Astrology is a revolutionary new Astrology, it is extremely important to understand the scope of its newness and the depth and breadth of what can be received from it that is beyond traditional astrology.

Chapter Five

THE SCOPE OF A RAY-CENTERED DELINEATION

The world we live in becomes smaller and smaller as technological progress makes it possible to fly half way around the earth in one day, to see on television via satellite things that are happening anywhere on the globe. There are more books, magazines, tape recordings, and records available in one large book store in one city than could be found in the entire world when the Piscean Age was young. More people have studied more subjects for more years in that one city than knew how to read a thousand years ago.

And yet in spite of all these sources of information, more people than ever are bewildered by such questions as, "Who am I?" "Why am I here?" "Do I have a real purpose for existing?" Few of them can find answers.

Because the Ancient Wisdoms are being brought to the light of day at last, these questions can now be answered through the study and practice of Ray-Centered Astrology—an Astrology of the Aquarian Age whose time is now. It is an Astrology of the planets, signs, and houses, but it is concerned primarily with seven kinds of energy, each of a different color which when seen together are the White Light that filled the Universe when God said "Let There Be Light." These seven energies are the Seven Rays which have their origin in the Seven Stars of Ursa Major, the Great Bear.

So that we will know why we are here, each of us receives one of the Seven Rays, the Soul Ray which determines our life plan. It is governed by one's abilities, strengths, weaknesses, and aspirations, and is calculated in reference to one's Ascendant sign.

Each person is also given a Personality Ray which supplies the particular kind of energy needed in outer life as an aid in achieving his Soul's purpose. It is calculated in reference to his Sun sign.

Key-words for each of the Rays follow.
Ray One—will and power
Ray Two—love and wisdom
Ray Three—intellectual creativity
Ray Four—harmony through conflict
Ray Five—the logical concrete mind
Ray Six—idealism and devotion
Ray Seven—order and rhythmic living

It is true that on a random basis every forty-ninth person would have the same Soul and Personality Rays, yet there are many differences among them. One difference may be the Ascendant signs, and another may be the Sun signs. Though two persons have identical Ascendant and Sun signs, many differences still are found in their charts that make each unique in that no one else can contribute to humanity in the same way. The reason is that no two people have had identical past lives and experiences or have developed the same abilities and strengths. They have not created the same problems in past lives which are to be solved in this life. Uniqueness is revealed not only through a detailed interpretation of a person's Soul and Personality Rays, but by other criteria. One of these is the interpretation of the Ascendant and Sun signs which includes a three-category guide for determining the level of Soul evolvement—average, advanced, or very advanced. Sufficient information is found in each category to enable a person to become aware of where he is now and to discover how he must change in order to advance to the next level.

Two Ray-Centered horoscopes, numbered two and three, are constructed and delineated, both of which accentuate the person's uniqueness. Horoscope Two depicts both the specific planetary energies essential to the Soul's purpose and the specific planetary energies essential to the personality serving the Soul. The delineation of this horoscope deals with the planets, the Rays each planet rules, the signs of each planet, the aspects, and the house positions for each group of planets designating the Soul life and the personality life serving the Soul, and the relationship between the two groups.

Horoscope Three depicts the major problem that needs to be resolved in this life time. The planets depicting the Soul life in Horoscope Two are also used in Horoscope Three. While the personality planets serving the Soul were used in Horoscope Two, the personality planets indicating self-centered desires are used in Horoscope Three. The same depth of meanings are extracted here as in Horoscope Two.

Yet in both horoscopes, cognizance is taken of the balance of positive and negative Rays or the predominance of either. The energy of the odd-numbered Rays is comparable to the masculine gender characteristics—power, assertiveness, and intellect. The energy of the even-numbered Rays is comparable to the feminine characteristics—love, sensitivity, and concern for others.

An in-depth interpretation of the two Ray-Centered horoscopes and of the Soul and Personality Rays is particularly revealing. To interpret the total essence of the person's being, the delineation of the planets and houses of the natal chart not covered in the Ray-Centered Horoscopes and the delineation of the Nodes are added. Though they assume less importance than the Ray-Centered Horoscopes, they are carried out in the same manner.

The planet nearest the zenith of the natal chart and the Ray it rules signify where the entity's consciousness was before the present earth life. The abilities derived from that experience and how they can be applied to this life are indicated.

The planet or planets most influential in the total life of the person are determined by their prominence in the natal chart and by the signs the planets tenant. This determination is made for any one planet through the prominence of the signs that planet rules exoterically, esoterically, and hierarchically.

Color has an important place in Ray-Centered Astrology, not only for enhancing the energies consonant with the Soul and Personality Rays, but also to help a person overcome certain weaknesses. Since each Ray has a specific color, and each color has its own rate of vibration, we are affected differently by each color.

Before a person can benefit optimally from Ray-Centered Astrology, he must have some knowledge of two concepts which have their origin in the Ancient Wisdom upon which much of the understanding of the self rests. Reincarnation and Karma presently are widely believed in by people throughout the world.

Reincarnation is the concept that each of us has had many lives, learning, progressing, and evolving spiritually from one to the next, each life having a definite purpose or plan. Until we discover why we are here and until we begin actualizing what we came to accomplish, we shall experience frustration and unhappiness. Because no two people have had identical past lives, no two of us can contribute to humanity in the same way. The challenge to each person to find his special niche can be met through Ray-Centered Astrology.

The concept of Karma is that for every action there is a consequence. The Bible defines it, "As you sow, so shall you reap." For every wrong thought, word, and action of past lives and in this life, we experience difficulties until the inherent lessons have been learned. By learning the lessons, we can avoid the difficult karmic experiences. This is often referred to as, "The Grace of God." Further, for every right thought, word, and action in past lives and in this life, we reap rewarding karmic experiences. In essence, Karma tells us that we are our own creators—that we are responsible for the situations we find ourselves in now, and that the sooner we take responsibility for situations that are not to our liking, the more energy and time we shall have to create a better tomorrow.

In a Ray-Centered Astrology delineation, the progressed natal chart is interpreted as a primary step toward determining our deep psychological and inner spiritual stirrings in the present and in the near future. It is interpreted esoterically using the knowledge of the Rays and planets involved, and the rulers of the signs and the cusp signs of the houses they tenant. This reveals the specific planetary energies, Ray energies, and areas of life with which we will be dealing. By fusing this knowledge with that of the rest of the delineation, we can come to accept and use the total interpretation in a way that is meaningful in light of the progressed aspects.

We should become aware that any challenging aspect that will become partile in the near future, especially if it involves the same planets with a natal challenging aspect, indicates a tendency to use the extra energy unwisely. Because we are all creatures of habit, we continue to exhibit the same weaknesses over and over again when the planetary positions cyclically indicate these periods unless an effort is made to change undesirable habits. We can avoid the karmic suffering resulting from our weaknesses if we make a determined effort to overcome them by constructively using our energies. In trying to overcome a weakness, we must be aware that the energy formerly used in the weakness must go somewhere. Energy never ceases to exist—it can only change its form. If self-discipline is used to eradicate a weakness without directing the energy constructively, the character weakness may slip from the conscious to the unconscious mind and cause repressions resulting in additional suffering. Therefore we should first become aware of our weaknesses, especially when aspects provide more energy for intensifying the weaknesses. Then we can transmute the energy formerly used in weaknesses into strengths and constructive thoughts and actions. We should visualize the wise use of this energy, then act as though we have always used it wisely. Because energy follows thought, there is much power in this visualization. Examples of certain challenging aspects, the weaknesses they indicate, and the strengths and constructive uses of the energies to which they can be transmuted are found in the Appendix. Chapter Three describes the strengths into which various specific weaknesses can be transmuted.

Because success breeds success, when we have mastered the wise use of one of our challenging aspectual energies, we can easily move on to another. As we progress we find ourselves more in tune with our inner nature and with the universe. This attunement results in a better functioning of the glandular system, bringing about better emotional and physical health, a higher level of Soul evolvement, and success and joy in life work.

Because every seventh year of one's life is a year of change, of crisis, and of opportunity, it is advisable to know our last year of opportunity and assess how we handled it. This can help us learn from our mistakes and thus take better advantage of the next year of change and opportunity.

It is an esoteric fact that we are greatly influenced by the four signs of the cross of our Sun at birth. The sign of the Sun, the sign opposite it, and the two signs at right angles make the cross. The time periods when the Sun is in one of the signs of our cross should be elucidated according to the meanings of the signs, their esoteric rulers, and the houses they tenant.

When we have completed our Ray-Centered delineation, we should study the information provided. As we formulate our life plan consonant with our Soul and Personality Rays as well as with the rest of our Ray-Centered delineation, it is advisable to reassess our motivation.

To attain success and joy in our life plan, the motivation must be love for humanity and the aspiration to serve others in the way only each of us can do.

Chapter Six

STEPS IN INTERPRETATION OF RAY-CENTERED ASTROLOGY

The study and delineation of any Ray-Centered astrological work should be preceded by prayer. Each of us should formulate the nature of our prayer from our own shortcomings. The tenor and acuity of the entire delineation rests on the level of Soul evolvement of the astrologer. The more highly evolved he is, the sharper his perception, the more pure his motivation, and the more gentle and loving his mode of delivery. The astrologer's reputation rests on the degree to which his clients are led to spontaneously initiate self-change.

Step 1. Find the approximate level of Soul evolvement by studying the pattern in the natal chart. The simpler the geometric pattern, the more integration between planets and cardinal points, and the smaller the orbs of the aspects, the more highly evolved we are. Very advanced souls tend to have a 9-pointed star pattern, a 6-pointed star pattern, a 7-pointed star with a grand trine, or a 5-pointed star with a grand trine. Charts of these types are extremely rare. The 9-pointed star is 3 grand trines with 9 novile aspects of approximately 40° each. The 6-pointed star is 2 grand trines of 6 sextile aspects of approximately 60° each, often referred to as the Star of David because the biblical David had a chart of this type. The 7-pointed star is 7 septile aspects of approximately 51° each. The 5-pointed star is 5 quintile aspects of approximately 72° each. Advanced souls tend to have a well-integrated chart and a fairly simple geometric pattern. There may be 2 grand trines, not necessarily structured like the Star of David, but with their planets distanced unequally from each other. There may be 1 grand trine with its planets aspecting the rest of the chart. Even if there are many challenging aspects of oppositions, squares, semi-squares, or sequi-quadrates, the chart still indicates an advanced Soul if there is fairly small-orbed aspectual integration with all planets and cardinal points. Only a highly evolved Soul would be permitted to be born at a time in which there were many challenging aspects, indicating difficult karmic experiences to help him overcome his weaknesses. One who is less highly-evolved would not be allowed a chart of many difficult karmic experiences, but would need at least two lives to learn the lessons needed for overcoming those weaknesses. None of us is allowed to take on more lesson-teaching karma in one life time than we are able to handle and learn from.

Step 2. Study the progressed natal chart for the coming year and find the aspects that will become exact during the year between all progressed planets, natal planets and the slower-moving transitting ones. Progressed aspects indicate deep psychological and spiritual stirrings, and are of relatively long duration. The aspects from slow-moving transitting planets, being of longer duration than those from the fast-moving planets, have some significance because they indicate the way in which the environment may affect the native. In addition to the interpretation of the planets, signs, and houses concerned in the aspects, the Ray each aspecting planet rules and the esoteric rulers of the signs should be considered. If there are any challenging aspects, especially if the planets of those aspects also have natally challenging aspects, we should try to determine the constructive use of these energies and how we can benefit from changing any character weaknesses signified by the challenging aspects into strengths. Culminating aspects, whether progressed or transitting bring potent energies consonant with the signs and with the planets and the Rays they rule, with the expenditure of these energies usually taking place in the houses the planets tenant. If one has an aspect signifying a character weakness becoming partile in the coming year, the aspectual energies will intensify the weakness because we are all victims of habit. This intensification brings with it lesson-teaching karmic effects. The best way to eliminate these difficulties is to change the pattern of use of these energies that habit has created; we should change the pattern by awareness, visualization of the right pattern, and by self-discipline. The added energy, rather than being an inhibiting influence to our work, relationships, and well-being, will then be beneficial. Drawing an analogy between the progressed chart and a garden, the chart should be considered as a seed which when cared for lovingly and wisely by watering and removing weeds, will produce nourishing and beautiful fruit. The weeding and watering is analogous to the eradication of the weakness and the visualization and practice of the strength the weakness can be transmuted into, to be started as long a time as possible before the aspect becomes exact. The aspects that are exact or approaching exactness should be considered seriously in light of the succeeding steps in delineation. The present energies and needs that are shown by these aspects dictate the focus of the interpretation.

Step 3. Find the Soul Ray by following the calculations in Chapter 2, and use the information in Chapter 3 pertaining to the Soul Ray. This information will provide a basis on which to build a life plan which is the activation of the Soul's purpose of serving others.

Step 4. Study the Ascendant sign in Chapter 4. This supplements the Soul Ray information for the Soul's purpose in this life, and differentiates one person from another wherein the Soul Rays are alike but Ascendant signs are different (other dissimilarities will be discussed later). The integrative relationships between the Ascendant sign information and the Soul Ray information, including the masculine and or feminine genders which are the positive and negative polarities should be understood. All odd-numbered Rays are of the masculine gender or positive polarity, and all even-numbered Rays are of the feminine gender or negative polarity. All fire and air signs (Ascendants) are masculine; water and earth signs (Ascendants) are feminine. If a person's Soul Ray and Ascendant are both masculine, his Soul's purpose would tend to be extrovertive, intellectual, and powerful in its expression. Fear would not be a barrier, but lack of love, which he should try to cultivate, might be. If the Soul Ray and Ascendant are both feminine, the Soul's purpose would tend to be introvertive and concerned with the inner life. A lack of love would more than likely not be a barrier, but fear, which can be eradicated by thought control, might be. If the Soul Ray and Ascendant are of opposite genders, the Soul's purpose could combine both the fearless, extrovertive, intellectual, and powerful expression with the sensitivity, love, and concern for others which the introvertive inner life provides. This does not mean that someone with both a masculine Soul Ray and Ascendant or someone with both a feminine Soul Ray and Ascendant does not possess both the masculine and feminine qualities; it means only that his Soul's purpose in serving others has to do mostly with the masculine or feminine part of his nature.

Step 5. Find the Personality Ray from the calculations in Chapter 2, and study the information pertaining to the Personality Ray in Chapter 3. The type of personality thus revealed should be regarded as a contributor to the Soul Ray's purpose. Show how the Soul Ray is the master and how it can use the Personality Ray as a servant or means of expression.

Step 6. Study the Sun sign in Chapter 4. This information supplements that of the Personality Ray found in Step 5. It differentiates the personality of one person from another whose Personality Rays are alike but whose Sun signs differ. The blending of the Sun sign, which has less importance, with the Personality Ray gives a more complete picture of one's personality. Include the gender or polarity of the Personality Ray and the Sun sign (see Step 4 for details).

Step 7. Study the interaction of the Soul Ray supplemented by the Ascendant with the Personality Ray supplemented by the Sun sign, and draw indicated conclusions, keeping in mind that the Soul Ray should have a more potent influence than the Personality Ray. The general meaning of the Soul Ray supplemented by the Ascendant designating the Soul's purpose for one's life plan should be combined with the Personality Ray supplemented by the Sun sign designating how the Soul's purpose should be carried out.

If one has a Ray 2 Soul, a Pisces Ascendant, a Ray 4 Personality and an Aries Sun, the Soul's purpose would be to acquire wisdom and disseminate it with love in a compassionate fashion. His personality's function is to serve his Soul's purpose. When he has resolved some of his conflicts, the harmony he has acquired will enable him to enthusiastically pioneer new methods or systems in which the wisdom he has acquired can be used by others.

Study the polarity interaction of the Soul Ray and the supplementary Ascendant with the Personality Ray and the supplementary Sun sign. A suggested procedure is to use M for an odd-numbered Soul or Personality Ray (masculine) and F for an even-numbered Soul or Personality Ray (feminine); use m for a masculine Ascendant or Sun sign (fire and air signs) and f for a feminine Ascendant or Sun sign (water and earth signs); underline the gender initials for the Soul Ray and Ascendant, thus emphasizing that they are more important than those of the Personality Ray and Sun sign. Using the previous example: A Ray 2 Soul is F, a Pisces Ascendant is f, a Ray 4 Personality is F, an Aries Sun is m—$\underline{Ff}$ Fm. Not only are three of the four genders feminine, but so are both of the Soul indicators. This points strongly to sensitivity and love and concern for others, but a possible lack of confidence in oneself. He should do his best to activate his Aries Sun characteristics to eradicate any lack of confidence he may feel. When there is a predominance of negative polarities, as in this case, there is a tendency to psychic sensitivity, charisma, introversion, and love and concern for others, all of which are a part of the feminine nature associated with the "yin" of the "I Ching" and the "anima" of Jung.

With a predominance of positive polarities, there is a tendency to be strong willed with intense power in thoughts, words and actions, to extroversion, to intellectuality, and to one-pointedness, all of which are a part of the masculine nature which is correlated with the "yang" of the "I Ching" and the "animus" of Jung.

For the average and even the advanced person with either a predominant negative or positive polarity, there is a tendency toward certain shortcomings. For the negative polarity, a major one is a lack of self-confidence. For the positive polarity, a major one is a lack of love and concern for others. For the very advanced person, neither a lack of self-confidence nor a lack of love and concern for others manifests itself. For the average or advanced person with the same polarity for his Soul Ray and Ascendant but the opposite for his Personality Ray and Sun sign, there is apt to be a lack of rapport between the Soul and personality.

The very advanced person with this configuration does not

feel a lack of rapport but uses the energies of his Soul and personality in a complementary fashion to foster unity between his Soul's purpose and his personality expression of his life plan. The very advanced person has overcome most or all weaknesses and uses the qualities of each of the 7 sub-Rays of both his Soul and Personality Rays when the occasion demands it. It is important to work toward this advanced status.

It requires effort to change an habitual weakness into one or more strengths. There must be awareness of the weakness, an aspiration for change, a visualization of the desired strengths, the discipline for achievement, and the provision of time to make the effort. Certain environmental aids can be used to hasten the achievement of the goal; one is the judicious use of color. It has long been known that different colors affect us in different ways because of the variance of the rate of vibration of each color. A person with a masculine predominance who finds a lack of love and sensitivity in his being along with strong aggressive tendencies can benefit from using green for relaxation, blue for sensitivity, and pink to feel more love toward others. Someone with a feminine predominance who is too emotional and lacks confidence can benefit from the vibrations of white which will help him feel more confident, yellow which will help him be guided more by his perceptive mind rather than his emotions, indigo which will help him use his logical mind rather than his emotions, and violet which will help him attain a more rhythmic and organized style of living conducive to peace. It is advisable for all people to avoid red which has the lowest vibration and can precipitate impulsiveness, irritability, anger, passion, or violence, especially when there is a challenging Mars aspect. Black, which is the absence of color and therefore acts as a sponge, should be avoided by all sensitive persons, especially when they are in the presence of low-vibrational people. Unless your thoughts are on a high level, black will tend to draw undesirable thoughts of others. Orange is beneficial for those who lack physical strength. It is a blend of the excitable, energetic red and the mental yellow, providing energy without impulsiveness. Blue, the color of the heavens and symbolic of love and wisdom, helps raise one's level of consciousness because it fosters less self-centeredness and more love and concern for others.

Step 8. Set up a Ray-Centered horoscope showing the inner Soul life and the outer personality life expressing the Soul's purpose. This is Horoscope 2; Horoscope 1 is the natal horoscope.

To find the inner Soul life, find all the esoteric planetary rulers of the natal Ascendant by using Chart 4. This is done by finding the primary esoteric ruler of the Ascendant, then the esoteric ruler of the sign that ruler falls in, then the esoteric ruler of the sign the second planet falls in, and so on until all esoteric rulers have been found. The energies of these planets influence the inner Soul life.

Find the esoteric rulers of the Sun sign in the same way as for the Ascendant. The energies of these planets influence the outer personality life by showing how the Soul's purpose can be expressed.

In setting up this Ray-Centered horoscope, use the same house cusps as used natally. In this horoscope insert only those planets which were found to be the esoteric rulers of the Ascendant and Sun signs. They will be in the same positions as found in the natal horoscope. To differentiate those planets depicting the inner Soul life from those depicting the outer personality life serving the Soul, two different colors should be used. I use blue for the inner Soul life planets and yellow for the outer personality life planets serving the Soul. To get a clear picture, I also make the symbols for the Ascendant and Sun and their primary esoteric rulers larger than the symbols for the other esoteric rulers.

Calculate any aspects these planets make to each other and indicate them in the horoscope with connecting lines. It is suggested that different colors be used for different types of aspects in order to see the whole picture at once. I use red lines for challenging aspects of oppositions, squares, semi-squares, and sesqui-quadrates; green for easy aspects of trines, sextiles, and semi-sextiles; yellow for quintiles and their derivatives; violet for septiles and their derivatives; a broken violet line for quincunxes. The quintile aspects of 72°, 144°, 36°, and 108°, denoting potential genius capacity and the septile aspects of 51°, 103°, and 154° denoting creative capacities, each within an orb of one degree, should be included in the aspects.

Through the study of this horoscope, the inner life and its

outer life expression can be seen easily. In the interpretation, special attention must be given to the Soul rulers versus the personality rulers. These planets, the Rays they rule, the aspects to each other, and the signs and houses they tenant are all important in the delineation of this Ray-Centered horoscope. Use Chart 5 to find the Rays these planets rule, and Chapter 3 for an explanation of the Rays concerned. This horoscope should be studied intensively for its optimum interpretive value.

Designate which planet or planets, if any, and the Rays they rule are supplying energies for both the subjective life of the Soul and the outer life of the personality, and how these energies are a point of contact between the Soul and the personality in expressing the Soul's purpose.

In the interpretation of the house positions of the Soul and personality ruling planets, attention should be paid to the esoteric rulers of the cuspal signs and the Rays they rule, as well as the signs in which these planets are found and the Rays they rule. Fundamental to the house interpretations are the spiritual connotations of each house. These houses have meaning for those who are beginning to contact their Souls. It must be remembered, however, that as one manifests more deeply on a Soul level, the house interpretations or areas of life are less and less accurate until they are no longer accurate at all. At that time there are no limitations in the areas of life in which one manifests any of his planetary energies. Until that time comes, which may be a long period for most of us, the following Chart 27 should be useful. These are the meanings I intuitively perceived. In the course of your work, you may want to add to them or perhaps substitute your meanings for mine. I, too, in the course of my work may add to these meanings or substitute others. However, this can be used as a start, and if you feel good with it you will keep it; if not, you will add or substitute when the time is right. Each of us is the result of many lives, experiences, and development of abilities so different from those of another person, that what feels right for me may not be right for you, and vice versa. We must be true to ourselves and give to others what we are and what we have.

The delineation of this Horoscope 2 shows the inner Soul life and its purpose for this incarnation as well as the outer personality life in light of how it can serve the Soul's purpose.

CHART 27

SPIRITUAL MEANINGS OF THE HOUSES AND THE ESOTERIC RULERS OF THE CONVENTIONAL SIGNS OF THE HOUSES WITH ARIES ON THE FIRST HOUSE

HOUSE ESOTERIC
RULER
MEANING

HOUSE	ESOTERIC RULER	MEANING
1	☿	The Soul and its expression, divine ideas to be used in serving others
2	♈	Help to achieve spiritual illumination and better attitudes and values, powerful energy and its uses
3	♀	The kind of intellect, reason, logic, understanding
4	♆	Help to attain Soul depth, foundations of the Soul, awareness of past lives
5	☉	Help to integrate the personality, self-realization through Soul contact
6	☽	Help in perfecting oneself by changing weaknesses into strengths, service to family and or community
7	♅	Kinds of relationship experiences necessary to weigh the benefits from materialistic desires versus spiritual aspirations
8	♂	Types of intense energy for temptations, testing, and spiritual regeneration
9	⊕	Types of experiences and goals needed for understanding and adhering to Universal Laws and spiritual truths
10	♄	Ways of raising the consciousness level, manifesting the Soul's purpose through the career
11	♃	Kinds of Aquarian Age philosophies that can be best understood and used with love, types of successful world service

12   ♇   Type of power which can bring repressed feelings and weaknesses from the unconscious to
the conscious in order to eradicate them and
help others do the same, the kind of help received from the spirit plane

Step 9. Set up another Ray-Centered horoscope to find the
problem for this lifetime—Horoscope 3. Each life brings with
it a problem from past lives which is the main reason for incarnation. Until one finds his main problem and overcomes it,
he experiences difficult karma in order to change weaknesses
into strengths. This horoscope enables one to find and resolve
the problem. The problem is shown in the horoscope by the
conflict between the inner Soul aspiration and the self-centered
personality desires.

In constructing this horoscope, use the same cusps found in
the natal horoscope. Insert the Ascendant and the esoteric rulers of the Ascendant as found in Step 8. These depict the inner
Soul life. Insert the Sun sign and insert all the exoteric rulers
of the Sun in the same way as with the esoteric rulers of the
Sun in Step 8. These depict the self-centered personality desires. Two different colors should be used for the symbols, one
for depicting the inner Soul life and the other for the self-
centered personality desires. I use blue for the inner Soul life
planets, and red for the self-centered personality desire planets.
As in Step 8, I suggest that the symbols for the Sun and Ascendant and their primary rulers be made larger than other
symbols in order to emphasize their greater influence. Aspects
between all planets in this horoscope should be calculated and
indicated in the horoscope by colored lines as in Step 8. Use
Chart 27 for the spiritual meanings of the house positions of
the planets. As in Step 8, delineate this horoscope using the
planets, aspects, signs, houses, and Rays which the planets
rule. In the interpretation of the houses, attention should be
paid to the esoteric rulers of the signs in which the planets and
cusps are found, as well as the Rays these planets rule.

Determine whether one or more planets are both esoteric
rulers of the Ascendant and exoteric rulers of the Sun. If so,
this planet or planets are the point or points of contact between
the Soul and the self-centered personality desires. Through

these planetary energies, the self-centered personality desires can be most easily transmuted into spiritual aspirations.

This horoscope shows the inner Soul life aspiration as it conflicts with the self-centered personality desires, revealing the most difficult problem of this life and indicates ways in which the problem can be solved.

Step 10. From the natal chart, interpret the meanings of the Moon's Nodes and those houses and planets not interpreted in Steps 8 or 9. Using Chart 27 for the esoteric meanings of the houses, include the aspects and the Rays these planets rule, the cuspal signs and their esoteric planetary rulers and the Rays these planets rule, and the aspects between planets found in Horoscopes 2 and 3 and the rest of the planets and the Moon's Nodes.

Step 11. Find the planet closest to the zenith in the natal chart and the Ray it rules. Between earth lives, each of us inhabits one or more planets to learn what those planets can teach us. What we learn from the last planet we inhabit can make our present life more fulfilled. The last one is the planet closest to the zenith. Note both the planet's capacities and the qualities of the Ray it rules as beneficial in this life, noting what role that planet played, if any, in Horoscopes 2 and 3.

Step 12. Find the planet or planets in the natal chart that are the most influential. Use the following chart showing the signs each planet rules in an exoteric, esoteric, and hierarchical capacity. Note that some planets rule one, two, three, or four signs. A planet is influential by virtue of having three planets or important points of the natal chart in the sign or signs it rules. If the planet found in Step 11 is included here, greater importance should be given it. Interpret this step not only as to the meanings of the planets, but of the Rays they rule. Using Horoscopes 2 and 3, find the specific influence of each planet as it relates to the Soul life, the personality serving the Soul, the self-centered personality desires, or none of these.

CHART 28

SIGNS PLANETS RULE EXOTERICALLY, ESOTERICALLY, AND OR HIERARCHICALLY

☿ – ♊ ♍ ♈ ♏   ♅ – ♒ ♎ ♈

♀ – ♎ ♊ ♉ ♑   ☽ – ♋ ♍ ♒

⊕ – ♉ ♐ ♊   ♆ – ♓ ♋

♂ – ♈ ♍ ♐   ♇ – ♏ ♓

♃ – ♐ ♒ ♍   ☉ – ♌

♄ – ♒ ♑ ♎   ♈ – ♉

Step 13. Change, crises, and opportunity occur in a 7 year-cycle throughout one's life. Thus it is advisable to know the last cycle year in order to assess how it was handled and how it might have been handled better. This retrospection should help one take better advantage of the next cycle year for which a progressed horoscope would be helpful. These years occur at ages 7, 14, 21, etc.

Step 14. Determine the general tendencies of the various periods in one's life. Fourteen years was chosen for each period because it coincides with changes precipitated by aspects of transitting Uranus to natal Uranus and with karmic lessons to be learned from aspects of transitting Saturn to natal Saturn. This step should portray the stirrings of one's psyche, inner life, Soul and the prompting for the general trend of thoughts, words, and actions in any particular period. Only the progressed planets, using a day for a year, aspecting the natal planets are used. They determine the general types of energies that are most potent in each period. The total span of years covered by all the periods used is approximately equivalent to the Uranus return, the third Saturn return, and the frequently publicized actuarial span of 84 years for women. This age span is shorter for men according to the published findings. However, increasing numbers of both sexes are living beyond these spans.

Find the exact major aspects of conjunction, opposition, square, trine, and sextile of the progressed planets to natal planets in each period, disregarding the progressed Moon. The progressed Moon's effect is important in a detailed analysis, but because the approximate duration is only one month, it is not desirable in this general overview. Compare the number of aspects in the various periods to determine in which periods one receives little energy, more energy, or much energy. List the number of easy versus challenging aspects to determine the smooth-sailing of one's Soul's purpose of helping others versus the karmic lesson-teaching experiences in each period. It is not that the easy aspects are more fortunate than the challenging or vice versa, but that they are both fortunate for different purposes, and are both necessary for Soul evolvement.

The challenging aspects usually denote periods of karmic responsibility or difficulties in which to learn certain lessons, while the easy aspects usually denote periods in which one, being relatively free of karmic difficulties, can more easily serve others in a career or hobby synonomous with his Soul Ray.

For each period, consider the planets of each aspect pair, list the Rays that rule each planet, and then tabulate in descending order of frequency the number of times each Ray is listed. From the Ray meanings in Chapter 3, find the general trend of the various periods, noting which Rays are prominent and which are not, indicating the types of thoughts and activities one is inclined to engage in during each period.

Step 15. Find the four periods of each year when one is greatly influenced. Each person is significantly influenced by the four signs of the cross the Sun was in at his birth. The four time periods each year when the Sun is transitting the mode of one's Sun sign, whether it is cardinal, fixed, or mutable, should be recorded and elucidated so that one can avail himself of certain opportunities in each period. The elucidation should include the meaning of the sign, the esoteric planetary ruler of the sign, the meaning of the Ray that planet rules, and the house or houses that sign tenants.

Step 16. One should formulate a plan for his life work consonant with the Soul and Personality Rays and also with the rest of the Ray-Centered delineation. This should be attempted only after one has made an in-depth study of the previous 15 Steps. During this formulation it is advisable to reassess one's motivation. If it is not because of a love for humanity and an aspiration to serve others in his unique way, he would do well to work on transmuting his weaknesses into strengths and forget about his Soul's purpose until he acquires love for others and the aspiration to serve them. When his motivation for his life plan becomes spiritually oriented, the following steps are important to assure success and joy in his work.

1. A strong intention of carrying it through by focusing his ideas in his mind.
2. Visualization by impressing on his mind what he wants to do.
3. Projection which is the willing of his life plan by his mind. Because energy follows thought, strong thoughts can energize his ideas for his life plan to actualization. Projective techniques differ with each Ray. The major projection should be synonomous with one's Soul Ray, yet tied in with the Personality Ray projective technique in a subsidiary manner. These techniques are found in the following chart.

CHART 29

PROJECTION TECHNIQUES OF THE RAYS
TO BE USED IN WILLING THE LIFE PLAN

Ray 1. Assert the intent of your life plan because of knowledge, conviction, and love.

Ray 2. See your life plan with intense concentration in relation to your understanding of God's Plan on earth.

Ray 3. Concentrate on yourself as being your life plan or purpose for which you came into this life through achieving mental silence.

Ray 4. Concentrate on your personality and Soul merging to achieve your life plan.

Ray 5. Assert that your lower concrete mind and your higher intuitive mind unite with the Universal Mind.

Ray 6. Sustain the highest light of which you are capable, preferably love, then idealism, then devotion, and let it control your life plan.

Ray 7. Assert that spirit and matter can meet because spirit becomes matter at its lower vibration and matter becomes spirit at its highest vibration.

Step 17. If one has the Sun, Moon, and Saturn in one house, one is ready to receive an initiation (the raising of the consciousness to a higher level and the demonstration of intuitive understanding put to practical application). This configuration is only one index of readiness to receive an initiation. A lack of this configuration does not, by any means, indicate that one cannot raise his consciousness to a much higher level. In this case, if a Ray-Centered Astrologer is preparing a delineation for a client, it is advisable to omit this step because there is power in words.

Step 18. Certain aspects between Jupiter and Pluto are conducive to the successful study and teaching of esoteric wisdoms—the trine, sextile, semi-sextile, septile, quintile, and quincunx. Success results because Jupiter is the esoteric ruler of Aquarius, and Pluto is the esoteric ruler of Pisces, and these signs indicate service to help humanity evolve spiritually in this, the Aquarian Age. This is only one index to successful teaching of esoteric wisdoms, therefore, lacking this aspect does not mean one would be unsuccessful. However it would be advisable, in this case, to omit this step if an astrologer is preparing a delineation.

The supportive research data on which Ray-Centered Astrology is based encompasses the study of the charts of all my clients over the past ten years. From that number I have chosen a chart for a detailed Ray-Centered delineation in each of the three combinations that can occur when the Soul and Personality Rays are considered from the point of view of their gender polarity. Chapter Seven deals with the chart of an entity having both Soul and Personality Rays odd-numbered. Chapter Eight is that of an entity having both Soul and Personality Rays even-numbered. Chapter Nine delineates the chart of an entity with one Ray odd-numbered and the other even-numbered.

CASE STUDY 1—NATAL & PROGRESSED
HOROSCOPE 1

RAY 7 SOUL, RAY 1 PERSONALITY

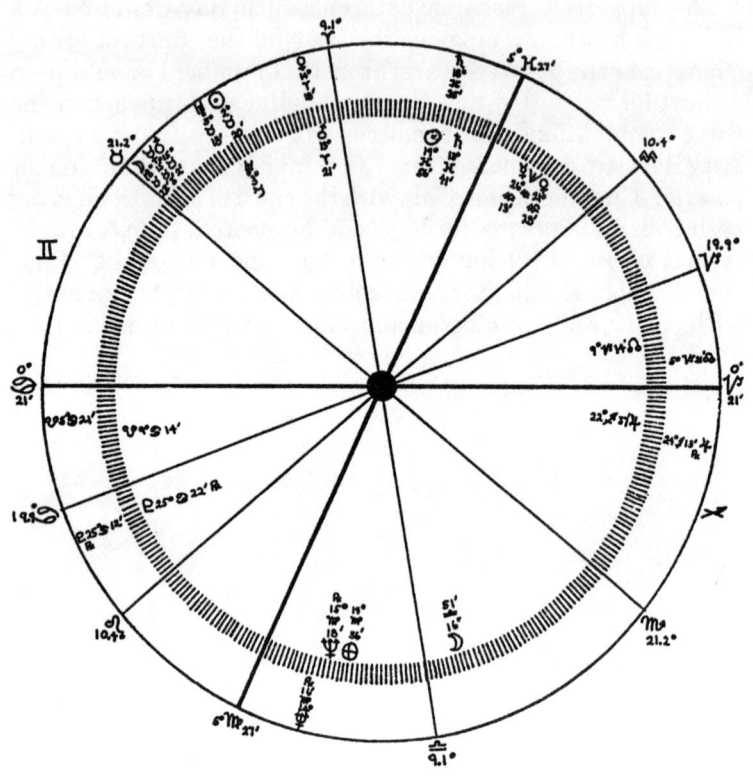

Chapter Seven

CASE 1

Step 1. Find the approximate level of Soul evolvement.
This person's chart indicates a high level. There is a fairly close aspectual relationship between all planets, denoting a good integration in which the personality is not fragmented but can operate as a unit with the mind in control of the emotions and physical body. This entity was born at a time he chose to accept responsibility for much lesson-teaching karmic experience as revealed by the many challenging aspects, another indication of a highly evolved Soul. No entity is allowed to take on any more lesson-teaching experiences in a particular life than he is capable of handling. He has a Finger-of-God aspect—two quincunxes from a single planet to two planets which sextile each other, signifying a special spiritual mission. This lifetime is not an easy one for him, but one with great potential for spiritual growth which can bring him much joy as he works on his progression.

Step 2. Study the progressed natal chart for the coming year.
In considering this chart as a seed that can blossom into fruit, it is no surprise that he requested astrological help at that particular time. He had six progressed planets in the eleventh house, all making partile aspects that year. These exact aspects gave him varied and strong energies for Aquarian Age philosophies and goals to be of service to mankind. Every progressed aspect that became exact during the year is concerned with the eleventh house.
His progressed Sun conjunct Uranus in Taurus in the eleventh house shows intuition (Uranus), vitality (Sun), and a determined urge (Taurus) to serve humanity (eleventh house) as a result of illumination (Taurus) and to make a clean and sudden break with the old way of living, being now in tune with the Aquarian Age philosophies (eleventh house and Uranus). He accomplished this by breaking contact with his former acquaintances, taking a new name, moving to a new location, taking a different job, and spending much time in

179

meditation and contemplation of his inner Soul life. Because the Sun is a ruler of Ray Two of love and wisdom, and Uranus is the ruler of Ray Seven of order and powerful thoughts, and the esoteric ruler of Taurus is Vulcan, this aspect deals with the ability to bring to the conscious mind, after crystallization in the unconscious, any repressions, guilt feelings, or other weaknesses to eradicate through powerful thoughts that are used in a wise and loving manner. With the aid of Vulcan's rulership of Ray One, his Personality Ray, he has much will power to accomplish this goal.

The progressed Neptune retrograde in Virgo in the fourth house quincunx progressed Venus in Aries in the eleventh house shows frustration until there is a concerted effort to serve humanity (eleventh house) in an original, enthusiastic, (Aries), loving, harmonious manner (Venus), yet in a detailed analytical way (Virgo) through the logical mind (Venus) and the psychic inspirational capacity (Neptune). Because Neptune is a ruler of Ray Six of idealism and devotion, and Venus is the ruler of Ray Five of concrete knowledge, his logical reasoning capacities should be used in a dedicated and idealistic way. Because the esoteric ruler of Aries is Mercury, a ruler of Ray Four of harmony through conflict, and the esoteric ruler of Virgo is the Moon, also a ruler of Ray Four, there will be added frustration until he begins to overcome his weaknesses and resolve his conflicts.

Progressed Mercury conjunct progressed Mars in Taurus in the eleventh house trine Neptune retrograde in Virgo in the fourth house shows great mental courage (Mercury conjunct Mars), determination and illumination (Taurus), and analytical work (Virgo) with his Soul progress (fourth house) pursuits in rapport with his psychic capacity (Neptune) and his Soul urges (fourth house). This aspect helps him to perfect himself and serve others (Virgo) with the illumination (Taurus) that he receives from his Soul (fourth house). Mercury is a ruler of Ray Four of harmony through conflict, and both Mars and Neptune are rulers of Ray Six of idealism and devotion. This shows that through strong idealistic urges, he can attain harmony by working through his conflicts and becoming aware of and eradicating character weaknesses. The esoteric ruler of Taurus is Vulcan, the ruler of Ray One of power and will, and the esoteric ruler of Virgo is the Moon, the ruler of Ray Four of harmony through conflict, giving him the power to attain harmony by overcoming weaknesses.

His progressed Moon in Taurus in the eleventh house will go into his twelfth house three months after his birthday and will make partile aspects with five natal planets and two progressed planets within the year. Even though the duration of the effects of each aspect is only one month, these aspects, because there are five of them, indicate a determination to understand himself on a deeper level, followed by illumination and service to others.

A summary of his progressions in this year of his life, indicates that he is an ideal candidate for a Ray-Centered astrological delineation because not only would he be very frustrated if he did nothing during the year concerning his Soul evolvement, but because he has a compelling urge to serve humanity and a strong need for the awareness and eradication of his weaknesses.

Step 3. Find the Soul Ray by following the calculations in Chapter Two.

The calculations show that his Soul Ray is Ray Seven. Study the information in Chapter Three pertaining to Ray Seven carefully. All the information in that section is important to this person's welfare. To understand this case study more thoroughly, it is suggested that the reader review the Ray Seven information.

In general, his life work or Soul's purpose should be one in which organization or peaceful rhythmic order is paramount, brought about through the power and one-pointedness of his thought forms.

Uranus is the ruling planet of Ray Seven and makes a partile conjunction during the year with his progressed Sun; therefore, this is an ideal time to break with the old and begin his Soul's life work. An urge for involvement in Aquarian Age goals is shown by all his progressed aspects and by his Ray Seven Soul and its ruler, Uranus, the exoteric ruler of Aquarius.

He will be affected more and more by Ray Seven energy because it is becoming more potent as we move deeper into the Aquarian Age. Having a Ray Seven Soul, he has powerful thoughts which can be either very harmful or very beneficial to himself and others. Therefore, the primary goal in Case 1 should be the transmutation of any thoughts of less than high vibration to the higher level. To help him attain this level, he would do well to develop a greater understanding of the various levels of Soul evolvement of different people, and realize that only through accepting and loving them where they are, can he help them to evolve. His life work should be concerned with one or more of the following: esoteric astrology, esoteric psychology, esoteric psychiatry, or any other science which relates the body to spirit, organizational or executive work, work toward a universal religion, occult work, or helping minerals or animals to evolve.

Step 4. In Chapter Four, study the Ascendant sign, Cancer, thoroughly and supplement this with his Ray Seven Soul information.

In generalizing, his Cancer Ascendant gives him the urge to nurture those who, for the time being, cannot fend for themselves. He has the psychic sensitivity to become aware of his problems and those of others and their possible causes. All the Cancer information found in Chapter Four should be merely supplementarily influential in the choice of his Soul's purpose or life work. Whichever of the services listed under Step 3 he feels impelled to choose for his Soul's purpose, this service should be carried out in a sensitive and nurturing way so that he can become attuned to his inner being.

His Cancer Ascendant of the water element is feminine, and his Ray Seven Soul, being odd-numbered, is masculine. Since the gender of his Soul Ray is opposite that of his Ascendant, his Soul's purpose could combine the fearlessness of his extrovertive, powerful expression with an introvertive love and concern for others.

Step 5. Find the Personality Ray from calculations given in Chapter Two.

He has a Ray One Personality. In Chapter Three carefully study the information pertaining to Ray One for the personality as the servant carrying out the Ray Seven Soul's purpose.

In generalizing, Case One's Soul purpose of establishing order, rhythm, and/or organization in a sensitive and nurturing fashion is aided by his Ray One Personality of will and power, giving him leadership capabilities. He can easily destroy hatreds, religious and racial antagonism, and feelings of isolation, and substitute, after an in-depth, long-term study, certain wisdoms, some Universal Laws, and a dawning sense of world consciousness.

Step 6. Study his Sun sign in Chapter Four.

The energies of his Pisces Sun supplement his Ray One Personality to depict more clearly his type of personality. Although in traditional astrology, Pisces is associated with only one ruler, Neptune, which may give a lack of confidence and willpower, this is true only when he has not yet contacted his Soul. Just the opposite is true for a person with a Pisces Sun when the natal chart shows Soul contact as it does in the chart of Case One. Pluto, the esoteric ruler of Pisces, gives him immense power to destroy outworn concepts, ideas, religions, educational systems, and government laws and projects, and substitute new ones in harmony with Aquarian Age philosophies. Until this person establishes strong contact with his Soul, he should transmute any residual selfish urges for power and domination over others to dedication and sacrifice for the upliftment of all peoples.

His odd-numbered Ray One Personality, denoting the masculine gender, supplemented with his Pisces water-element Sun, denoting the feminine gender, give his personality as it does his Soul, a fearless, extrovertive, powerful expression tinged with an introvertive love and concern for others.

It is important to study thoroughly the Pisces sign information in Chapter Four in the light of his personality expression. In general, his Pisces Sun energy will enable his Ray One powerful personality to use this power in a gentle compassionate way with the motivation of uplifting others.

Step 7. Study the interaction of the Soul Ray supplemented by the Ascendant with the Personality Ray supplemented by the Sun sign, keeping in mind that the Soul Ray indicates his purpose in life, and that the Personality Ray indicates his manner of expressing his Soul's purpose.

184

He has a Ray Seven Soul and a Cancer Ascendant. His Soul's purpose is to serve others through his powerful one-pointed thoughts, words, and actions in a rhythmic, ordered way, along with his innate nurturing capacity and with the help of his psychic sensitivity.

He has a Ray One Personality and a Pisces Sun. He can express his Soul's purpose in a powerful manner, yet with compassion and kindness for the suffering.

As far as gender is concerned, using *M* for masculine gender of the Rays, *F* for feminine gender of the Rays, and *f* and *m* for the Ascendant and Sun sign genders, and underlining the Soul Ray and Ascendant genders indicating the Soul's purpose to indicate its greater influence, we have the following: *Mf* Mf. This shows that both his Soul's purpose and his personality expression are basically strong willed, with intense power in thoughts, words, and actions that are one-pointed, and intellectually oriented. However, both his Soul and his personality in a supplementary but also complementary way in this case, indicate psychic sensitivity, receptivity, magnetism, and love and concern for others. The gender combinations show great rapport between the Soul's purpose and the personality expression of that purpose. The *Mf* and Mf show an excellent balance between the masculine and feminine elements of his being. This indicates an easier acquisition of a feeling of wholeness within himself than in the average person.

Because the Rays of one's Soul and personality have a much stronger influence than the Ascendant and Sun signs, and because both his Rays are of the masculine gender, he is a self-starter. There is a strong assertiveness within his being, not only to manifest according to his Soul Ray and its purpose, but to express his Soul's purpose according to his Personality Ray.

Even though it is wise for all persons to avoid red and black in their surroundings, it is especially important that he does so. A Ray Seven Soul combined with a Ray One Personality indicates powerful thoughts and strong action-orientation. If red is added, it might be more than he could handle well, which tends to produce irritation and impulsive behavior. A Cancer Ascendant and a Pisces Sun combination indicates a very sensitive and receptive nature. The color black would add to his receptivity, and its use when in the company of those of a low vibration at the time his was not at a high level, could cause him to receive many negative thoughts because black is a color of absorption.

Step 8. Set up a Ray-Centered Horoscope showing the inner Soul life and the outer personality life expressing the Soul's purpose. Use Chart 4 to find the esoteric rulers of the Ascendant and Sun signs. See the natal horoscope (Horoscope 1) for positions of the planets to be used in this horoscope (Horoscope 2).

To find the inner Soul life, use the natal Ascendant and all its esoteric planetary rulers.

The primary esoteric ruler of the Cancer Ascendant is Neptune which is in Virgo; the esoteric ruler of Virgo is the Moon which is in Libra; the esoteric ruler of Libra is Uranus which is in Taurus; the esoteric ruler of Taurus is Vulcan which is in Aquarius; the esoteric ruler of Aquarius is Jupiter which is in Sagittarius; the esoteric ruler of Sagittarius is Earth which is in Virgo. We stop here because we have already found the esoteric ruler of Virgo.

To find the personality life that is serving the Soul, use the Sun and all its esoteric rulers. The primary esoteric ruler of the Sun sign, Pisces, is Pluto which is in Cancer; the esoteric ruler of Cancer is Neptune which is in Virgo; the esoteric ruler of Virgo is the Moon which is in Libra; the esoteric ruler of Libra is Uranus which is in Taurus; the esoteric ruler of Taurus is Vulcan which is in Aquarius; the esoteric ruler of Aquarius is Jupiter which is in Sagittarius; the esoteric ruler of Sagittarius is Earth which is in Virgo. We stop here because we have come full circle.

Entering the Ascendant and Soul life planets and the Sun and personality life planets that are serving the Soul produces a picture of Case One's Soul life and Soul-serving personality life. Each of these two groups is inserted in a different color in Horoscope 2, using the same cusps as in the natal horoscope and different colored lines to denote different types of aspects. The specific planetary energies designated for the Soul's purpose consonant with his Ray Seven Soul are shown, and those specific planetary energies designated for the personality expression of his Soul life consonant with his Ray One Personality which help him in his outer life to manifest his Soul's

CASE 1—HOROSCOPE 2

INDICATES THE SOUL'S PURPOSE AND ITS EXPRESSION USING SOUL LIFE PLANETS AND PERSONALITY PLANETS SERVING THE SOUL

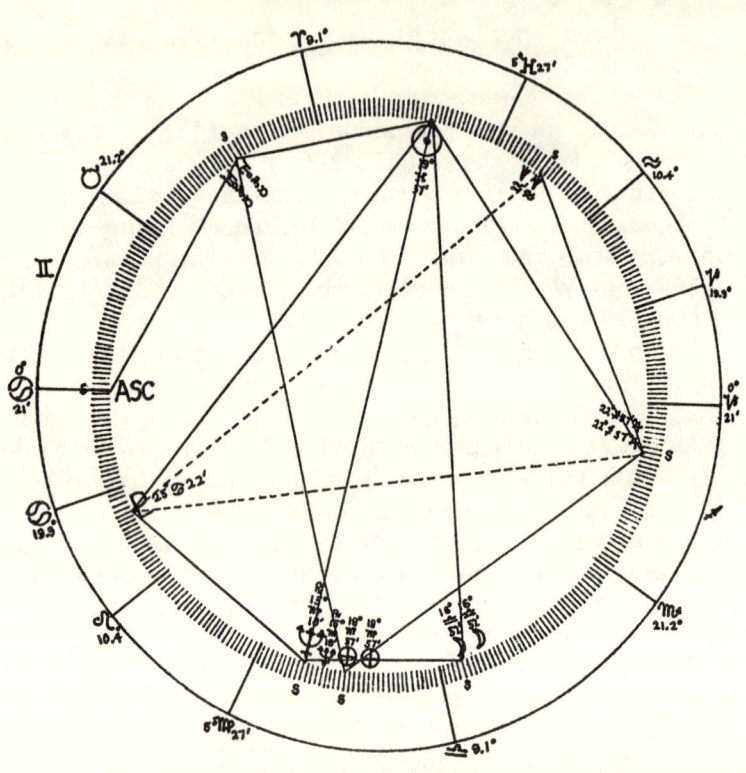

purpose are also shown. The interaction between these two groups is especially significant in noting which planets, if any, are used in both groups in pinpointing which planetary energies are combined through aspects, and the identity of those aspects. There is a good balance between the number of planetary energies for the Soul life and the personality life that is serving the Soul. Seven planetary energies are used for the Soul life and eight for the personality life that is serving the Soul. It is very unusual and significant that six of these planetary energies are used for both the Soul and the personality that is serving the Soul. This indicates a close rapport between his Soul and the personality expression of his Soul's purpose.

The most important house is the fourth because it is the only house which tenants two planets, both of which designate the Soul life and the personality life that serves the Soul. This gives him the energy to look into the depths of his Soul and to become aware of past lives. Because Neptune is one of the planets in the fourth house, the psychic sensitivity for Soul growth is accentuated. Neptune is a ruler of Ray Six, giving him an idealism which impels him to attainment. Neptune septile Pluto gives him intense psychic power. Because Earth is the other planet in the fourth house, it will be his lot to have many karmic experiences from which to learn his needed lessons. Due to a sesqui-quadrate from Earth to Uranus, these karmic experiences often come to him when he least expects them. His Earth square Jupiter shows that they will be numerous. The Earth, being a ruler of Ray Three of the higher mind, helps him to more easily learn the lessons from his karmic experiences. Because the cusp of the fourth house is Virgo and both planets are in Virgo, he has a deep need to perfect himself, and a strong urge to work toward overcoming his weaknesses. The esoteric ruler of Virgo, the Moon, is a ruler of Ray Four of harmony through conflict, which repeats that only by resolving his conflicts can he attain any degree of harmony.

His fifth house holds the Moon, a planet of both the Soul and its personality expression. In Libra, the Moon shows that relationships are very important in learning his karmic lessons. Fifth house tenancy of the Moon shows that self-realization could be attained primarily through the energies of the Moon, but also through the Sun and Neptune because of aspects to them, and through Uranus because it is the esoteric ruler of Libra in which the Moon is posited and which is the fifth house cusp. The Moon makes a semi-sextile to Neptune, giving him inspirational capacity and the ability to contact his Soul in depth, both helpful to self-realization. The Moon tri-septiles the Sun in the tenth house, which is an energizing planet only for the personality that is serving the Soul, showing creative capacity which can easily be expressed through a career in a compassionate and kind fashion (Sun in Pisces).

Because Uranus energizes both the Soul life and the personality life that is serving the Soul, and because it is in Taurus in the eleventh house, Aquarian Age philosophies and illumination can be closely linked with his self-realization and his Soul's purpose. Eleventh house matters of Aquarian Age philosophies and humanitarian service are influenced strongly by Uranus which is the ruler of Ray Seven, his Soul Ray. He is able to express his Soul's purpose through his outer life in an organized rhythmic way because Uranus is a planet of both the Soul life and the personality that is serving the Soul. The only aspect to the Cancer Ascendant is a sextile from Uranus which gives a powerful impetus from his Soul for eleventh house matters, although these matters are not altogether easy. A sesqui-quadrate from Uranus to Earth shows unexpected difficult karmic experiences from which he needs to learn. A semi-square from Uranus to Sun shows tendencies to rebellious and erratic behavior.

In discussing his tenth house, his rebellious and erratic tendencies just referred to, can be overcome through the trine of Pluto to the only planet tenanting the tenth house, the Sun. Because Pluto is in Cancer in the second house and the Sun is in Pisces and because both planets depict only the personality life that is serving the Soul, he has an enormous reservoir of psychic power at his command to demonstrate desirable attitudes quickly on an outer expression. It is as though he receives instant illumination when the occasion demands it. Because the esoteric ruler of the tenth house cusp and the esoteric ruler of the sign of its only occupant is Pluto, the above statement not only becomes doubly strengthened, but applies potently to career matters.

The single trine in his chart is between Pluto and the Sun, both planets influencing only the outer personality life that is serving the Soul, and collaborates with and strenghtens his Ray One Personality of power and will. To serve his Soul's purpose, he has a very powerful personality because both the Sun and its primary esoteric ruler, Pluto, designating the personality serving the Soul, are the only planets in this chart that are not rulers of the Soul life. All the other planets in Chart 2 are rulers of both the Soul and personality life that serve the Soul. Though powerful and used for his outer life expression, this trine aspect is not assertive power, but the power of the water element, a power exercised easily and beneficially because of his psychic sensitivity to others' feelings, thoughts, and needs and the ability to satisfy those needs through his career and through spiritual illumination.

The Sun, a ruler of Ray Two, indicates that any of his love and/or wisdom can be showered on others through his career. The opposition of the Sun to Neptune shows some confusion between his inner life and his personality expression of it through his career. The square of his Sun to Jupiter in Sagittarius in the sixth house shows a tendency to look at career matters through rose-colored glasses. Help from both of these challenging aspects can be received from the solitary trine.

His second house is very important not only because it harbors Pluto, the primary ruler of his outer personality life planets that are serving the Soul, but also because it is the focal planet of his Finger-of-God aspect. This aspect gives the added information for a spiritual mission that he decided to carry out in this lifetime. This spiritual mission will be expressed mainly through his outer life because Pluto is a planet of the outer life expression only. Yet the inner Soul life plays a large part in this mission because the other two planets that complete this aspect pattern are of both the inner and the outer life. The quincunx of Jupiter to Pluto shows frustration until he, through love and wisdom, tries to overcome his weaknesses and change those attitudes in need of changing. The quincunx of Vulcan to Pluto shows frustration until he uses the energies of these, the two most powerful planets in the heavens, to crystallize the weaknesses and guilt feelings in his unconscious and bring them into the conscious mind to remove them. Because Vulcan in the ninth house in Aquarius, and Jupiter in the sixth house in Sagittarius are sextile, Universal Laws and Aquarian Age concepts can be used advantageously to achieve self-perfection and carry out his spiritual mission of serving others. The release point of this aspect falls in Capricorn in the eighth house. The constructive activation of this aspect brings spiritual regeneration, with a high level of consciousness upliftment, but it cannot be accomplished without hard, persistent work and discipline. He finds that as he makes progress in his own regeneration, he is able to aid others in raising their own consciousness to a higher level. Both Pluto, which is the focal point of the Finger-of-God aspect, and the second house cusp are in Cancer. Neptune, being the esoteric ruler of Cancer, plays an important role in this aspect. It is septile Pluto, giving much psychic sensitivity and inspirational capacity for his spiritual mission.

There are two significant signs in sixth house matters because of an interception. Scorpio and Sagittarius give him one-pointedness, enthusiasm, and intensity in overcoming his weaknesses and in serving others. The esoteric ruler of Scorpio, Mars, does not appear in Horoscope 2; therefore its energy is not especially influential to the Soul life and its outer life expression. However, the esoteric ruler of Sagittarius, Earth, is doubly influential because it is both a ruler of the Soul life and the personality which serves it, and is the sign in which Jupiter, the only planet tenanting the sixth house, is found.

Earth, a ruler of Ray Three of intellectual activity, located in Virgo in the fourth house, is square Jupiter. This reveals the possibility of many karmic difficult experiences taking place before good judgment is attained to assess the value of the lessons learned. Jupiter square Sun in Pisces shows he has a tendency to look at life through rose-colored glasses. Yet the sextile from Vulcan in Aquarius in the ninth house to Jupiter, a ruler of Ray Two of love and wisdom, reinforces the innate qualities of Jupiter. This aspect urges him to blend Aquarian Age philosophies with love and wisdom so that his many karmic experiences will not only be the fiber of his Soul's purpose, but can also be the means through which his personality carries out the Soul's purpose in serving others and perfecting himself.

The ninth house holds Vulcan in Aquarius. As a ruler of Ray

One, Vulcan gives him immense power to understand Aquarian concepts and Universal Laws, and use them in such a way that he can crystallize his buried wrong thoughts and bring them to the light of day in order to rid himself of them. Vulcan is a planet of both the Soul life and personality life that serves the Soul, which makes this process easier. The esoteric ruler of both Vulcan's sign and the cusp of the ninth house, Aquarius, is Jupiter which is in sextile aspect to Vulcan, giving an expansive quality to Vulcan's power to crystallize, and to the strength of the Finger-of-God aspect. This will help him change his tendencies toward unawareness of lessons that his many karmic experiences are trying to teach him, as signified by a T-square of Jupiter to Sun and Earth, to an awareness. When he uses these capacities at an optimal level in his own life, he will be able to help others use them for their spiritual regeneration.

In his Finger-of-God aspect, both Pluto and Vulcan are rulers of Ray One of will, power, and purpose, and Jupiter is a ruler of Ray Two of love and wisdom. These rulerships indicate that his spiritual mission is concerned with immense power and a definite purpose to be carried out through love and wisdom.

The Soul life planets and the Rays they rule are: Ascendant—Ray Seven, Neptune—Ray Six, Moon—Ray Four, Uranus—Ray Seven, Vulcan—Ray One, Jupiter—Ray Two, and Earth—Ray Three. The only Ray not represented is Ray Five of science and the concrete mind, which indicates that his Soul life is not concerned with scientific or logical pursuits. The only Ray represented more than once is Ray Seven which here corroborates and strengthens his Ray Seven Soul's purpose as shown in an earlier step. He has well-balanced and diversified energies contributing to his Soul's purpose, which give him a rich inner life.

Those personality life planets which can carry out his Soul's purpose and the Rays they rule are: Sun—Ray Two, Pluto—Ray One, Neptune—Ray Six, Moon—Ray Four, Uranus—Ray Seven, Vulcan—Ray One, Jupiter—Ray Two, and Earth—Ray Three. Rays One and Two are doubled. The doubling of Ray Two endows the element of his personality that is serving his Soul with much love and wisdom. The doubling of Ray One confers immense power and will to carry out his Soul's purpose. The only Ray not represented is Ray Five of science and concrete knowledge.

That there is rapport between his inner life and its outer expression, is shown by the fact that the only Ray missing from these two groups of rulerships is Ray Five of science and concrete knowledge which indicates that his Soul life and its personality expression will not be concerned with his reasoning mind but with all other aspects of his being.

Step 9. Set up another Ray-Centered Horoscope to find the main problem for this lifetime as shown by the conflict between the inner Soul aspiration and the self-centered personality desires. This is designated as Horoscope 3. In this horoscope, use the same house cusps as in Horoscopes 1 and 2. Insert the Ascendant and all its esoteric rulers as found in Step 8. The Ascendant and these planets depict the inner Soul life. Find the exoteric rulers of the Sun sign.

The exoteric ruler of the Pisces Sun is Neptune which is in Virgo. The exoteric ruler of Virgo is Mercury which is in Aquarius. The exoteric ruler of Aquarius is Uranus which is in Taurus. The exoteric ruler of Taurus is Venus which is in Aquarius. Insert in this horoscope these planets and the Sun which depict the self-centered personality desires. It would be advisable to place these planets in the horoscope in a color that is different from the Soul life planets.

It would be advisable to enlarge the abbreviation for "Ascendant" and the symbol for "Neptune," the primary esoteric ruler, because they have more power than the other Soul life planets. Also, it would be advisable to enlarge the symbols for "Sun" and for "Neptune" of the self-centered personality for the same reasons. Seven planets are very influential to the inner Soul life and five to the self-centered personality desires. This is to his credit, making it easier to attain Soul evolvement than if the numbers were reversed.

The self-centered personality desire planets and the Rays they rule are: Sun—Ray Two, Neptune—Ray Six, Mercury—Ray Four, Uranus—Ray Seven, and Venus—Ray Five. All Rays are represented except Rays One and Three. The absence of Ray One is fortunate in this rulership grouping because it shows that there is not a great deal of power directed toward his self-

CASE 1—HOROSCOPE 3

INDICATES FOR THIS LIFE THE CONFLICT BETWEEN SOUL LIFE PLANETS AND SELF-CENTERED PERSONALITY PLANETS AND ITS RESOLUTION

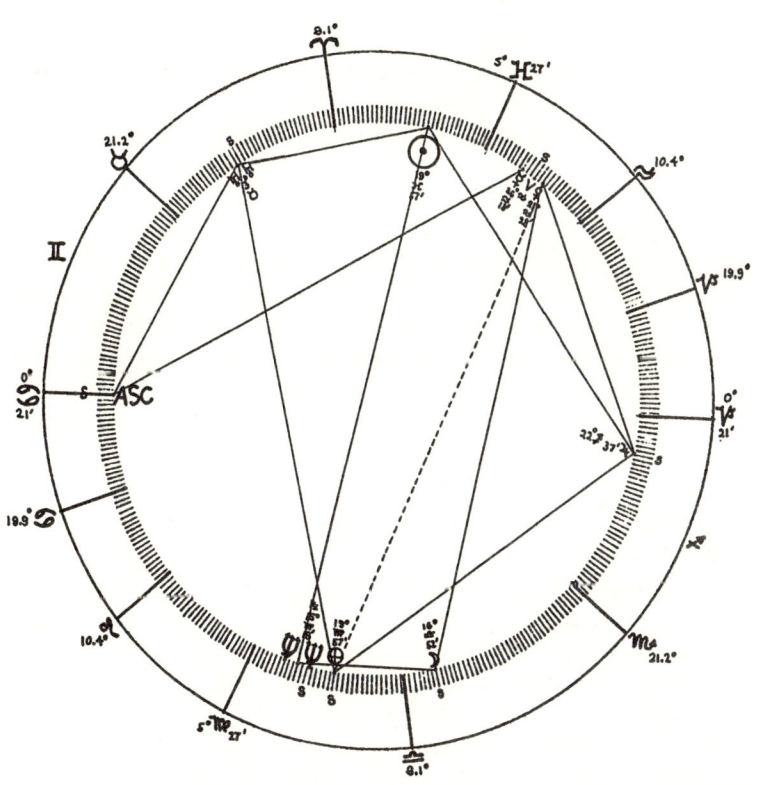

centered desires; therefore it will be fairly easy for him to transmute these self-centered desires to Soul-infused aspirations. The absence of Ray Three is also fortunate because it predicates little or no desire for new experiences solely for self-centered reasons. Yet, as shown in a previous step, he will have many experiences, but mainly as karmic lessons to be learned from the past. Three of the five Rays are feminine, denoting sensitivity, concern for others, and passivity. Two of the Rays are masculine, denoting assertiveness, intellect, and extroversion. The ratio of three to two shows a good balance of the masculine/feminine polarity of the planetary energies of his self-centered personality desires.

In Step 8 we found the planets and the Ascendant and their Rays which influence the inner Soul life. They are: Ascendant—Ray Seven, Neptune—Ray Six, Moon—Ray Four, Uranus—Ray Seven, Vulcan—Ray One, Jupiter—Ray Two, and Earth—Ray Three. Only Ray Five is missing, which means his logical mind is not important to his inner Soul life. A double Ray Seven indicates that organization, order, and rhythm are necessary for his Soul life and purpose. Three of these Rays are of negative polarity and four are positive. Like the foregoing, they are in good balance. Two masculine Rays are missing in one group and one in the other group, yet all feminine Rays are represented in both groups, indicating that his problems are concerned mostly with the feminine part of his nature—his feelings and his sensitivity.

His problem for this lifetime is definitely challenging. It concerns a T-square involving a semi-square and a sesquiquadrate to planets of the T-square. His Sun in Pisces in the tenth house, a personality desire planet, squares Jupiter in Sagittarius in the sixth house, a Soul life planet. This indicates a self-centered, subtle desire for career prominence, and at the same time, a Soul urge to work toward perfecting himself and serving others with strong goal direction congruent with Universal Laws. Both Sun and Jupiter are rulers of Ray Two of love and wisdom. Because Jupiter denotes his Soul, he aspires to serve others with love and wisdom in an unattached way. The Sun, denoting the personality, indicates a desire for honor and attachment to the monetary fruits of his labor. This is a challenging problem, yet he receives help from a tri-septile between the Sun and the Moon in Libra in the fifth house, which gives a high level of creative talent for four reasons: (1) the tri-septile in itself is a donor of creativity; (2) Ray Four, ruled by the Moon, is a donor of creativity; (3) the fifth house, tenanting the Moon, is a house of creativity and self-realization; (4) the sign Libra, tenanting the Moon, is a donor of rhythm, beauty, and balance. The Moon makes two other aspects in this horoscope, one to Neptune and one to Venus, which emphasize the Moon's instrumentality in resolving Case One's problems. The semi-sextile to Neptune in Virgo in the fourth house gives psychic energy to delve deeply into the past to help him better understand the undesirable habits that should be changed. Because Neptune is a planet of both the Soul life and the self-centered desires, and the Moon is a planet of the Soul life only, the preponderance of energy directed toward the Soul life indicates this aspect is extremely helpful in diverting energy that was previously used for self-centered desires to Soul aspirations. Moon trine Venus, a self-centered planet, indicates the ease of using his logical mind to understand Aquarian Age principles and Universal Laws so that he can make a wise choice in deciding whether it is to his advantage to spend time and energy in self-centered indulgence or in Soul evolvement. The square of Jupiter to Earth in Virgo in the fourth house, two planets influencing the Soul life, indicates a seeming though not actual difficulty in perfecting himself and in serving others because of the many karmic experiences that must be his until he learns his needed lessons. His Sun opposite Neptune in Virgo in the fourth house indicates some confusion with reference to his Soul evolvement and his desire for career prominence. This is a most challenging aspect, not only for this reason, but mainly because while only Neptune is a Soul life planet, both the Sun and Neptune are planets of self-centered personality desires. Awareness that his many karmic experiences are not a deterrent to Soul growth helps to lessen his confusion a great deal. Jupiter square Neptune shows a tendency toward poor judgment in that he feels to some degree that his Soul evolvement, even though his urges are strong, is a lot easier than it actually is. This, too, adds to his confusion, yet with both planets' energies directed to the Soul life, and only Neptune's energy directed toward self-centered desires, this aspect is not too difficult to work through. Neptune, a ruler of Ray Six of idealism and devotion, indicates a need for a less emotional approach to his spiritual urges. Because his Uranus in Taurus in the eleventh house is semi-square his Sun, there is a tendency to be stubbornly rebellious in a subtle way in career matters, making it difficult for him to follow orders of a superior. The sesquiquadrate from Uranus to Earth shows unexpected karmic experiences coming from friends. Earth quincunx Venus in Aquarius in the ninth shows frustration until he is aware that the freedom without responsibility he desires in his affectional relationships is one cause of his difficult experiences.

Two planets, Neptune and Uranus, act as major points of contact between the inner Soul life and the outer self-centered personality desires. It is through these planets and the easy aspects they make to other planets, and that these other planets make to additional planets that much help is given him. The Uranus energy he uses in self-centered personality desires is erratic and unpredictable with his friends and in his goals. Yet the Uranus energy he uses for his inner Soul life is much in tune with Aquarian-Age philosophy. Because Uranus is sextile his Cancer Ascendant and because Uranus is the ruler of Ray Seven which is his Soul Ray (Ascendant), there is much psychic sensitivity, contemplation, and rhythmic power in his thoughts, all of which contribute to a rich and powerful Soul life which can be used optimally in attaining illumination and engaging in humanitarian service. The power in his Soul life also benefits him in working out the previously mentioned conflicts.

After he becomes aware of his problems, he is able, through perception and sensitivity, to visualize himself as he wants to be—his thoughts of visualization have much power in helping him to actually become that which he visualizes. His Ascendant, which signifies his Ray Seven Soul, is trine his Mercury, a ruler of Ray Four of harmony through conflict, in Aquarius in the ninth house. The Ascendant, being the primary indicator of his Soul life, is stronger in this trine than Mercury, a planet of his self-centered personality desires, which is the source of much conflict in his mind. The strength of the Ascendant thus shows that his self-centered thoughts can easily be changed to strong Soul-infused ones, caring for all regardless of race, religion, sex, age, color, or level of Soul evolvement.

It is to be noted that the phenomenon will occur in this and in other charts in which a single planet carries a two-fold power in a single aspect. In this case, the aspect is Neptune opposite Sun. The Neptune energy of self-centered personality desires indicates emotional confusion between career and home life; the Neptune energy of his Soul life confers a capacity to look deeply into his psyche for self understanding. His Neptune, a ruler of Ray Six of idealism and devotion, semi-sextile Moon, a ruler of Ray Four of harmony through conflict, in Libra in the fifth house is a second example of the twin-powered aspect referred to above. The Neptune energy of self-centered desires semi-sextile the Moon of Soul aspirations shows a mild tendency to become irritated by the weaknesses of others. The Neptune energy of the inner Soul life semi-sextile the Moon of the Soul life shows the possibility of creative capacity and harmony from resolving conflicts, enabling him to make life more harmonious for others.

The Moon is trine Venus, a ruler of Ray Five of concrete knowledge, in the ninth house, enhancing his creative capacity through unattached love for others and through understanding and using Universal Laws. His Venus is sextile Jupiter, accentuating the previous aspect showing his love for Universal Laws coupled with a reasoning mind, making it easier to raise his level of consciousness and to help others do the same. His Vulcan, a ruler of Ray One of power and will, a Soul life planet, is in the ninth house in Aquarius. This indicates the power he can exercise through understanding Universal Laws to crystallize his unconscious weaknesses, and bring them to the surface and eradicate them. Jupiter, the esoteric ruler of Aquarius which is not only the cusp of the ninth house but the sign of all three planets therein, is an esoteric ruler of his Soul. It enhances the understanding of spiritual truths in this New Age so he can use them for his own Soul growth and that of others.

The fourth house of the Soul and the ninth house of the understanding of Universal Laws and spiritual truths are the strongest houses in this chart, indicating that his problems should be solved to the depth of his Soul and with the strong implementation of spiritual truths.

In summary, his main problem is the conflict between his personality, on a subtle level, for fame and honor, and his Soul's aspiration to use his psychic capacity not only to understand his weaknesses better and eradicate them, but also to serve others through his spiritual understanding and his own Soul growth.

Step 10. From his natal horoscope (Horoscope 1) complete that part of the delineation begun in Steps 8 and 9 with Horoscopes 2 and 3. Include in this delineation the Moon's Nodes and all aspects not found in Horoscopes 2 and 3. Determine the esoteric planetary rulers of the cuspal signs and the meaning of the Ray each planet rules.

The first house, signifying the Soul and its expression, is tenanted solely by the South Node of the Moon. A square from the South Node in Cancer to Mars, a ruler of Ray Six of idealism and emotionalism, in Aries in the eleventh house indicates that certain friends may use physical energy impulsively and impatiently either toward him or in some way to cause him problems. If they do, his feelings will be hurt until he has learned a karmic lesson, having its origin in a past life in which he acted the same way toward others. He brought that tendency into this life, but when he has learned, through receiving the same treatment from others, to overcome this weakness in his own nature, he will no longer receive this lesson-teaching treatment. This aspectual energy then will be transmuted to the esoteric rulers of Cancer and Aries which are Neptune, a ruler of Ray Six of idealism and devotion, and Mercury, a ruler of Ray Four of harmony through conflict. This transmutation blends the idealistic urges of Neptune with the activity of the mind to attain harmony.

The esoteric ruler of the Ascendant is also Neptune which conjuncts Earth, a ruler of Ray Three of the higher mind, in Virgo in the fourth house. This reinforces a previous statement that Earth experiences are crucial for perfecting himself and getting in touch with his Soul.

The third house with no tenanting planets has Leo on its cusp. The esoteric ruler of Leo is the Sun, a ruler of Ray Two of love and wisdom, which is in Pisces in the tenth house. His logical reasoning mind easily can be filled with love, a combination of head and heart which can spell wisdom. When this combination is used with compassion for and kindness toward the suffering in a career capacity (Sun in Pisces in the tenth house), self-realization is assured.

His seventh house of many relationships that are necessary for weighing benefits of materialistic self-centered desires versus spiritual aspirations, is tenanted only by the North Node in Capricorn. This fact, coupled with Capricorn on the cusp, indicates the importance of persistent effort in weighing the forementioned benefits and gives him the self-discipline to overcome undesirable habits, leading to a higher level of consciousness. The trine from the North Node to Neptune shows an urge toward idealism. The trine from the North Node to Uranus, the ruler of Ray Seven of order and strong thoughts, shows an ease of construction of positive thought forms. These two aspects acting in concert enable him to make a wise decision as to which will benefit him most—self-centered desires or spiritual aspirations. The esoteric ruler of both the seventh house cusp and the sign of the North Node is Saturn which is in Pisces in the tenth house. Saturn, a ruler of Ray Three of intellectual activity, indicates a career in helping the unfortunate through his abstract mind. Such a career will aid him in making a wise choice between self-centered desires and spiritual aspirations because of the suffering he sees in these persons as a result of their self-centered desires, and it also enables him to fulfill karmic obligations of the past.

The cusp of the tenth house, Pisces, predicates a career in which compassion and kindness for the suffering is paramount. The esoteric ruler of Pisces is Pluto, a ruler of Ray One of power and will. This signifies intense energy directed toward the Soul's purpose through his career. Pluto in Cancer in the second house shows sensitivity toward spiritual illumination, especially useful for career matters. It is mainly through Pluto, the primary ruler of the personality, that aid can be given the Soul and its purpose. Saturn, a ruler of Ray Three of the higher mind, in the tenth house is quincunx the Moon, a ruler of Ray Four of harmony through conflict, in Libra in the fifth house and is opposite Neptune in Virgo in the fourth house. This shows a tendency to occasional fearful and fuzzy thinking which causes conflicts. However, his Mars in Aries in the elev-

enth house making an exact semi-sextile to Saturn gives him
the energy and the mental capacity to clarify the emotionally
colored confused thoughts. With this clarification comes the
realization of the interdependence between his career and Soul
evolvement.

These clearer thoughts can result also from Aquarian Age
philosophies because of Mars' situation in the eleventh house.
Mars, a ruler of Ray Six, is opposite the Moon, a ruler of Ray
Four, in the fifth house. This shows a tendency to be angry,
impatient, and impulsive and then to forget how he behaved.
Mars square the Nodes shows that others will be impatient and
angry with him as karmic lessons-teaching experiences. Mars
quincunx Neptune shows a tendency to the confused use of this
Martian energy; Mars septile Venus gives him creative talent
in Aquarian Age projects and Mars semi-sextile Saturn gives
him courage and self-confidence to serve humanity through his
career. Since the quincunx from Mars to Neptune indicates the
expenditure of much psychic energy in his thoughts and actions, it is very important that he make strong efforts to mon-
itor his thoughts and change them when necessary. His Mars
bi-septile Pluto gives him not only will power to change negative thoughts, but the realization of the desirability of good
thoughts. The esoteric ruler of Aries, the sign of Mars and the
cusp of the eleventh house, is Mercury, a ruler of Ray Four of
harmony through conflict. The type of Aquarian philosophies
he could most successfully use to help others attain harmony
would be those concerned with divine ideas. These ideas would
relate strongly to such Universal concepts as Reincarnation
and Karma, and could be given one-pointedly to reach the
minds of others.

The eighth house has no tenanting planets. Its cusp is Capricorn as is the cusp of the seventh house, conferring discipline
and the urge to work diligently and persistently to overcome
temptation and to regenerate spiritually. The esoteric ruler,
Saturn, a ruler of Ray Three of the higher mind, ties his career
very strongly to his Soul evolvement as it does in seventh house
matters, but as esoteric ruler of the eighth house cusp, Saturn
shows that his contemplative capacity is the instigator of his
spiritual regeneration. Saturn opposite Neptune may confuse
him as to whether he should spend most of his time working

toward a career or toward Soul evolvement until he realizes they can be combined. Saturn semi-sextile Mars, a ruler of Ray Six of idealism and devotion, in Aries in the eleventh house gives courage, energy, and enthusiasm which can be devoted to a pioneering type of career in rapport with Aquarian Age philosophy which may be conducive to his spiritual regeneration. Another aspect favoring his spiritual regeneration is Saturn, a ruler of Ray Three, septile Uranus, the ruler of Ray Seven, pointing toward a creative talent that can be used in his career to make intuitive Aquarian philosophies workable. Courage and enthusiasm for implementing Aquarian Age philosophies in his career and in his own life can be his stepping stone to understanding himself more clearly and to passing the many tests that his Soul gives him.

The twelfth house has no tenanting planets, but it has an interception. The esoteric ruler of its cusp, Taurus, is Vulcan in Aquarius in the ninth house, a ruler of Ray One of will and power. The Taurus cusp indicates that through meditation he can receive much illumination of Universal Truths and Aquarian-Age philosophies. This illumination, coupled with Vulcan's power to crystallize repressions, guilt feelings, and other blockages and weaknesses of the unconscious, brings hidden difficulties into the conscious mind where they can be eradicated. The esoteric ruler of Gemini, which is the intercepted sign of the twelfth house, is Venus, the ruler of Ray Five of the logical mind. It is in Aquarius in the ninth house conjunct Vulcan, a ruler of Ray One. This shows that he is capable of understanding Universal Truths logically, then using them with Vulcan's capacity to bring blockages from the unconscious to the light of day. This dual capacity of Vulcan and Venus helps rid him of buried problems of the past and brings to the conscious mind all that needs to be eradicated.

There are two aspects involving Horoscopes 2 and 3 yet to be interpreted. One of the three planets, Pluto, is in Horoscope 2 while the other two planets, Mercury and Venus, are in Horsocope 3. Pluto, a ruler of Ray One of will and power in Cancer in the second house is quincunx Mercury, a ruler of Ray Four of harmony through conflict, in Aquarius in the ninth house. Because Pluto is a ruler of the personality to serve the Soul, and Mercury is a ruler of the personality for self-centered desires, there is a conflict between a tendency to force his opinions referring to Aquarian philosophical spiritual truths on others and using his will power to study, understand, and pass on to those who are ready for these same truths. Until this conflict is resolved by adhering to the latter, he experiences much frustration. Pluto, a ruler of Ray One of will and power tri-septiles Venus, the ruler of Ray Five of the logical mind, in Aquarius in the ninth house. This enhances his sensitivity for creative projects and for their practical use in rapport with Aquarian Age philosophy. This very enhancement encourages the transmutation of the Venus energies formerly used in irresponsible affectional experiences to experiences for Soul growth. Pluto gives him much power to make this change.

Step 11. Find the planet closest to the zenith in the natal chart and the Ray it rules. Because this is the last planet his consciousness was on before his present life, explain the abilities derived there to be applied in this life.

Saturn, a ruler of Ray Three of intellectual activity of the higher mind, was his last planet of occupancy before this life. The obstacles and restrictions he encountered and the discipline he was taught there are beneficial in this life to help him accept and learn quickly from difficult karmic experiences.

Step 12. Find the planet or planets in the natal chart that are most influential. Use Chart 28 showing all signs each planet rules. A planet is influential by virtue of having three planets or important points in the sign or signs it rules.

Seven planets are especially influential. The degree of influence of each is shown in Horoscopes 2 and 3. Uranus, the ruler of Ray Seven of order and rhythm, and Neptune, a ruler of Ray Six of idealism and devotion, have the strongest influence. They are influential in the Soul life, the personality life expressing the Soul's purpose, and in the self-centered personality life.

Two other planets are influential in two categories—Jupiter, a ruler of Ray Two of love and wisdom, and the Moon, a ruler of Ray Four of harmony through conflict, are influential in the Soul life and in the personality life expressing the Soul's purpose.

Two other planets are influential in only one category—Pluto and Venus. Pluto, a ruler of Ray One of will and power is influential in the personality expressing the Soul's purpose, and Venus, the ruler of Ray Five of the logical mind, is influential in the self-centered personality.

The last influential planet, Saturn, a ruler of Ray Three of intellectual activity of the higher mind, shows no specific influences in these three categories, yet it is influential throughout all facets of his life because, as noted in Step 11, it is the last planet on which his consciousness resided before this life.

The fact that each of these seven most influential planets rules a Ray different from any of the other planets makes this a most unusual and complete representation of Ray energy usage and influence, giving him a unique opportunity for Soul growth. Uranus and Neptune, which are influential in all three categories, indicate inspirational capacity and the ability to use powerful thoughts to produce ordered and rhythmic living. Jupiter and the Moon, which are influential in two categories, show that he has the potential to use his inspirational and powerful thoughts in a sensitive, loving, and wise manner. Of the two planets influential in only one category, Pluto gives him intense power to express his Soul's purpose in his outer life, yet Venus may create difficulties for him when he rationalizes irresponsible affectional relationships, a definite weakness. Saturn's influence can release instant difficult lesson-teaching karma to eliminate that weakness when the higher abstract perceptive mind takes precedence over the rationalizing mind.

Step 13. Every seventh year there is a significant change in one's life, a possible crisis, and a good chance for opportunities. Find his age when his last opportunity year occurred and when the next one will occur. He can then look back to assess how he handled it and contemplate how he might have handled it better so that he can take full advantage of the next year of opportunity.

His age during the last year of opportunity was forty-two in 1978 and the next will be forty-nine in 1985.

Step 14. Determine the general tendencies of each 14-year period to age 84. Using a day for a year, find the exact major aspects (conjunction, opposition, square, trine, and sextile) of all progressed planets except the Moon to natal planets for each period. From this information in the various periods, compare the number of total aspects, the number of. easy versus challenging aspects, the Ray each planet making an aspect rules, and the number of times each Ray is activated. From this comparison indicate the general trend of thoughts and activities in the various periods of his life. Exact aspects give extra energies of the Rays and planets involved. Because this step is not a detailed one, but is a general overview, and because Ray-Centered Astrology and the progressions are concerned mostly with the inner life, the progressions and the Rays ruled by the aspecting planets are stressed.

AGE—0 TO 14 YEARS FOR CASE 1

Progressed Planets' Positions	Partile Aspects	Easy	Challenging	Rays Planets Rule
☉ 19 ♓ 57—3 ♈ 50	P ☉ □ ♃		✗	2, 2
☊ 9 ♑ 14—8 ♑ 29	P ☉ △ ♆	✶		2, 1
☿ 26 ♒ 13—18 ♓ 15	P ☿ ✶ ☊	✶		4
♀ 21 ♒ 28—8 ♓ 42	P ☿ ☌ ♄	✗		4, 3
♂ 13 ♈ 21—23 ♈ 53	P ☿ ✶ ♅	✶		4, 7
♃ 22 ♐ 57—23 ♐ 59	P ☿ ✓ ♆		✶	4, 6
♄ 13 ♓ 41—15 ♓ 22	P ♀ ✓ ☿	✶		5, 4
♅ 3 ♉ 0—3 ♉ 42	P ♀ ✶ ♃	✗		5, 3
♆ 15 ♍ 18 ℞ —14 ♍ 54 ℞	P ♀ ✶ ♅	✗		5, 7
♇ 25 ♋ 22 ℞ —25 ♋ 12 ℞	P ♂ ✶ ♀	✗		6, 5
	P ♂ △ ♃	✗		6, 2
	P ♂ ✓ ☽		✗	6, 4
	P ♄ ✓ ♆		✗	3, 6

7 Rays # Found	7 Rays Frequency
1 — 1	4 — 6
2 — 5	2 & 6 — 5
3 — 2	5 — 4
4 — 6	3 & 7 — 2
5 — 4	1 — 1
6 — 5	
7 — 2	

AGE—14 TO 28 YEARS FOR CASE 1

Progressed Planets' Positions	Partile Aspects	Easy	Challenging	Rays Planets Rule
☉3 ♈ 50—17 ♈ 40	P ☉ □ ☊		x	2
☊8♈ 29—6 ♆ 54	P ☉ ☌ ♂	x		2, 6
☿18♓ 15—14♈ 34	P ☉ ☍ ☽		x	2, 4
♀8♓ 42—25♓ 52	P ☿ ☌ ☉	x		4, 2
♂23♈ 53—4♉ 15	P ☿ □ ☊		x	4
♃23♐ 59—24♐ 25	P ☿ ☌ ♂	x		4, 6
♄15♓ 22—16♓ 59	P ☿ □ ♃		x	4, 2
♅3♉ 42—4♉ 27	P ☿ △ ♇	x		4, 1
♆14♍ 54℞ —14♍ 34℞	P ♀ ☌ ☉	x		5, 2
♇25♋ 12℞ —25♋ 9℞	P ♀ ✶ ☊	x		5
	P ♀ □ ♃		x	5, 2
	P ♀ ☌ ♄	x		5, 3
	P ♀ ☍ ♆		x	5, 6
	P ♀ △ ♇	x		5, 1
	P ♂ ✶ ☿	x		6, 4
	P ♂ ☌ ♅	x		6, 7
	P ♂ □ ♇		x	6, 1

7 Rays	♂ Found		7 Rays	Frequency
1 —	3		2 & 4 —	7
2 —	7		5 & 6 —	6
3 —	1		1 —	3
4 —	7		3 & 7 —	1
5 —	6			
6 —	6			
7 —	1			

AGE—28 TO 42 YEARS FOR CASE 1

Progressed Planets' Positions	Partile Aspects			Easy	Challenging	Rays Planets Rule
☉17 ♈ 40—1 ♉ 22	P ☉	✶	☿	✗		2, 4
☊ 6 ♑ 54—5 ♑ 37	P ☉	✶	♀	✗		2, 5
☿14 ♈ 34—13 ♉ 37	P ☉	△	♃	✗		2, 2
♀ 25 ♓ 52—13 ♈ 4	P ☉	□	♇		✗	2, 1
♂ 4 ♉ 15—14 ♉ 28	P ☿	△	☊	✗		4
♃24 ♐ 26℞ —24 ♐ 15℞	P ☿	✶	☿	✗		4, 4
♄16 ♓ 59—18 ♓ 29	P ☿	✶	♀	✗		4, 5
♅ 4 ♉ 27—5 ♉ 15	P ☿	△	♃	✗		4, 2
♆14 ♍ 34℞ —14 ♍ 17℞	P ☿	☌	♆	✗		4, 7
☋ 25 ♋ 9—22 ♋ 12	P ☿	☍	♇		✗	4, 1
	P ☿	☌	☽		✗	4, 4
	P ♀	□	☊		✗	5
	P ♂	△	☊	✗		6
	P ♂	✶	♄	✗		6, 3

7 Rays # Found		7 Rays Frequency
1 — 2		4 — 10
2 — 6		2 — 6
		5 — 3
3 — 1		
4 — 10		1 & 6 — 2
5 — 3		3 & 7 — 1
6 — 2		
7 — 1		

AGE—42 TO 56 YEARS FOR CASE 1

Progressed Planets' Positions	Partile Aspects			Easy	Challenging	Rays Planets Rule
⊕ 1 ♉ 22—14 ♉ 58	P ⊕	△	♌	✗		2
☊ 5 ♈ 37—4 ♈ 33	P ⊙	✳	♄	✗		2, 3
☿ 13 ♉ 37—5 ♊ 58	P ⊙	☌	♅	✗		2, 7
♀ 13 ♈ 4—0 ♉ 16	P ☿	✳	⊙	✗		4, 2
♂ 14 ♉ 28—24 ♉ 31	P ☿	□	☿		✗	4, 4
♃ 24 ♐ 16℞ —23 ♐ 29	P ☿	□	♀		✗	4, 5
♄ 18 ♓ 29—19 ♓ 47	P ☿	✳	♄	✗		4, 3
♅ 5 ♉ 15—6 ♉ 3	P ☿	△	♆	✗		4, 6
♆ 14 ♍ 17℞ —14 ♍ 5℞	P ☿	✳	℞	✗		4, 1
♇ 25 ♋ 12—25 ♋ 19	P ♀	✳	☿	✗		5, 4
	P ♀	✳	♀	✗		5, 5
	P ♀	☌	♂	✗		5, 6
	P ♀	△	♃	✗		5, 2
	P ♀	□	℞		✗	5, 1
	P ♀	☌	☽		✗	5, 4
	P ♂	✳	⊙	✗		6, 2
	P ♂	□	♀		✗	6, 5
	P ♂	✳	♄	✗		6, 3
	P ♂	△	♆	✗		6, 6

7 Rays ♀ Found		7 Rays Frequency
1 — 2		4 & 5 — 9
2 — 6		6 — 7
3 — 3		2 — 6
4 — 9		3 — 3
5 — 9		1 — 2
6 — 7		7 — 1
7 — 1		

AGE—56 TO 70 YEARS FOR CASE 1

Progressed Planets' Positions	Partile Aspects	Easy	Challenging	Rays Planets Rule.
☉14 ♉ 58--28 ♉ 29	P ☉ ✶ ⊕	x		2, 2
☊ 4 ♈ 33--3 ♍ 54	P ⊕ □ ☿		x	2, 4
☿ 5 ♊ 58--14 ♊ 3	P ☉ □ ♀		x	2, 5
♀ 0 ♉ 16--17 ♉ 27	P ⊕ △ ♆	x		2, 6
♂ 24 ♉ 31--4 ♊ 25	P ⊕ ✶ ♇	x		2, 1
♃ 23 ♐ 29℞ --22 ♐ 12℞	P ☿ ✶ ♂	x		4, 6
♄ 19 ♓ 47--20 ♓ 54	P ☿ □ ♄		x	4, 3
♅ 6 ♉ 3--6 ♉ 50	P ♀ △ ☊	x		5
♆ 14 ♍ 5℞ --14 ♍ 0 ℞	P ♀ ✶ ♄	x		5, 3
⚷ 25 ♋ 19--25 ♋ 31	P ♀ ☌ ♅	x		5, 7
	P ♀ △ ♆	x		5, 6
	P ♂ □ ☿		x	6, 4
	P ♂ ✶ ♇	x		6, 1
	P ♃ ☌ ♃	x		2, 2
	P ♄ ☌ ⊕	x		3, 2
	P ♇ ☌ ♇	x		1, 1

7 Rays # Found	7 Rays Frequency
1 -- 4	2 -- 9
2 -- 9	5 & 6 -- 5
3 -- 3	1 & 4 -- 4
4 -- 4	3 -- 3
5 -- 5	7 -- 1
6 -- 5	
7 -- 1	

AGE—70 TO 84 YEARS FOR CASE 1

Progressed Planets' Positions	Partile Aspects	Easy	Challenging	Rays Planets Rule
☉ 28 ♉ 29--11 Ⅱ 56	P ♅ ⚹ ♂	X		4, 6
☊ 3 ♈ 54--3 ♈ 36	P ♅ □ ♄		X	4, 3
☿ 14 Ⅱ 3 ℞ --8 Ⅱ 40 ℞	P ♀ ⚹ ☉	X		5, 2
♀ 17 ♉ 27--4 Ⅱ 37	P ♀ □ ♅		X	5, 4
♂ 4 Ⅱ 25--14 Ⅱ 9	P ♀ □ ♀		X	5, 5
♃ 22 ♐ 12 ℞ --20 ♐ 35 ℞	P ♀ ⚹ ♇	X		5, 1
♄ 20 ♓ 54--21 ♓ 44	P ☍ ⚹ ♂	X		6, 6
♅ 6 ♉ 50--7 ♉ 54	P ♂ □ ♄		X	6, 3
♆ 14 ♏ 0 ℞ --14 ♏ 0	P ♃ ⚹ ♀	X		2, 5
♇ 25 ♋ 31--25 ♋ 46				

7 Rays ♂ Found		7 Rays Frequency	
1 -- 1		5 -- 6	
2 -- 2		6 -- 4	
3 -- 2		4 -- 3	
4 -- 3		2 & 3 -- 2	
5 -- 6		1 -- 1	
6 -- 4		7 -- 0	
7 -- 0			

SUMMARY OF RAY ACTIVATION FOR CASE 1
DERIVED FROM 6 AGE-PERIOD CHARTS

Age Period	Total	Aspects Easy	Challenging	Frequency per Ray per Period 10	9	8	7	6	5	4	3	2	1	0
0 to 14	13	9	4					4	2 6	5		3 7	1	
14 to 28	17	10	7				2 4	5 6			1	3 7		
28 to 42	14	10	4	4				2		5	2 6	3 7		
42 to 56	19	14	5		4 5		6	2		3	1	7		
56 to 70	16	12	4		2				5 6	1 4	3	7		
70 to 84	9	5	4					5		6	4	2 3	1	7

There was only one period in which all Seven Rays were not manifested (shown by rulership of planets of exact aspects), and in that period only one Ray was missing. This is significant in that it indicates a fairly good balance of the various Ray energies to help him throughout his life. Even though every period has more easy than challenging aspects with a relatively low variance of one and one quarter to three times, this is not an easy life for him. Many difficult karmic experiences will be his until needed lessons are learned because Ray Four of harmony through conflict is the strongest Ray in his life and also the strongest Ray in every period but the last two. Yet the indications show a potential high degree of Soul evolvement. One reason is that the more lesson-teaching experiences one has, the sooner he overcomes his weaknesses. This puts Case 1 in a position to better serve others with more time, ability, and with the energy of Ray Two of love and wisdom, the second strongest Ray he receives from his exact aspects. Ray Five of the concrete mind is third in strength, enhancing his ability to acquire knowledge, develop reason, and learn to use logic. This will enable him to better understand such Universal Laws as Reincarnation and Karma, so important to him because of Ray Four's strength. Rays Four, Two, Five, and Six are the strongest in that order, and because three of these are even-numbered and the odd-numbered one falls next to the last, the energies supplied him from partile aspects are more of the sensitive, psychic, loving nature than of the intellectual and extrovertive.

From birth to age fourteen is the period in which his sensitivity, introversion, and loving, nurturing feeling are the most prominent of all six periods because Rays Four, Two, and Six are the strongest. Of these three, Ray Four, heading the list, indicates a period of many lesson-teaching experiences. Because there are two and one-quarter times more easy than challenging aspects, he receives much help in learning his karmic lessons. The next three periods are the most challenging of all six periods.

The second period, age fourteen to twenty-eight, is perhaps the most challenging in that it has the potential for overcoming many weaknesses. This period closely follows the sixth in the smallest ratio of easy to challenging aspects, yet it has the second largest number of aspects of any period, and no other Ray affects him more than Ray Four of harmony through conflict.

The third period of age twenty-eight to forty-two shows that Ray Four energy has the most input of any period, and also by far the most in this period. The total number of partile aspects is rather small compared to the previous and succeeding periods, yet the ratio of easy to challenging aspects is comparatively high. Therefore he receives much help in learning from his conflicts which, though perhaps not as numerous as in some other periods, will be his major concern in this period.

The fourth period from age forty-two to fifty-six has the most partile aspects and is therefore the time of highest energy input. Even though it is second of all periods in the highest ratio of easy to challenging aspects, no Ray energy he receives is stronger than Ray Four. This indicates a time of immense energy input, a great portion of which is lesson-teaching experiences, yet much help is given him in learning quickly from these experiences in many ways. The most outstanding way is through his logical reasoning because the strength of Ray Five of the concrete mind ties with Ray Four. This is the period in which he could do well to study and contemplate Reincarnation and Karma. He will not only be able to grasp well the meanings in a logical manner during this period, but can easily benefit from their application to his own life. This and the two previous periods show the greatest potential for Soul evolvement through difficult lesson-teaching experiences resulting in the overcoming of weaknesses.

The fifth period from age fifty-six to seventy will undoubtedly be the period of his greatest service to others for a number of reasons. One reason is that the ratio of easy to challenging aspects is the highest of all periods. Another is that this is the first period in which Ray Four of harmony through conflict is topped by other Ray energies in the number of times it reaches him through partile aspects. Its strength is comparatively small because it is topped by three Rays and tied by one. The more lessons he has learned in the previous challenging periods, the less will be his difficult karma in this period. For these reasons and because he has a relatively high number of exact aspects, he has the time and energy for making this period one of greater service to others consonant with his Soul Ray's purpose, resulting in a sharply increased level of Soul evolvement. Personal karmic responsibilities must always be met before one can use all his time in serving humanity. Because Ray Two is by far the strongest Ray in this period, its energies of love and wisdom can truly help him to be of great services to others.

The sixth period of age seventy to eighty-four finds by far the least number of exact aspects, thereby giving him less energy than in any other period. Even though Ray Four is topped by two other Rays in the number of times its energy reaches him, this is not an easy period because the ratio of easy to challenging aspects is the lowest of all periods. Yet having lived through five periods and hopefully having overcome many weaknesses, some of the so-called challenging aspects will not bring difficult experiences to him. With regard to those difficult experiences for which he has not yet overcome the corresponding weaknesses, he is fortunate in that Ray Five of the concrete mind has the highest energy input. Therefore it should not be difficult for him to understand logically certain Universal Laws and profit from them, thus lessening the challenging experiences. This is the only period in which a Ray is missing—Ray Seven of order and rhythmic living. This lack which appears here rather than in an earlier period, is fortunate in that this placement suggests that an order and rhythm established from five previous periods should have become habitual by this time.

Step 15. Each person is influenced greatly by the four signs of the cross that the Sun was in at his birth. Elucidate the specific opportunities during the four periods. Include for each sign its meaning, the meaning of the esoteric planetary ruler of the sign and the Ray that planet rules, and the house or houses the sign tenants.

1. The last week of February and the first three weeks of March, the Sun is in Pisces in his ninth and tenth houses. The esoteric ruler of Pisces, Pluto, is a ruler of Ray One of will and power. For about the first five days much power is at his command to understand himself better on a deep level, releasing buried blocks, repressions, and guilt feelings when the Sun is in his ninth house. During the rest of the period, while it is in his tenth house, he can improve career matters in a kind yet subtly powerful way.

2. During the last week in May and the first three weeks in June, the Sun is in Gemini in his twelfth house. The esoteric ruler of Gemini is Venus, the Ruler of Ray Five of the logical mind. This is a good time for him to bring from the unconscious to the conscious level, repressed feelings and other weaknesses to eradicate them through logical reasoning.

3. During the last week in August and the first three weeks in September, the Sun is in Virgo in his third and fourth houses. The esoteric ruler of Virgo is the Moon, a ruler of Ray Four of harmony through conflict. In only about the first five days of this period is the Sun in his third house when his conscious mind can analyze and learn from any difficult karmic lessons he is experiencing and thus overcome a weakness. During

the rest of the period when the Sun is in his fourth house, he could profitably meditate on a Soul level as to what he must do to resolve his conflicts and attain more harmony.

4. During the last week of November and the first three weeks of December, the Sun is in Sagittarius in his sixth house. The esoteric ruler of Sagittarius is Earth, a ruler of Ray Three of intellectual activity. Many experiences at this time help him to become aware of his weaknesses. At this time, efforts to understand Universal Truths could overcome some of his weaknesses, and through his enthusiastic one-pointed manner, help others do the same.

Step 16. When he has formulated a plan for his life work, he should reassess it periodically in terms of his motivation because lasting success is not possible without proper motivation. If his plan is not to serve others to the best of his ability because of his love and concern for them, he had best spend time becoming aware of his weaknesses as elucidated in this delineation, endeavoring to transmute them into strengths, especially those strengths of his Ray Seven Soul and Ray One Personality as found in Chapter Three. If his motivation is right and is strong, he can expect success and joy in his work as he follows these steps in carrying out his life plan:

1. A strong intention to carry it through by focusing his ideas in his mind.
2. Visualization by imagination and impressing on his mind what he wants to do.
3. Projection which is the willing of his plan by thought because energy follows thought. This projection must be carried out in a way that is consistent with his Soul and Personality Rays. From Chart 29 we find his Soul predicates a projection in line with the awareness that spirit and matter must meet because energy is spirit at its highest vibration and becomes matter at its lower vibration. His Ray One Personality indicates he must, through knowledge, conviction, and love, assert in his mind his life plan.

Step 17. One can successfully study and teach esoteric wisdom if in his natal chart he has a trine, a sextile, a semi-sextile, a quincunx, a quintile, a quintile derivative, a septile, or a septile derivative between Jupiter and Pluto.

Because this entity has a quincunx between Pluto and Jupiter, he is capable of successfully studying and teaching esoteric wisdom. This aspect between Pluto, a ruler of Ray One of power and will and the esoteric ruler of Pisces, with Jupiter, a ruler of Ray Two of love and wisdom and the esoteric ruler of Aquarius, indicates a strong urge to help humanity evolve spiritually in this, the Aquarian Age. Pluto is the focal planet in his Finger-of-God aspect pattern; it is found in the second house of spiritual illumination. These factors indicate more than a strong urge to esotericism—they indicate a destiny. All quincunx and septile aspects are fated, which means that those individuals possessing them willed so strongly, before birth, that the energy of those planets be used in specific spiritual ways in the coming life, that the Soul, often with the personality unaware, sees to it that actualization takes place.

218

CASE STUDY 2—NATAL & PROGRESSED
HOROSCOPE 1

Ray 2 Soul, Ray 4 Personality

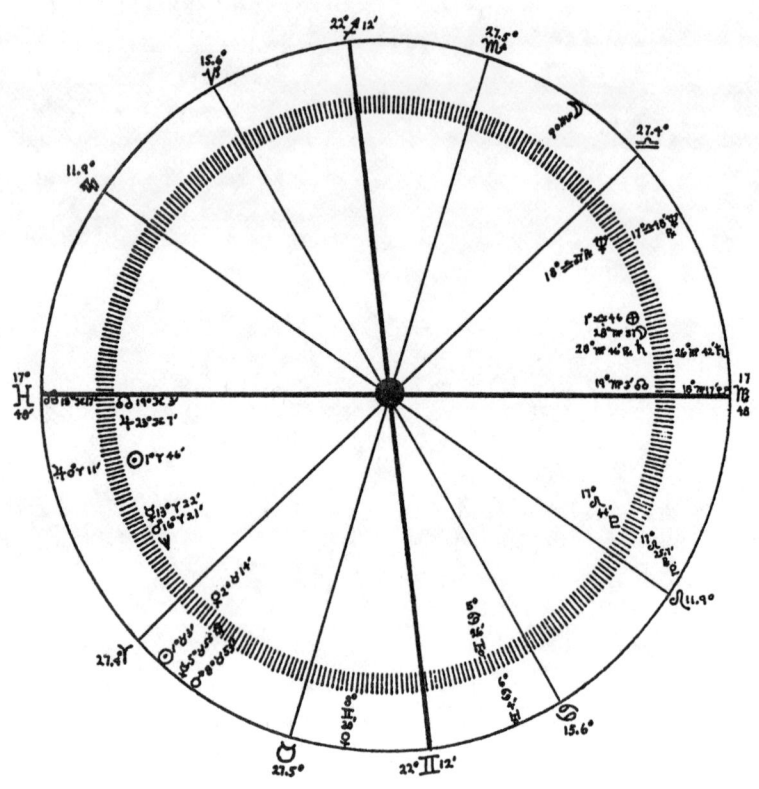

Chapter Eight

Case 2

Step 1. Find the approximate level of Soul evolvement. Case 2 is an advanced Soul. There are two Finger-of-God aspects indicating that a special spiritual mission is her destiny. Though not small-orbed, a grand trine exists. A fairly close aspectual relationship between all planets shows her personality is integrated and can act in a unified way. Many challenging aspects, signifying her character weaknesses, indicate that she is highly enough evolved to learn the karmic lesson these aspects can teach her. If this were not so, she would have been born at another time and place. A less-advanced Soul would not have been permitted to enter that physical body, for none of us is allowed to take on more than we are able to handle. The first part of her life will not be easy. Yet it can be a fulfilled and joyful life if she becomes aware of the Laws of Karma and Reincarnation and in her awareness realizes that each of us is our own creator because of past thoughts, words, and actions. Then she will assume full responsibility for her difficulties and will not blame others. In accepting her difficult karma in this light, she will learn her needed lessons more quickly, and as she overcomes her weaknesses she can be of immense help to others.

Step 2. Study the progressed natal chart for the coming year. In seeing it as a seed that can blossom into fruit, we find three partile aspects taking place during the year. There is an excellent opportunity this year for spiritual illumination, followed by a change of attitudes and values because of the major emphasis in her second house—three progressed planets making exact aspects are located in the second house, more than in any other house. One of the planets of each of two exact aspects is located in the second house. The third partile aspect has both planets tenanting the second house.

Of secondary influence, the third and fourth houses each have a planet making an exact aspect with a second house planet. The primary concern of second house spiritual illumination tied in with secondary concerns for communication, study, and the reasoning capacity of the third house and the building of a good foundation for her total being of the fourth house, show the areas of life in which there will be strong energy flow.

Progressed Mars in Taurus in the second house semisextile progressed Venus in Gemini in the third house gives her a great deal of energy and courage (Mars) and reasoning capacity (Venus) to break through the outworn concepts that hinder her Soul's progress toward true illumination (second house) and also gives her the one-pointedness (Mars) to understand (third house) and enjoy (Venus) the results of illumination which can be forthcoming. Because Mars is a ruler of Ray Six of idealism and devotion, and Venus is the ruler of Ray Five of concrete knowledge, her logical reasoning capacity will be accentuated, coupled with her urge to follow idealistic goals. The esoteric ruler of Taurus is Vulcan which gives her power to crystallize weaknesses from her unconscious, to surface them, and eradicate them. Since Venus is in Gemini and is the esoteric ruler of Gemini, the aspect of Venus to Mars strengthens her sense of logic and reason, making it easier for her to understand the intricacies of the illumination she can receive.

Progressed Mercury in Taurus in the second house sextile progressed Uranus in Cancer in the fourth house gives her energy for intuition (Uranus) and psychic sensitivity (Cancer) in original ideas (Uranus) concerning spiritual illumination (second house) in rapport with her logical mind (Mercury). These ideas can very well change her current attitudes and values advantageously, leading to Soul growth at a deep level (fourth house). Mercury, a ruler of Ray Four of harmony through conflict, favorably aspecting Uranus, the ruler of Ray Seven of order and rhythm, indicates a year in which she can more easily become aware of the karmic lessons she needs to learn and can learn them in a rhythmic way with little anxiety. The esoteric ruler of Taurus is Vulcan, a ruler of Ray One of will and power, which gives her the ability to crystallize unconscious weaknesses, surface them, and eradicate them. The esoteric ruler of Cancer is Neptune, a ruler of Ray Six of idealism and devotion, which gives her the sensitivity and the idealistic urge to understand herself better and to change that which needs changing.

Progressed Sun conjunct Venus in Taurus in the second house gives her vitality (Sun) and a feeling of love and joy (Venus) in attaining illumination (second house), and in applying it in her life. Through the combined energies of the power of Vulcan, the esoteric ruler of Taurus, and Ray Two of love and wisdom (the Sun being its ruler) and of Ray Five of concrete knowledge (Venus being its ruler), she has the power, when used with love, to convert her knowledge, acquired through logic, into wisdom so that beneficial changes can come into her life.

It is interesting that the progressed Moon in Scorpio in the ninth house was exactly trine her Uranus in Cancer in the fourth house when the writer, a woman engaged in esoteric research (Moon in Scorpio), was impressed to use her chart for publication (ninth house) through Astrology (Uranus) to give her added information to help her in her deep Soul searching (fourth house). In view of the interpretations of the preceding three partile progressed aspects, the year of progression was an excellent time for a Ray-Centered delineation. It was not a coincidence that she asked me to do astrology work for her at that time. Not only should her intuitive and psychic capacity be enhanced for a better understanding of this delineation but she would enjoy contemplating it, learning from it, and impelled to implement the findings in her life.

The unusual conjunction of the transitting Sun, Moon, Mars, and Venus at fourteen degrees Aries on April 4, 1981 fell within a degree of her Mercury in her first house where she has a stellium of Aries planets. Because the first house is of the Soul and its expression, we can see the powerful Arian energy which can be harnessed for Soul evolvement. The enthusiasm and courage of the Arian energy gives her the potential to raise her consciousness so she can become more aware of the importance of karmic responsibilities and the lessons to be learned as a means of Soul growth.

Step 3. Find the Soul Ray by following the calculations of Example Horoscope 7 in Chapter Two. As shown therein, this client has a Ray Two Soul. Study carefully the information in Chapter Three pertaining to Ray Two. All the information in that section is important to the client's welfare.

In general, her life plan or Soul's purpose is consonant with

222

love and wisdom. All Ray Two Souls approach the Spiritual Path through intense and earnest study of spiritual teachings until these teachings become so much a part of their consciousness that they also become a part of their daily living. As Case 2 applies the results of her spiritual studies to her life, she will find that others are magnetically drawn to her through her love and wisdom. Her Soul's purpose should be serving others by the healing of the spirit, mind, or body through religion, health, education, or esotericism. The major weaknesses to which she may.be susceptible are the manifestation of fear and of selfish desires which can be transmuted into positive thinking and unattached love.

Step 4. Study the Ascendant sign, Pisces, thoroughly in Chapter Four and supplement this to her Ray Two Soul information. In generalizing, her Pisces Ascendant gives her the capacity to serve others in a kind, compassionate, and empathetic manner. She has the ability to dissolve her separative feelings, rid herself of her ego, and become At One with All.

The Pisces information, though important, should be supplemental in the choice of her Soul's purpose or life work. The main focus is consonant with her Ray Two Soul. Her Pisces Ascendant of the water element is feminine and her Ray Two Soul, being even-numbered, is also feminine. Her Soul's purpose, therefore, would be concerned with the inner life. If a lack of self-confidence occurs, it is important that she work with positive thoughts. She would not draw to her those she would serve by aggressive extroverted behavior, but by love and magnetism.

Step 5. Find the Personality Ray by following the Example Horoscope 7 calculations in Chapter Two. As shown therein this client has a Ray Four Personality. In Chapter Three, study carefully the information pertaining to Ray Four as that which serves her Ray Two Soul's purpose. In generalizing, Case 2's Soul's purpose of healing others in spirit, mind, or body in a compassionate and empathetic way is aided by her Ray Four Personality of harmony through conflict.

It is paramount that she help those she serves attain harmony. Certain concepts, such as Reincarnation, Karma, and the power of thought should be a part of her working procedure so that those she serves will take the responsibility for their present conditions and change their thoughts, words, and actions for a healing and upliftment to take place.

Step 6. Study her Sun sign in Chapter Four. The energies of the Aries Sun supplement the Ray Four Personality to depict more clearly her personality. Mars, the exoteric ruler of Aries, influences her strongly until she begins working on her Soul evolvement. This gives her a tendency toward impulsiveness, aggression, and anger. As Soul contact is made, Mercury, the esoteric ruler of Aries, becomes more influential. There is then a shifting of her basic energy from the physical and emotional to the mental—her mind then becomes increasingly able to function as the controlling factor, replacing the emotions of an earlier time.

Her Ray Four Personality of harmony through conflict, supplemented by her Aries Sun with Mercury the esoteric ruler predominant, indicates a capacity to understand the Law of Karma and to benefit from it in order to attain the harmony desired. She could become aware that she alone is responsible for her present conditions and that she alone can create better ones. As an advanced Soul with Mercury, the esoteric ruler of Aries, predominating, she receives a higher vibration of Mars—energy and courage.

When she has attained a very advanced status of Soul evolvement, the hierarchical ruler, Uranus, will become the predominating influence. At that time she will become aware that intuition impelled by Uranus is more productive of further evolvement than the logical thought impelled by Mercury. The intuitional energy of Uranus tells her in a flash what is best in her thoughts, words, and actions to attain that harmony which her Ray Four Personality so strongly seeks.

Her even-numbered Ray Four Personality, denoting the feminine gender, supplemented by her Aries Sun, denoting the masculine gender, gives her personality a basic introvertive love and concern for others, colored by the power of extrovertive behavior and her intellect. Having both genders represented indicates a well-balanced personality.

It is important to study thoroughly the Aries information in

Chapter Four in light of her personality expression. Generalizing, her Aries Sun energy will stimulate the creation of original, pioneering ideas to solve conflicts and attain harmony for
herself and others.

Step 7. Study the interaction of the Soul Ray supplemented
by the Ascendant, with the Personality Ray supplemented by
the Sun sign, keeping in mind that the Soul Ray indicates her
purpose in life and that the Personality Ray indicates her manner of expressing her Soul's purpose. Her Ray Two Soul and
Pisces Ascendant show that her Soul's purpose is to serve others
by healing their bodies, minds, or Souls through acquired wisdom and with love in a compassionate, empathetic manner.

Her Ray Four Personality and Aries Sun show that she can
express her Soul's purpose through helping others resolve their
conflicts by utilizing such concepts as Reincarnation, Karma,
and the power of thought which can be done in an innovative
manner.

Gender has specific meaning in a delineation. Using M for
the masculine gender of a Ray, F for the feminine gender of a
Ray, f and m for the Ascendant and Sun sign genders, and
underlining the Soul's purpose to indicate its greater influence,
we have the following: $\underline{F}f\,\underline{F}m$. Not only are three of the four
genders feminine, but so are both of the Soul indicators. This
points strongly to sensitivity, love, and concern for others, but
a possible lack of confidence in herself. She should try to activate her only masculine indicator, her Aries Sun, to overcome
any lack of confidence she may feel. A predominance of the
negative polarities shows strong tendencies toward psychic sensitivity, charisma, introversion, and love and concern for others—all part of the feminine nature of her being, associated
with the "Yin" of the "I Ching" and the "anima" of Jung. She
has much to give with her sensitivity and love and concern for
others, but the will to give what she has is not as strong as it
might be. The wise use of her Aries energy in giving her confidence and enthusiasm coupled with that of Pisces to dissolve
her ego and feel At One with All, can bring to her a radiance
which attracts others so that she can give them what she is,
what she has accomplished.

White is the color that could be of most help as an aid in the development of her self-confidence. Yellow is of secondary importance in encouraging intellectual activity and emphasizing the mind as her guide rather than the emotions. Both red and black should be used as seldom as possible. With three of the four indicators of the feminine gender denoting a strong emotional nature, red would only tend to impulsiveness, irritability, and anger. Black would add to her strong receptivity. Its use when in the company of those of a low vibration at the time her vibration was also at a low level could cause her to receive many negative thoughts and impressions because black is a color of absorption.

Step 8. Set up a Ray-Centered horoscope showing the inner Soul life and the outer personality life expressing the Soul's purpose (Horoscope 2). Use Chart 4 to find the esoteric rulers of the Ascendant and Sun signs. See the natal horoscope (Horoscope 1) for positions of the planets to be used in Horoscope 2.

To find the inner Soul life, use the natal Ascendant and all its esoteric planetary rulers. The primary esoteric ruler of the Pisces Ascendant is Pluto which is in Leo; the esoteric ruler of Leo is the Sun which is in Aries; the esoteric ruler of Aries is Mercury which is also in Aries.

To find the Soul-serving personality life, use the Sun and all its esoteric rulers. The esoteric ruler of the Aries sun sign is Mercury which is in Aries. Because the ruler of the Sun sign is placed in its own sign, there is only one esoteric ruler for the personality life expressing the Soul's purpose.

Enter the Ascendant and Soul life planets, and the Sun and its solitary ruler as a personality expression of the Soul life, each group with a different color into Horoscope 2, using the same cusps as in the natal horoscope (Horoscope 1), and using different colored lines to denote different types of aspects, to produce a picture of Case Two's Soul life and Soul-serving personality life. The specific planetary energies designated for the Soul's purpose consonant with her Ray Two Soul are shown. Those specific planetary energies designated for the personality expression of her Soul life that are consonant with her Ray Four Personality, which help her in her outer life to manifest her Soul's purpose, are also shown.

CASE 2—HOROSCOPE 2

Indicates the Soul's Purpose and its Expression
Using Soul Life Planets and
Personality Planets Serving the Soul

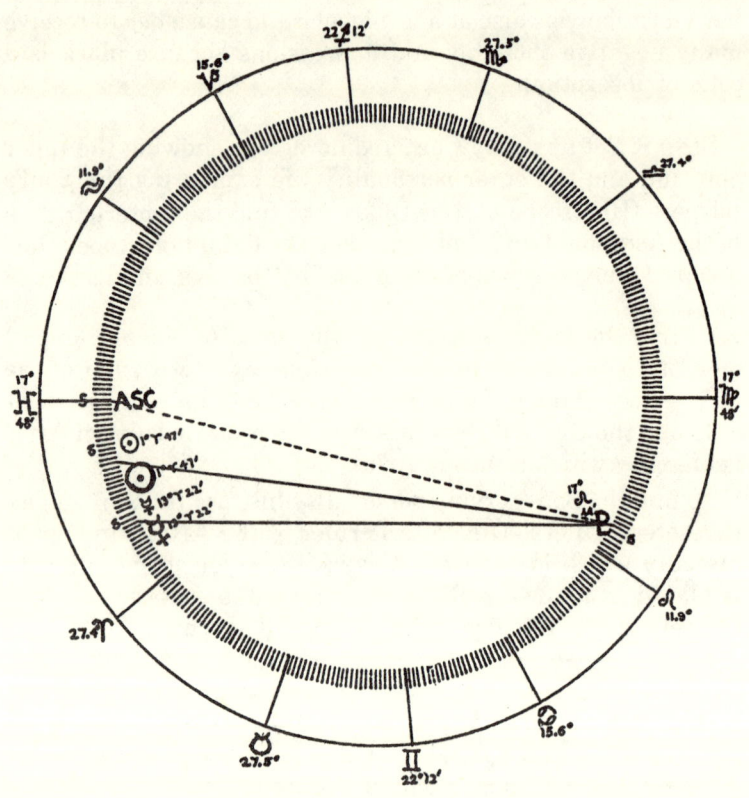

The interaction between these two groups is especially significant in pinpointing which planetary energies are combined· through aspects and the identity of those aspects. Her inner Soul life has double the number of planetary energies that her Soul-serving personality life has (for the purpose of explaining energy sources, the Ascendant which is not a planet will be referred to here as a planet). This indicates that her inner Soul urges have much more potency than her personality has to express them. Awareness of this fact tells her that special efforts must be made to manifest her Soul's purpose. In reality, this is not quite as·difficult as it may seem because the same two planets which indicate the Soul-serving personality expression are two of the. four planets indicating the Soul life, and both of these planets are found in Aries and in the first house giving them extra strength for expression. These two planets, the Sun, a ruler of Ray Two of love and wisdom, which is her Soul Ray, and Mercury, a ruler of Ray Four of harmony through conflict, which is her Personality Ray, indicate a third reason for a good rapport between her Soul life and her Soul-serving personality life.

Only two houses are influential because they tenant all planets. The first house is of primary importance because it tenants all but one planet and also signifies the Soul and its expression. The sixth house is of secondary importance, tenanting the remaining planet, and signifies transmuting one's weaknesses into strengths and serving others.

Because Pluto, a ruler of Ray One of will and power,· is in her sixth house, further corroboration of previous interpretation signifying her Soul's purpose should be healing of the Soul, mind, and or body is strongly reinforced here. Intense power to help herself and others rid themselves of weaknesses to the very depths of their beings is the mode of healing for her life work because for lasting healing to take place in the Soul, mind, or body, there must be Soul evolvement.

If she works diligently on her Soul's purpose, it will lead to self-actualization. There is an unusual rapport between her Soul life and her personality expression of it in that the esoteric ruler of Leo, the sign of Pluto's location, is the Sun which is a planetary energy of both groups and is found in Aries, the esoteric ruler of which is Mercury, also a planetary energy of both groups. Because Pluto makes an exact quincunx to the Ascendant, her inner life will be very frustrating until she acquiesces to its urges. Her Pisces Ascendant tells her that self-realization is not important, only compassion and feeling At One with All is important, yet her Pluto in Leo prompts her toward self-realization. This frustration can be relieved when she realizes that a healthy combination of the two can be effected by a true feeling of Oneness with All which leads to self-realization.

A sesquiquadrate from Pluto to the Sun shows powerful pressures from within and without for transmuting her weaknesses into strengths, and a trine from Pluto to Mercury shows a powerful, alert, keen mind that can understand and implement the necessary concepts of Karma and Reincarnation in her life. Because Mercury is a planet of both the Soul and personality, it bridges the two.

Except for the Ascendant, all planetary energies are in fire signs which put forceful spiritual energy at her command for her inner life and its expression. Even though the planetary energies of this horoscope are relatively few, their fire element predominance and their unusually high integrative factors increase the potency of these energies. The Sun and Mercury are in Aries and are indicators of both the Soul and its personality expression, showing that she is capable of spiritual ideas and could express them well through her personality.

The Soul life planets and the Rays they rule are: Ascendant—Ray Two, Pluto—Ray One, Sun—Ray Two, and Mercury—Ray Four. A double Ray Two shows that love and wisdom are paramount in her Soul life. Therefore it would be advantageous for her to study writings of the Masters so deeply that what she learns will become a part of her essence. The love and wisdom which is so necessary to her inner life will then be a part of her. Her Ray Four shows a strong need for harmony which can be hers as she learns her needed lessons from karmic experiences. Her Ray One gives her power and a strong will to accomplish in her inner life the goals she sets for herself.

The Soul-serving personality planets and the Rays they rule are the Sun, which rules Ray Two of love and wisdom, and Mercury which rules Ray Four of harmony through conflict. Her personality expression of her Soul life should be accomplished primarily through love and wisdom, which is true for all of us because the Sun is the primary indicator of everyone's personality. She has only one other indicator, Mercury, which shows that she must attain harmony through resolving conflicts by understanding the karmic causes and then making the necessary changes. Even though the primary indicators of the Soul-serving personality life are two even-numbered Rays showing a possible lack of self-confidence, the fact that both planets are in Aries in the first house indicates that the lack is filled to a certain degree.

Step 9. Set up another Ray-Centered Horoscope to find the main problem for this lifetime as shown by the conflict between the inner Soul aspiration and the self-centered personality desires. This is designated as Horoscope 3. Use the same house cusps in this horoscope as in Horoscopes 1 and 2. Insert the Ascendant and all its esoteric rulers as found in Step 8. The Ascendant and these planets depict the inner Soul life.

Find the exoteric rulers of the Sun sign. The exoteric ruler of the Sun is Mars which is in Aries. Since the exoteric ruler of the Sun is in the same sign as the Sun itself, there are, in this case, no other exoteric rulers of the Sun. Insert in this horoscope the Sun and Mars which depict the self-centered personality desires.

It would be advisable to (1) place the personality desire planets in the horoscope in a color different from the Soul life planets, (2) enlarge the abbreviation, "Asc." and the symbol for Pluto, the primary esoteric ruler, because they have more power than other rulers of the Ascendant, (3) enlarge the symbols for Sun and Mars indicating the self-centered personality desires to designate their power. Even though, in this case, there is only one exoteric ruler of the Sun, it is considered just as important as a primary ruler when there is more than one ruler.

There are four planets very influential to the inner Soul life, and only two are very influential to the self-centered personality desires. This two-to-one ratio makes it much easier to attain Soul evolvement than if these numbers were reversed.

The self-centered personality desire planets and the Rays they rule are: the Sun—Ray Two, and Mars—Ray Six. An ab-

230

CASE 2—HOROSCOPE 3

Indicates for this Life the Conflict Between Soul
Life Planets and Self-centered Personality Planets
and its Resolution

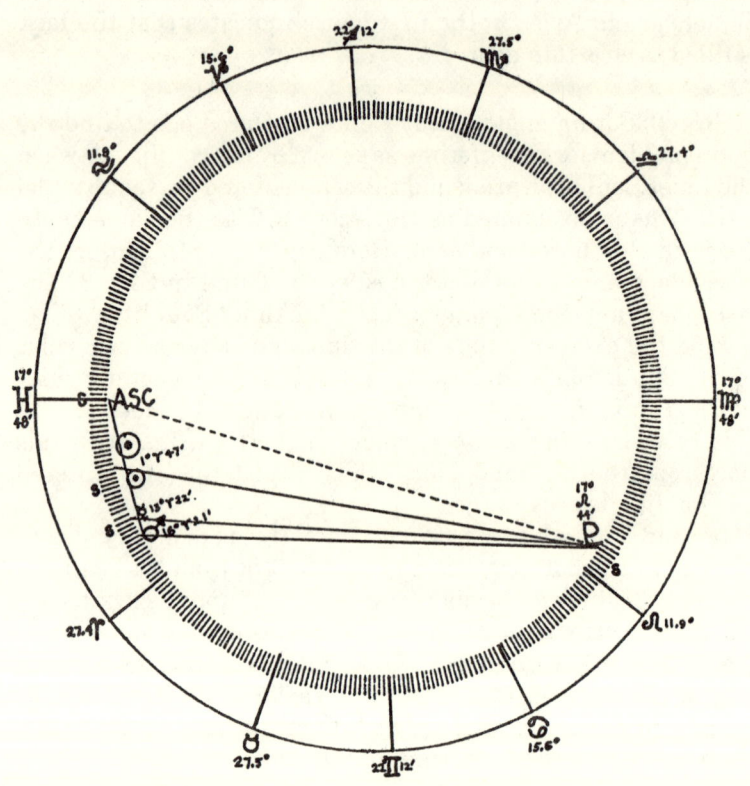

sence of odd-numbered Rays indicates that there is not a great deal of power directed toward her self-centered desires, which is fortunate. This makes it easier for her to transmute her self-centered desires to Soul-infused aspirations than if both planets were rulers of odd-numbered Rays. Rays Two and Six are feminine in gender denoting sensitivity, passivity, and emotionalism. However, because Mars is one of the planets which is of its essence, energy to be impulsively expended, and because both Sun and Mars are in Aries, normally the most powerful and aggressive of all signs, one might think these energies might be exhibited in an aggressive, extrovertive, or intellec- . tual manner. However, the opposite is the case in the life of this entity. She uses this energy in a strongly introverted and emotional way that is consonant with the meanings of even-numbered Rays. This phenomenon clearly demonstrates the immense power of the Rays over the power of the signs and planets.

In Step 8 we found the planets and the Ascendant and their Rays which influence the inner Soul life. They are: Ascendant—Ray Two, Pluto—Ray One, Sun—Ray Two, and Mercury—Ray Four. Three of the Rays are even-numbered (feminine) which indicates a strong predominance of love, sensitivity, and concern for others over the masculine qualities of the intellect and will.

This chart shows a conflict between her Soul's urge to heal others and the lack of self-confidence in her ability to do so. An exact quincunx between the Ascendant and Pluto, both of the inner Soul life, shows much frustration until she works toward her Soul's purpose.

A sesquiquadrate between the Sun, a ruler of Ray Two of love and wisdom in Aries in the first house, and Pluto, a ruler of will and power in Leo in the sixth house, reveals immense power and vitality, but a tendency to dissipate it in meaningless activity.

A trine from Mercury to Pluto, both planets of the Soul, shows that through the study of the Laws of Karma and Reincarnation (Mercury is a ruler of Ray Four of harmony which can be attained by the wise use of these Laws), she can successfully heal others.

Available energy which can be used toward her Soul's purpose is provided by a trine from Mars to Pluto and a semi-sextile from Mars to the Ascendant. It should not be difficult for her to succeed because of the multiplicity of factors involving Pluto, the primary esoteric ruler of the Soul life, a ruler of Ray One of will and power, located in Leo which is the sign of self-realization, in the sixth house of perfecting oneself and serving others, and having twice as many aspects as any other planet in this horoscope.

It is highly significant that the Sun is the only planet which influences both her Soul's purpose and her self-centered personality desires. Therefore her Aries Sun acts as a point of contact between the two. She must marshal her innate Aries characteristics which she sometimes uses for self-centered desires into the Soul's purpose of extroversion and leadership qualities for her powerful healing capacity to be activated. An Aries stellium in the first house of the Soul and its expression, Pluto in Leo in the sixth house of perfecting herself and serving others, and Pisces on the Ascendant combine to reveal fiery spiritual power at her command to solve her problem when she develops sufficient courage.

Step 10. From her natal horoscope, complete the part of the delineation that was begun in Steps 8 and 9, referring to Horoscopes 2 and 3. Include in this delineation the Moon's Nodes and all aspects not found in Horoscopes 2 and 3. Interpret the meanings of the houses, their cuspal signs, the esoteric planetary rulers of the cuspal signs, and the Ray each planet rules.

A grand trine between Mars, a ruler of Ray Six of idealism and devotion in the first house, Pluto, a ruler of Ray One of will and power in the sixth house, and the Midheaven indicates that it would be easy for her healing mission to become her life work. Because it is a fire trine, and because Pluto and Mars are included, there is a more than sufficient supply of energy for her Soul's purpose.

The bi-quintile between Pluto, a ruler of Ray One in Leo in the sixth house, and Jupiter, a ruler of Ray Two in Pisces in the first house, shows that her expansive and powerful psychic capacity can be combined advantageously with her intellect toward her Soul's purpose of healing others.

The North Node conjunct the Ascendant gives added energy

for the expression of the Soul's purpose. This conjunction is the focus of a Finger-of-God aspect comprising Neptune, a ruler of Ray Six of idealism and devotion in Libra in the seventh house, and Pluto, a ruler of Ray One of will and power in Leo in the sixth house. The Finger-of-God is a fated aspect but there is always much frustration until the spiritual mission that the Finger-of-God indicates is actualized. The frustration of the North Node conjunct Ascendant quincunx Neptune results in emotionalism in close relationships which impedes the Soul's purpose of healing others. The quincunx from the North Node conjunct Ascendant to Pluto causes frustration until this intense power that wells up within her is used for her Soul's purpose. Yet the sextile between Pluto and Neptune indicates the possibility of the wise use of this energy idealistically when her understanding of this Ray-Centered delineation deepens. The release point of this Finger-of-God aspect is the South Node, the most karmic point in the horoscope, and because it is in Virgo in the seventh house, close relationships are important to teach her karmic lessons. However, the learning will not be easy. In a past life she was critical of the weaknesses of her close companions. Thus her lesson-teaching karma is being criticized in close relationships. Hopefully, she will learn to accept and love others, no matter where they stand on the scale of Soul evolvement. The South Node in all charts indicates lesson-teaching karma. In her chart, because it is the release point of the Finger-of-God, two components of which are the Ascendant and Pluto, both indicators of the Soul life, it and her lesson-teaching karma are closely tied to her Soul's purpose.

The last aspect to be considered in the first house is the Sun, a ruler of Ray Two of love and wisdom in Aries, square Uranus, the ruler of Ray Seven of ceremonial order and strong thought forms, in Cancer in the fourth house of the foundation of the Soul. This signifies unpredictable behavior resulting from unleashed emotions which will continue until she uses her mind to control them.

The first and seventh houses are very important areas of her life because the Nodes, two of the three points of the Finger-of-God aspect, and all but three of the planets are located in them. She has a triangle composed of two bi-septiles and a tri-septile.

Two of the planets of the triangle are located in the first and seventh houses. For these reasons her main emphasis in life should be in the areas these two houses signify, namely, the Soul and its expression, weighing the advantage of manifesting on a Soul versus personality level, and close relationships.

The forementioned triangle is composed of Neptune, a ruler of Ray Six in Libra in the seventh house, tri-septile Jupiter, a ruler of Ray Two in Pisces in the first house, Neptune bi-septile Uranus, the ruler of Ray Seven in Cancer in the fourth house, and Uranus bi-septile Jupiter. This configuration has been found in large numbers in charts of spiritual leaders. It is an aspect of spiritual aspirations and of creativity. Pisces, Cancer, and Libra indicate psychic sensitivity, creativity, and relationships. The Rays these planets rule, Rays Two, Six, and Seven, indicate a potential for using strong thoughts in a rhythmic way, with idealistic motives and love and wisdom.

Virgo on the cusp of the seventh house reveals that she will attract critical and analytical people as close companions, and that she will carefully analyze the advantages of manifesting on a self-centered level versus a Soul level. The esoteric ruler of Virgo is the Moon, a ruler of Ray Four of harmony through conflict, which is found in the seventh house. Once more we find close relationships as a necessity for learning needed lessons to attain harmony.

Neptune opposite Mars, both rulers of Ray Six, shows a tendency of undue emotionalism in close relationships. This energy can be transmuted into idealistic behavior through the understanding of previous aspectual interpretations.

Earth, a ruler of Ray Three of the abstract mind in Libra, is quincunx Venus, the ruler of Ray Five of the concrete mind in Taurus in the second house. This indicates that many close affectional relationship experiences are necessary for spiritual illumination, which will occur first through logical understanding and later through contemplation.

Because Earth, a ruler of Ray Three, is square Uranus, a ruler of Ray Seven, many of her experiences will happen suddenly.

Her Moon, a ruler of Ray Four, and Saturn, a ruler of Ray Three, are conjunct in Virgo in the seventh house and opposite Jupiter, a ruler of Ray Two in Pisces, indicating much emotionalism and simultaneously an ability to use the higher mind to resolve conflicts and attain harmony through love and wisdom, combining the meanings of Rays Two, Three, and Four which these three planets rule. The esoteric ruler of the Virgo seventh house cusp is the Moon, a ruler of Ray Four, which is posited in the seventh house, which again tells us that there will be conflicts to be worked out in close relationships.

The opposition of her Moon to her Sun shows a lack of rapport between her conscious and unconscious minds. Pondering on the meaning of this delineation will, after a time, foster the beginning of a rapport between her conscious and unconscious minds.

The Aries second house cusp gives her enthusiasm and an impetus to change attitudes and values that need changing, which could lead to spiritual illumination. The esoteric ruler of Aries is Mercury, a ruler of Ray Four of harmony through conflict. It is through conflict that she will learn her lessons and thus alter her attitudes and values in order to attain harmony. Mercury is also in Aries and is in the first house of the Soul and its expression. Her alert mind can easily tune in to her Soul's purpose in an integrative manner and act as a vehicle of its expression. Mercury, a ruler of Ray Four, and Mars, a ruler of Ray six, both in Aries, give her the courage of her convictions and the impetus to use idealistic concepts to solve her conflicts.

Mercury, a ruler of Ray Four, opposite Neptune, a ruler of Ray Six in the seventh house, encourages difficult karmic relationships and often clouds her view of things. When she understands that we are our own creators and we attract only the people and conditions that help toward ultimate Soul growth, the confusion that is so characteristic of a challenging Neptune aspect will vanish.

Mercury, a ruler of Ray Four, is trine Pluto, a ruler of Ray One, giving her a powerful mind that can penetrate the depths of her being.

Venus, a ruler of Ray Five of the concrete mind in Taurus, tenants the second house, making easy aspects to the Sun, a ruler of Ray Two, and Uranus, the ruler of Ray Seven, bestows charisma and a loving nature and the ability to use her logical mind to understand spiritual illumination to establish a life of rhythm and order. When this takes place, others who are searching for illumination will be magnetically attracted to her.

Taurus on the third house cusp signifies that her thoughts often dwell on various attitudes and value systems. Because the esoteric ruler of Taurus, Vulcan, is a ruler of Ray One of will, power, and purpose, her thoughts are powerful and can easily be focused on a particular purpose or plan which may lead to her Soul's purpose because Vulcan is in the first house of the Soul and in Aries where this power can manifest with much energy and enthusiasm.

In helping her to manifest on a Soul level, which planets in the first house help bring about, Vulcan's power here aids in crystallizing repressions, guilt feelings, and weaknesses in her unconscious and bringing them to the conscious mind to eradicate them.

The Gemini fourth house cusp together with Venus, its esoteric ruler and the ruler of Ray Five of the reasoning mind, suggest not only a possible awareness in the depths of her being of the difference between personality desires and spiritual aspirations, but also the ability to use her logical concrete mind to distinguish between the two. Venus in Taurus in the second house shows that her reasoning capacity is useful in developing better attitudes and values which will enrich her at the very depths of her being.

Venus, the ruler of Ray Five, semi-sextile the Sun, a ruler of Ray Two in the first house, gives her the capacity to use logical thinking to understand spiritual illumination so that it reaches her on a basic level from whence true Soul expression can originate.

Uranus, the ruler of Ray Seven, is posited in Cancer in the fourth house, giving her the ability to direct powerful one-pointed thoughts to the very depth of her Soul. Its square to the Sun, a ruler of Ray Two in Aries in the first house, shows a tendency toward unpredictable and rebellious thoughts. The sextile of Uranus to Venus helps her to understand those thoughts. This understanding contributes to a rhythmic living pattern and a charisma which attracts those who can help her reach her Soul on a deep level.

Cancer on the fifth house cusp indicates that psychic and

nurturing capacity and the ability to become aware of others' needs are some of her tools for attaining self-realization. The esoteric ruler of Cancer, Neptune, a ruler of Ray Six, is in Libra in the seventh house. Its opposition to Mars, a ruler of Ray Six, and Mercury, a ruler of Ray Four, both in Aries in the first house, shows a tendency toward misplaced idealism in close relationships which acts as a deterrent to self-realization.

A tri-septile from Neptune, a ruler of Ray Six, to Jupiter, a ruler of Ray Two in Pisces in the first house, denotes the ability to understand the Law of Karma, so that she can become aware of the realistic expectations of close relationships, knowing that in accepting them and learning from the karmic lessons they are meant to teach, self-realization of her Soul's purpose can become a reality.

Neptune, a ruler of Ray Six, sextile Pluto, a ruler of Ray One in Leo in the sixth house, gives the needed extra energy to consummate this reality through healing the body, mind, or Soul of others.

Neptune quincunx the conjunction of Ascendant and North Node in Pisces signifies frustration from a lack of self-confidence in her capacity to express her Soul's purpose of service to others with a feeling of compassion and Oneness-with-All.

Leo on the cusp of the sixth house signifies fiery energy that can be harnessed to perfect herself and serve others. The esoteric ruler of Leo is the Sun posited in Aries in the first house, adding to the fiery energy that can be used for Soul evolvement. The single resident planet in the sixth house is Pluto, a ruler of Ray One of will and power and the primary esoteric ruler of her Pisces Ascendant (signifying the Soul). All of this adds up to powerful, intensive energies directed toward Soul expression.

The Libra eighth house cusp signifies that much testing via temptations concerned mainly with close relationships can lead to spiritual regeneration. The eighth house cusp also gives her the ability to weigh clearly the benefits of manifesting either on a self-centered personality level or on a Soul level. This insight could help her immensely in making wise choices that could be instrumental in her spiritual regeneration.

Uranus, the esoteric ruler of Ray Seven of order, rhythm, and powerful thoughts is in Cancer in the fourth house—thoughts which come to her as flashes of lightning can be powerful enough to reach the depths of her being to establish a changed but rhythmic life. Her Uranus placement enables her to fuse her thoughts with meditative psychic capacity to energize any decisions she might make.

The ninth house Scorpio cusp will impel her to rigorously test spiritual concepts before she accepts them as the basis of her religion as spiritual truths that will become the unshakable foundation at the depths of her being. Mars, the esoteric ruler of Scorpio and a ruler of Ray Six of idealism and devotion in Aries in the first house, confirms that whatever spiritual concepts she accepts will be those to which she is wholly devoted. Because Mars is part of a fire grand trine with Pluto and Midheaven, through her career, she will have the courage, energy, and enthusiasm to abolish outworn concepts handed down from generation to generation and replace them with New Age divine ideas so urgently needed now.

Sagittarius on the Midheaven denotes a strongly goal-oriented career in which the attainment of one goal leads to others ad infinitum. Her goal-oriented career in its many levels of advancement will be consonant with the many levels of consciousness-raising she attains. The esoteric ruler of Sagittarius is Earth, a ruler of Ray Three of the higher mind in Libra in the seventh house, indicating that relationships are important not only to raise her level of consciousness but also to advance her career. Earth conjunct Moon, a ruler of Ray Four of harmony through conflict, and Saturn, a ruler of Ray Three of the abstract mind and square Uranus, the ruler of Ray Seven of strong thoughts and order, together indicate that close relationships, though not always pleasant, are important in learning needed karmic lessons and to practice the career her Soul has planned for her. It is imperative that she not expect too much in personality desires from her relationships, but that she approach them with the thought of growing spiritually through them.

Capricorn on the eleventh house cusp indicates that she has a capacity to work hard and persistently with Aquarian Age concepts and through them raise her consciousness and that of others. The esoteric ruler of Capricorn is Saturn, a ruler of Ray Three of the higher mind through which she can understand and use Aquarian Age concepts, such as the freedom of the individual to act according to his own conscience and that each person creates his own environment. Her Saturn is in Virgo in the seventh house conjunct the Moon and opposite Sun and Jupiter, indicating a tendency to repress unpleasant feelings resulting from close relationships rather than face and deal with them. To deal effectively with the difficult experiences which arise from her relationships, she can successfully implement the above mentioned concepts and will understand that her Soul attracts to her the types of people necessary for evolvement. The ancient doctrine of Karma as the Aquarian Age is dawning is becoming increasingly a part of the belief not only of the Eastern world but also of the West and will become worldwide. This karmic doctrine indicates that we must have certain experiences to learn our needed lessons, and that we create our own environment by past thoughts, words, and actions. In this understanding she will be better able to accept disappointments in a Soul-elevating manner, knowing that these disappointments are the substance of an upliftment.

Saturn square Midheaven indicates career obstacles that will be overcome only when she has learned the lessons of her karmic responsibilities in relationships.

Saturn, a ruler of Ray Three of the abstract mind, quintile Uranus, the ruler of Ray Seven of rhythmic living and strong thoughts, is one facet of her capacity. Once her mind is saturated with Aquarian Age truths, she can easily use them in a practical way to work out her own problems and help others do the same.

Aquarius on the twelfth house cusp gives her the ability to use New Age philosophies advantageously once she has studied them and becomes convinced of their validity in order to bring from the unconscious to the conscious mind repressions, guilt feelings, and other weaknesses so she can eradicate them. When she becomes successful in this area, she can serve others in this all-important process that in some life each of us must engage.

The esoteric ruler of Aquarius is Jupiter, a ruler of Ray Two in Pisces in the first house, indicating an urge for Soul evolvement through a feeling of Oneness-Toward-All. Until she has worked out the conflicts of Jupiter square Midheaven and Jupiter opposite Moon and Saturn, the latent love and wisdom promised by Jupiter finds it difficult to manifest its potential. These aspects indicate a tendency to repress undesirable emotions, and in the repressing to erroneously think that an improvement is made, all of which negatively affects her Soul evolvement and career. Yet, if she uses wisely the psychic capacity given to her by Jupiter, a ruler of Ray Two, bi-quintile Pluto, a ruler of Ray One, and Neptune, a ruler of Ray Six, and bi-septile Uranus, the ruler of Ray Seven, she can become aware of the difficulties that result from repression, and can make changes so that she no longer represses undesirable emotions but begins to deal with them.

The novile between Jupiter, a ruler of Ray Two, and the Taurian Venus, the ruler of Ray Five, promises spiritual regeneration through illumination and the changing of attitudes and values if her logical mind is lovingly applied to the wise use of spiritual truths.

Step 11. Find in the natal chart the planet closest to the zenith and the Ray it rules. Because this is the last planet her consciousness was on before this life, explain the abilities derived there to be applied in her present life. Neptune, a ruler of Ray Six of devotion and idealism, was her last planet of occupancy before this life. She acquired a devotion to the attainment of ideal thoughts, words, and actions, a most helpful aid to Soul evolvement.

Step 12. Find the planet or planets in the natal chart that are most influential in an all-encompassing way. Use Chart 28 showing all signs each planet rules. A planet is influential by virtue of having three planets or important points in the sign or sign it rules. Interpret the functions of these planets, the functions of the Rays they rule, and the specific influence of each relating to the Soul's life, the personality serving the Soul, the self-centered personality desires, or none of these specific influences.

Eight planets are especially influential. The most influential of these is Mercury, a ruler of Ray Four of harmony through conflict. Mercury is influential in all three areas of her being—the Soul life, the personality life expressing the Soul's purpose, and the self-centered personality life as shown in Horoscopes 2 and 3.

Only two of the remaining seven planets are influential in any of these three categories. Pluto, a ruler of Ray One of will and power, is influential in only one category, the Soul life. Therefore there is immense inner power urging her to accomplish her Soul's purpose, while Mercury which has a threefold strong influence gives her energy to attain the necessary harmony through karmic experiences and learning from them, affecting her Soul life, the personality expression of her Soul, and self-centered personality desires. Even though this is not an easy confrontation, the fact that Mercury is in Aries in the first house shows that once she becomes aware of Aquarian concepts and applies them, she will learn quickly and evolve rapidly. Mars, a ruler of Ray Six of idealism, devotion, and emotionalism, is strongly influential in her self-centered personality desires. An impatience and impulsiveness to bring her self-centered personality desires to fruition may produce unpleasant karmic results because of Mercury's strong influence in this category also. This suffering can be ameliorated and in time dispensed with altogether through the application of Aquarian Age concepts to the center of her being.

The remaining influential planets, though showing no strong influence in any of the above three categories of her life, show an overall strong influence of secondary importance to Mercury, Pluto, and Mars.

Of these five planets, Neptune, a ruler of Ray Six of idealism, devotion, and emotionalism heads the list because it is also the planet closest to the zenith in the natal chart. It indicates the strength of her idealism and devotion to a person or cause that is meaningful to her.

The Moon, a ruler of Ray Four of harmony through conflict, suggests that emotional conflicts will fill her life until she understands that the difficult experiences are of her own creation and until she learns from them.

Uranus, the ruler of Ray Seven of rhythmic living and powerful thoughts, suffuses her life with these characteristics.

Venus, the ruler of Ray Five of the concrete mind, is influential in that logical reasoning capacities are paramount in her life style.

The last of these influential planets, Jupiter, a ruler of Ray Two of love and wisdom, pours its energy into her consciousness, strongly influencing a greater acquisition and expression of these qualities.

Of these eight most influential planets, the only Ray that none of these rule is Ray Three of the abstract mind. Each of two Rays is represented twice, Ray Four of harmony through conflict and Ray Six of devotion, idealism, and emotionalism, which show a strong tendency to be highly influenced by her emotions which create conflicts. In applying the reasoning capacity of her Venus energy in the understanding and application of Aquarian Age concepts, her emotionalism and conflicts will decrease and eventually cease to impose themselves.

Step 13. Every seventh year in one's life there is a significant change, a possible crisis, and potential opportunity. Find the age when her last opportunity year occurred, and when the next will occur. She can then look back to assess how she handled it and how she might have done better so that she can take full advantage of the next year of opportunity. Her age during the last year of opportunity was twenty-eight in 1979, and the next will be thirty-five in 1986.

Step 14. Determine the general tendencies of each fourteen-year period to age eighty-four. Using a day for a year, find the exact major aspects (conjunction, opposition, square, trine, and sextile) of all progressed planets, except the progressed Moon, to natal planets for each period. From this information, compare in the various periods the number of total aspects, the number of easy versus challenging aspects, the Ray each planet making an aspect rules, and the number of times each Ray is activated. From this comparison indicate the general trend of thoughts and activities in the various periods of her life. Exact aspects give a person extra energies of the Rays, planets, and signs involved. Because this step is not detailed, but is a general overview, and because Ray-Centered Astrology and the progressions are concerned mostly with the inner Soul life, the progressions and the Rays ruled by the aspecting planets are stressed.

AGE—0 to 14 years for CASE 2

Progressed Planets' Positions	Partile Aspects	Easy	Challenging	Rays Planets Rule
☉ 1 ♈ 46—15 ♈ 51	P ☉ ☌ ☿	x		2, 4
☊ 19 ♓ 3—18 ♓ 54	P ☉ □ ♅		x	2, 7
☿ 13 ♈ 22—4 ♉ 47	P ☿ ☌ ♀	x		4, 5
♀ 2 ♉ 14—19 ♉ 23	P ☿ ☌ ♂	x		4, 6
♂ 16 ♈ 21—27 ♈ 5	P ☿ ☍ ♆		x	4, 6
♃ 23 ♓ 7—26 ♓ 31	P ☿ △ ♇	x		4, 1
♄ 28 ♍ 46℞ —27 ♍ 41℞	P ♀ ⚹ ♅	x		5, 7
♅ 5 ♋ 26—5 ♋ 38	P ♀ □ ♇		x	5, 1
♆ 18 ♎ 37℞ —18 ♎ 14℞	P ♀ ⚹ ☊	x		5
♇ 17 ♌ 44℞ —17 ♌ 32 ℞	P ♂ ☌ ♆		x	5, 6
	P ♂ △ ♇	x		5, 1

7 Rays ⚷ Found		7 Rays Frequency	
1 — 3		4 & 6 — 5	
2 — 2		5 — 4	
3 — 0		1 — 3	
4 — 5		2 & 7 — 2	
5 — 4		3 — 0	
6 — 5			
7 — 2			

AGE—14 to 28 years for CASE 2

Progressed Planets' Positions	Partile Aspects	Easy	Challenging	Rays Planets Rule
☉ 15 ♈ 51—29 ♈ 34	P ☉ ☌ ♂	x		2, 6
☊ 18 ♓ 54—18 ♓ 27	P ☉ ∕ ♆		x	2, 6
☿ 4 ♉ 47—8 ♉ 33 (7 ♉ 0 ℞)	P ☉ △ ♇	x		2, 1
♀ 19 ♉ 23—5 ♊ 51	P ☿ ✶ ♅	x		4, 7
♂ 27 ♈ 3—7 ♉ 27	P ♀ ✶ ☉	x		5, 2
♃ 26 ♓ 31—29 ♓ 44	P ♀ ✶ ♃	x		5, 2
♄ 27 ♍ 41℞ —26 ♍ 45℞	P ♀ △ ♄	x		5, 3
♅ 5 ♋ 38—6 ♋ 0	P ♀ △ ☽	x		5, 4
♆ 18 ♎ 14℞—17 ♎ 51℞	P ♂ ☌ ♀	x		6, 5
♇ 17 ♌ 32℞—17 ♌ 26℞	P ♂ ✶ ♅			6, 7
	P ♃ ☍ ♄		x	2, 3
	P ♃ ☍ ☽		x	2, 4

7 Rays ♂ Found	7 Rays Frequency
1 — 1	2 — 7
2 — 7	5 — 5
3 — 2	6 — 4
4 — 3	4 — 3
5 — 5	3 & 7 — 2
6 — 4	1 — 1
7 — 2	

AGE—28 to 42 years for CASE 2

Progressed Planets' Positions	Partile Aspects	Easy	Challenging	Rays Planets Rule
☉ 29 ♈ 34—13 ♉ 11	P ☉ ☌ ♀	x		2, 5
☊ 18 ♓ 27—17 ♓ 43	P ☉ ⚹ ♅	x		2, 7
☿ 7♉ 0℞ —28 ♈ 59℞	P ☿ ☌ ♀	x		4, 5
♀ 5 ♊ 51—22 ♊ 24	P ☿ ⚹ ♅	x		4, 7
♂ 7 ♉ 27—17 ♉ 41	P ♀ □ ☊		x	5
♃ 29 ♓ 44—2 ♈ 49	P ♀ ⚹ ☿	x		5, 4
♄ 26 ♍ 45℞ —26 ♍ 3℞	P ♀ ⚹ ♂	x		5, 6
♅ 6 ♋ 0—6 ♋ 31	P ♀ △ ♆	x		5, 6
♆ 17 ♎ 51℞ —17 ♎ 30℞	P ♀ ⚹ ♇	x		5, 1
♇ 17 ♌ 26℞ —17 ♌ 25	P ♃ ☌ ☉	x		2, 2
	P ♃ ☌ ♀	x		2, 5
	P ♆ ⚹ ♇	x		6, 1

7 Rays ⚳ Found		7 Rays Frequency	
1 — 2		5 — 8	
2 — 5		2 — 5	
3 — 0		4 & 6 — 3	
4 — 3		1 & 7 — 2	
5 — 8		3 — 0	
6 — 3			
7 — ⚳			

AGE—42 to 56 years for CASE 2

Progressed Planets' Positions	Partile Aspects	Easy	Challenging	Rays Planets Rule
⊙ 13 ♉ 11--26 ♉ 38	P⊙ ⚹ ☊	×		2
☊ 17 ♓ 43--16 ♓ 27	P⊙ ⚹ ♃	×		2, 2
☿ 28 ♈ 59 ℞ (28 ♈ 21)--2 ♉ 4	P⊙ □ ♇		×	2, 1
♀ 22 ♊ 24--8 ♋ 24	P♀ □ ⊙		×	5, 2
♂ 17 ♉ 41--27 ♉ 45	P♀ ⚹ ♀	×		5, 5
♃ 2 ♈ 49--5 ♈ 39	P♀ □ ♃		×	5, 2
♄ 26 ♍ 3 ℞--25 ♍ 38 ℞	P♀ □ ♄		×	5, 3
♅ 6 ♋ 31--7 ♋ 9	P♀ ☌ ♅	×		5, 7
♆ 17 ♎ 30 ℞--17 ♎ 11 ℞	P♀ □ ☽		×	5, 4
♇ 17 ♌ 25--17 ♌ 29	P♂ ⚹ ☊	×		6
	P♂ ⚹ ♃	×		6, 2
	P♂ □ ♇		×	6, 1
	P♃ □ ♅		×	2, 7

7 Rays	# Found		7 Rays	Frequency
1	-- 2		2	-- 8
2	-- 8		5	-- 7
3	-- 1		6	-- 3
4	-- 1		1 & 7	-- 2
5	-- 7		3 & 4	-- 1
6	-- 3			
7	-- 2			

AGE—56 to 70 years for CASE 2

Progressed Planets' Positions	Partile Aspects	Easy	Challenging	Rays Planets Rule:
⊙ 26 ♉ 36—10 ♊ 9	P ⊙ ⚹ ⊙	✗		2, 2
☊ 16 ♓ 27—15 ♓ 13	P ⊙ △ ♄	✗		2, 3
☿ 2 ♉ 4—17 ♉ 11	P ⊙ △ ☽	✗		2, 4
♀ 8 ♋ 24—23 ♋ 50	P ☿ ☌ ♀	✗		4, 5
♂ 27 ♉ 45—7 ♊ 37	P ☿ ⚹ ♅	✗		4, 7
♃ 5 ♈ 39—8 ♈ 12	P ♀ △ ☊	✗		5
♄ 25 ♍ 38℞ —25 ♍ 33	P ♀ □ ☿		✗	5, 4
♅ 7 ♋ 9—7 ♋ 52	P ♀ □ ♂		✗	5, 6
♆ 17 ♎ 11℞ —16 ♎ 57℞	P ♀ △ ♃	✗		5, 2
♇ 17 ♌ 29—17 ♌ 39	P ♀ □ ♆		✗	5, 6
	P ♂ ⚹ ⊙	✗		6, 2
	P ♂ △ ♄	✗		6, 3
	P ♂ △ ☽	✗		6, 4

7 Rays # Found		7 Rays Frequency	
1 — 0		2 & 5 — 6	
2 — 6		4 & 6 — 5	
3 — 2		3 — 2	
4 — 5		7 — 1	
5 — 6		1 — 0	
6 — 5			
7 — 1			

AGE—70 to 84 years for CASE 2

Progressed Planets' Positions	Partile Aspects	Easy	Challenging	Rays Planets Rule
☉ 10 ♊ 9—23 ♊ 32	P ☉ □ ☊		✕	2
☊ 15 ♓ 13—15 ♓ 34	P ☉ ⚹ ☿	✕		2, 4
☿ 17 ♉ 11—11 ♊ 3	P ☉ ⚹ ♂	✕		2, 6
♀ 23 ♋ 50—8 ♌ 32	P ☉ □ ♃		✕	2, 2
♂ 7 ♊ 37—17♊12	P ☉ △ ♆	✕		2, 6
♃ 8 ♈ 12—10 ♈ 23	P ☉ ⚹ ♇	✕		2, 1
♄ 25 ♍ 33—25 ♍ 48	P ☿ ⚹ ☉	✕		4, 2
♅ 7 ♋ 52—8 ♋ 40	P ☿ ⚹ ☊	✕		4
♆ 16 ♎ 57℞ —16 ♎ 48℞	P ☿ ⚹ ♃	✕		4, 2
♇ 17 ♌ 39—17 ♌ 54	P ☿ △ ♄	✕		4, 3
	P ☿ □ ♇		✕	4, 1
	P ☿ △ ☽	✕		4, 4
	P ♀ △ ☉	✕		5, 2
	P ♀ □ ♀	✕		5, 5
	P ♀ ⚹ ♄	✕		5, 3
	P ♀ ⚹ ☽	✕		5, 4
	P ♂ ⚹ ☿	✕		6, 4
	P ♂ ⚹ ♂	✕		6, 6
	P ♇ ☌ ♇	✕		1, 1

7 Rays # Found	7 Rays Frequency
1 — 4	2 & 4 — 10
2 — 10	5 & 6 — 5
3 — 2	1 — 4
4 — 10	3 — 2
5 — 5	7 — 0
6 — 0	
7 — 0	

SUMMARY OF RAY ACTIVATION
FOR CASE 2
Derived from 6 Age Period Charts

Age Period	Total	Easy	Challenging	10	9	8	7	6	5	4	3	2	1	0
0 to 14	11	7	4						4 6	5	1	2 7		3
14 to 28	12	9	3				2		5	6	4	3 7	1	
28 to 42	12	11	1			5			2		4 6		1 7		3
42 to 56	13	6	7			2	5				6	1 7	3 4		
56 to 70	13	10	3					2 5	4 6			3	7	1
70 to 84	19	15	4	2 4					5 6	1		3		7

In this case there is never a decrease in exact aspects from any period to the following one. There is either an increase or the same number in each succeeding period. This is fortunate because the added maturity gained from the passing years helps her use the increased energies more beneficially. An exceptional variance of easy versus challenging aspects is found throughout the six periods, ranging from one and one-sixth times as many challenging as easy ones in one period, to eleven times as many easy as challenging in another. This may tend to cause upheavals, especially in her case in which these two periods are consecutive, with the extremely challenging one following the extremely easy one.

After fourteen years of an excess of easy aspects (the easiest of all periods), she is confronted with an excess of challenging ones (the most challenging of all periods). Yet a Ray-Centered delineation such as this can help her and others who may have this same aspect distribution to become aware of the sudden shift from easy to challenging or vice versa, and make plans for the radical differences.

The most prominent Ray when considering the six periods as a unit is Ray Two of love and wisdom, her Soul Ray, which makes it easier to accomplish her Soul's purpose of serving others. Ray Five of the concrete mind is the second most prominent Ray, helping her use logic and reason in her Soul's purpose. She is also fortunate that the third most prominent Ray is Ray Four of harmony through conflict, her Personality Ray. This indicates that there will be more than sufficient energy for her personality to carry out her Ray Two Soul's purpose, and that the learning from the many karmic difficulties she experiences will be extremely helpful in her service to others.

The first period from birth to age fourteen is the second most challenging of the six periods. Yet, having the smallest number of aspects of all periods, it provides the least energy of all, which should mitigate the difficult karma. Rays Four and Six are equally the strongest, presaging many karmic lesson-teaching experiences and showing a tendency toward emotionalism and lack of self-confidence. Ray Three of the higher abstract mind is missing, which should cause no undue hardship in childhood when to be literal is normal. In this case the abstract mind would not function precociously.

The second period from age fourteen to twenty-eight finds the energies of all Rays coming to her, allowing her life to be better balanced. A slight increase in aspects and therefore energies over the first period helps her become aware of her Soul and its purpose because Ray Two, her Soul Ray, is the most prominent. Ray Five is the second most prominent, helping her acquire knowledge and the capacity to think logically, thus understanding certain Universal Laws and the desirability of adhering to them and benefiting from them.

Even though Ray Three of the abstract mind is missing again in the third period from age twenty-eight to forty-two, indicating a time of little creativity, this is by far the easiest of all six periods. There is a very unusual ratio of one challenging aspect to eleven easy ones. Because Ray Five of the concrete mind is the most prominent, followed by Ray Two of love and wisdom, her Soul Ray, it would be advisable for her to study deeply in the areas of her Soul's purpose. This is a period in which she can learn well from writings and lectures of others, applying the discriminative logical powers which this period gives her. After sufficient competency is acquired in this area, this is an ideal time to begin serving others consonant with her Soul Ray's purpose. She should have ample time and energy for Soul evolvement through service because very few karmic experiences will impede her. This fourteen-year relief from difficult karmic experiences, and the attainment of a higher level of Soul evolvement, if she takes advantage of this auspicious time for serving others, can prepare her for the abrupt change of the next period.

The fourth period of age forty-two to fifty-six is the most challenging of all. If she takes life easy in the previous period with no thought of serving others, but only indulging herself (which she can easily do because of the types of energies of that period and because of free will), this will be an extremely difficult time for her. If she does take advantage of the previous period in serving others, she will receive much help in overcoming her weaknesses through learning from the karmic difficulties she will experience. Not only are there one and one-sixth times more challenging than easy aspects, the number of challenging aspects has increased from the previous period by seven times. Challenging aspects, though difficult, are a means of Soul evolvement through learning lessons in overcoming weaknesses. This is especially true for her in this period because of the prominence of her Ray Two Soul of love and wisdom, followed closely by Ray Five of the concrete mind. Continuing to serve others which it is hoped she had started in the last period could be accomplished as she experiences her karmic lessons and learns quickly from them. These experiences and her success in learning from them through the understanding of Universal Laws could be a source of help to many others. No Ray energy is missing, giving her a diversification of energies for not only helping overcome many weaknesses, but at the same time helping her serve others according to her Soul's purpose. Because this is the most challenging of all periods, it does not necessarily mean that her many difficult karmic problems will be long-lasting unless she makes no effort to understand the character weaknesses which precipitate them and does not use self-discipline to overcome them. Challenging experiences do not occur unless we have a lesson to learn from them. Once we have learned the lesson, the difficult karma is lifted from us, and the energy from the so-called challenging aspect is used in constructive ways.

The fifth period from age fifty-six to seventy is a drastic change from the previous period and is much easier. The ratio of more challenging to easy aspects of the previous period now reverses to three and one-third times more easy than challenging. Rays Two and Five, the most prominent in the last period, are also the most prominent in this period. Sufficient energy for a continuation of her Soul Ray's purpose and a great deal of logic and understanding is supplied her. Perhaps more than a continuation will be accomplished because the time and energy she devoted to learning from her increased difficult experiences of the last period can be used here for her Soul's purpose of serving others. It is fortunate that Ray One of will and power is missing in this, rather than the previous period in which the willpower so helpful to discipline was given her.

The sixth period from age seventy to eight-four has a still higher ratio of easy to challenging aspects than the previous period. Ray Seven of strong thought and order is missing, indicating a trend toward a period of little organization. It is fortunate that this lack appears in this period rather than in an earlier one because she will then have had many years in which to organize her life so that the habitual continuation of her ordered rhythmic living will leave ample time and effort for Soul evolution which this period so aptly provides. Rays Two and Four, her Soul and Personality Rays, are by far the most prominent, providing much energy for service consonant with her Soul's purpose and for her personality to aid in its achievement. This period shows a sharp increase in number of aspects from the previous period which had the highest number of any up to that time. This added energy is conducive to a greater accomplishment in her Soul's purpose.

Step 15. Because each person is influenced greatly by the four signs of the cross the Sun was in at his birth, elucidate the specific opportunities during the four periods. Include for each sign the meaning and esoteric planetary ruler, the Ray that planet rules, and the house or houses that sign tenants. (1) During the last week of March and the first three weeks of April, the Sun is in Aries in her first house. The esoteric ruler of Aries is Mercury, a ruler of Ray Four of harmony through conflict. This is an excellent period for Soul growth through difficult karmic experiences and learning from them. Her energy, enthusiasm, optimism, and self-confidence are on a relatively high level, all of which can contribute to her Soul evolvement. (2) During the last week of June and the first three weeks of July, the Sun is in Cancer in her fourth and fifth houses. The esoteric ruler of Cancer is Neptune, a ruler of Ray Six of idealism and devotion. The first half of this period is a time for Soul growth on a very deep level through a devoted nurturing of those in her environment who cannot fend for themselves, and through meditation for contacting her Soul. The second half of this period is an ideal time for inspirational creativity. (3) During the last week of September and the first three weeks of October, the Sun is in Libra in her seventh house. The esoteric ruler of Libra is Uranus, the ruler of Ray Seven of order, rhythm, and powerful thoughts. This is an auspicious time for close relationships and an opportunity to learn much from them. She can weigh the advantages of self-centered desires versus those of spiritual aspirations in a true Libran fashion. If she finds that focusing to a greater extent on one rather than the other brings more rhythm and order into her life, thus producing serenity, her powerful thoughts can make her choice more pronounced. (4) During the last week of December and the first three weeks of January, the Sun is in Capricorn in her tenth and eleventh houses. The esoteric ruler of Capricorn is Saturn, a ruler of Ray Three of the abstract mind. The first half of this period will bring an urge to work hard and consistently on certain career matters toward which her contemplation leads her. The last half of this period is an ideal time to devote to humanitarian concerns. She may work hard and for long hours in the way her higher mind suggests.

Step 16. When she has formulated a plan for her life work, she should reassess it periodically in terms of her motivation because lasting success is not possible without proper motivation. If her plan is not to serve others to the best of her ability out of love and concern, she should spend time becoming aware of her weaknesses as elucidated in this delineation, endeavoring to transmute them into strengths, especially those strengths of her Ray Two Soul and Ray Four Personality as found in Chapter Three. If her motivation is right and strong, she can expect success and joy in her work as she takes these following steps in carrying out her life plan:

1. A strong intention to carry it through by focusing her ideas.
2. Visualization by imagination and impressing on her mind what it is she wants to do.
3. Projection—the willing of her plan by thought because energy follows thought. This projection must be carried out in a way that is consistent with her Soul and Personality Rays. From Chart 29 we find that her Ray Two Soul predicates intense concentration in seeing her life plan in relation to the whole of God's Plan on Earth. Her Ray Four Personality indicates concentration on the merging of her personality and Soul to achieve her life plan.

Step 17. Check her natal chart for a trine, sextile, semisextile, quincunx, septile, septile derivative, quintile, or quintile derivative between Jupiter and Pluto. There is a bi-quintile indicating that she is capable of studying and teaching esoteric wisdoms. This aspect between Pluto, a ruler of Ray One of will and power and the esoteric ruler of Pisces, and Jupiter, a ruler of Ray Two of love and wisdom and the esoteric ruler of Aquarius, indicates a strong urge to help humanity evolve spiritually in this Aquarian Age. In addition to the power of Pluto in its own essence, it increases its power appreciably in her life. In her Horoscopes 2 and 3 it is found to be the most influential planet contributing to her Soul life because it is the primary ruler of the Ascendant (Soul) and is the only planet that aspects all other planets in these horoscopes. Jupiter has much strength and Soul power because of its close conjunction with the Ascendant (Soul) and North Node. In addition, both her Pluto and Jupiter were found in Step 12 to be influential in an all-encompassing way because of the prominence in her natal horoscope of the signs they rule.

CASE STUDY 3—NATAL & PROGRESSED HOROSCOPE 1

Ray 1 Soul, Ray 4 Personality

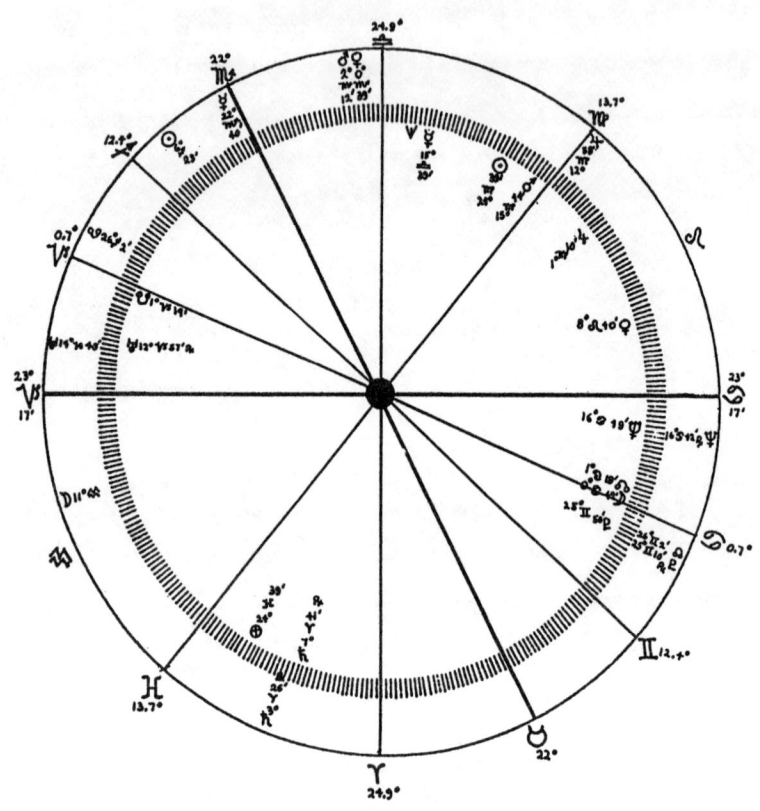

Chapter Nine

Case 3

Step 1. Find the approximate level of Soul evolvement. Case 3 is indeed an advanced Soul. A Finger-of-God aspect indicates a special spiritual mission is her destiny. Her natal planets are well integrated through an unusually large number of aspectual relationships which shows that all the facets of her being can easily work in unison. Having more challenging than easy aspects means she has brought a great deal of lesson-teaching karma into this life. Only an advanced Soul would be allowed to have this birth time because one can take on only that amount of lesson-teaching karma in one lifetime that she is able to handle. This will not be an easy life for her but one of great Soul evolvement if she determines it to be. Her spiritual mission will not begin until she has learned a high percentage of the needed lessons from her difficult karmic experiences that will confront her when challenging aspects are partile. By that time she will have hopefully conquered many weaknesses. Hopefully her life will become spiritually oriented and thus she will contribute to the Soul evolvement of others, resulting in self-realization and joy.

Step 2. Study the progressed natal chart for the coming year. In seeing it as a seed that can blossom into fruit, we see that this is an auspicious time for a Ray-Centered delineation. This is an extremely important year, with powerful combinations of energy coming to her from six exact aspects, and an additional three which, though not partile this year, are very close to partile and are powerful enough to affect her.

One of these is progressed Pluto square Sun approaching 31' from exactness during the year. Because this aspect is shown in her natal chart with an orb of only 71', and because Pluto moves very slowly, making its effects felt for a long period before it becomes partile, this progressed aspect will be very strong and pervasive in this particular year. Her progressed Pluto retrograde in Gemini in the fifth house square Sun in Virgo in the eighth house shows a tendency to impose her will on others in a detailed manner, sometimes in a dictatorial and exhibitionistic way, and at other times manipulative, but always with great intensity. This weakness shown in her chart prevails, as do all of our characteristics shown by our natal charts because of the way the energy was used in past lives. Because her chart indicates advanced Soul status, she undoubtedly is urged to transmute this energy to a higher level—intense power (Pluto is a ruler of Ray One) coupled with love and wisdom (Sun is a ruler of Ray Two) in serving others (Virgo) through comunicative skills (Gemini), leading to self-realization (fifth house) and ultimately spiritual regeneration (eighth house).

The only other challenging aspect is a quincunx between progressed Mars in Scorpio in the ninth house and progressed Saturn in Aries in the second house. This energy can produce frustration until she learns to use it advantageously. Its energy is intensely psychic and can be used for understanding and implementing Universal Truths in making the needed changes in attitudes and values which will help deflate her strong ego and separative feelings and help her feel At One With All. Because Saturn is a ruler of Ray Three of the higher mind, and Mars is a ruler of Ray Six of idealism and devotion, it can be done with contemplation and idealism.

She is fortunate in that she has the following seven easy progressed aspects to help with the two previous challenging ones. Of these seven, the first three can be instrumental in transmuting the energy of her progressed Pluto square Sun to better use.

Her progressed Mars in Scorpio in the ninth house is conjunct progressed Venus, indicating an enjoyment of psychically receiving Universal Truths. Because Mars is a ruler of Ray Six of idealism and devotion, and Venus is the ruler of Ray Five of the reasoning mind, the knowledge received can be both idealistically and logically applied.

The trine of progressed Sun in Sagittarius in the tenth house to Saturn retrograde in Aries in the second house will culminate very shortly after the year ends, but its energies will be strong during the year. The Sun is a ruler of Ray Two of love and wisdom, and Saturn is a ruler of Ray Three of the abstract mind. The synchronization of these energies shows a possible breakthrough with originality and one-pointedness toward a career, and the alteration of those attitudes and values that need changing. Even though this energy is fiery in its sources, giving it integrity and action orientation, it can be expressed in a cautious and disciplined way as a result of intuitive knowledge wisely applied with love.

Her progressed Mercury in Scorpio will conjunct the Midheaven and later in the year sextile her Sun in Virgo in the eighth house. The Sun is a ruler of Ray Two of love and wisdom, and Mercury is a ruler of Ray Four of harmony through conflict. These combined energies give her a heightened ability through love and wisdom to attain harmony by becoming aware of how certain of her weaknesses are bringing difficult experiences to her, and then by changing these weaknesses into strengths. This awareness can be reached through her psychic capacity (Scorpio) and in an analytical manner (Virgo), and will not only help her attain a certain degree of spiritual regeneration (eighth house), but impressive career benefits (tenth house).

Because the next three aspects are concerned with Venus, the ruler of Ray Five of concrete knowledge, this is an auspicious year to make use of her accumulated knowledge. Her progressed Venus has become exceptionally important by entering a new sign, Scorpio, after having been in Libra for many years. Therefore this year is the beginning of a new phase of her existence characterized by the capacity to bring from the depth of her being accumulated knowledge of philosophy, spiritual concepts, universal truth, and other ninth house matters. The unique ability conferred by her progressed Venus in the ninth house trine Moon in Cancer in the sixth house enables her to utilize her psychic capacity and her emotions to aid in the retrieval of the stored knowledge, referred to above, so that she can be of service to others in a nurturing and caring way. Because the Moon is a ruler of Ray Four of harmony through conflict, this aspect can be very influential in building the bridge from her personality to her Soul.

Her progressed Venus in Scorpio in the ninth house sextile Jupiter, a ruler of love and wisdom in Virgo in the seventh house, shows that the forementioned ability can easily demonstrate love and understanding which will enhance the seventh house proclivity for making wise choices. The decision whether to manifest solely on a personality level or to begin manifesting on a Soul level can be made wisely.

Her progressed Venus in Scorpio in the ninth house being trine the North Node in Cancer in the sixth house can reverse the nodal polarity, thereby inducing the manifestation of loving, sensitive, caring feelings in serving others through the understanding of spiritual concepts.

The last progressed aspect that influences her this year is a separating one by only six-tenths of a minute. It is progressed Jupiter in Virgo in the eighth house trine Uranus in Capricorn in the twelfth house. Since Jupiter is a ruler of Ray Two of love and wisdom, and Uranus is the ruler of Ray Seven of strong thoughts, the trine between them offers the opportunity to take advantage of smooth blending of their powers so that she can reach the unconscious levels of her mind, become aware of buried repressions and guilt feelings, and through that awareness purge them by conscious recognition. The result can be a true cognizance of her weaknesses that they will be transmuted into strengths.

Step 3. Find the Soul Ray by following the calculations of Example Horoscope 6 in Chapter Two. As shown therein this person has a Ray One Soul. Study carefully the information in Chapter Three pertaining to Ray One—all the information in that section is important to the person's welfare.

In general, her life plan or Soul's purpose is to destroy outworn concepts and ideas and substitute those which are more workable and in attunement with the Aquarian Age. All Ray One Souls approach the spiritual path by sheer force of will. If she uses her Ray One Soul energy of will and power unwisely, she will be prideful, dominating, and lacking in love toward others, creating havoc in their lives and even more in her own. If she uses this immense energy wisely she will have a healthy feeling of independence, courage and dedication, the ability to identify with the rhythm of the universe, and an eventual understanding of God's Plan for Earth.

Step 4. Study thoroughly the Ascendant sign, Capricorn, in Chapter Four and supplement this with her Ray One Soul information.

In generalizing, her Capricorn Ascendant gives her the discipline and persistence necessary for transmuting weaknesses into strengths which results in the raising of her level of consciousness and a possible spiritual initiation. All Capricorn information, though important, should be supplemental in the choice of her Soul's purpose or life work. The main focus is consonant with her Ray One Soul.

Her Capricorn Ascendant of the earth element is feminine, and her Ray One Soul, being odd-numbered, is masculine. Her Soul's purpose, therefore, is basically concerned with the intellect, power, and extrovertive behavior, but in a practical way that is in rapport with earthly needs. Both the masculine and feminine characteristics of her nature can be utilized in her Soul's purpose, giving her the potential for courage and self-confidence supplemented by practicality and calmness.

Step 5. Find the Personality Ray by following the calculations of Example Horoscope 6 in Chapter Two. As shown, this person has a Ray Four Personality. In Chapter Three carefully study the information pertaining to Ray Four which serves her Ray One Soul's purpose.

In generalizing, Case 3's Soul's purpose of destroying outworn ideas and concepts and substituting workable ones is aided by her Ray Four Personality of harmony through conflict. For her personality to carry out her Soul's purpose it is necessary that she attain the harmony that is so important for optimal manifestation of her physical, emotional, and mental bodies. To attain this needed harmony, an understanding of Reincarnation, Karma, and the power of thought is paramount so she can resolve her conflicts, thus lessening difficult karmic experiences and giving her the capability of performing her Soul's purpose.

Because her Ray One Soul gives her power to destroy concepts, ideas, and material forms that are no longer needed, and because her Ray Four Personality, after attaining the necessary harmony, can act as a bridge between the three lower kingdoms (mineral, plant, and animal) and humanity, her personality, after acquiring the necessary harmony, can aid her Soul's purpose by improving forms in the three lower kingdoms. This may be her Soul's task if certain of the earth changes and catastrophies that many have predicted occur. This dormant power can be activated only when enough spiritual progress is made for her thoughts and motivations to be high enough so that nothing but good can result from her work. With a Ray Four Personality, only through self-control and discipline can she bring tranquility to the warring forces of her nature, at which time her Soul will allow her personality to serve its purpose.

Step 6. Study her Sun sign in Chapter Four. The energies of her Virgo Sun supplement her Ray Four Personality to depict her personality more clearly. Mercury, the exoteric ruler of Virgo, influences her strongly until she begins working on Soul evolvement. The mind with its rationalization and maneuvering tendencies often works overtime from the energies of Mercury as an exoteric ruler of a sign. As Soul contact is made, the esoteric ruler of Virgo, the Moon veiling Vulcan and Uranus becomes more influential. Vulcan's energies will help her crystallize buried weaknesses including guilt feelings, and bring them from her unconscious to her conscious mind where they are dealt with and eradicated. As she advances in Soul evolvement, the energy of Uranus will enhance her intuition, leading to instant awareness in many areas. Her Ray Four Personality of harmony through conflict supplemented by her Virgo Sun with the esoteric ruler, the Moon veiling Vulcan and Uranus predominant, indicates power at her command to resolve conflicts and attain the harmony she needs. As an advanced Soul she continues to receive the energies of the exoteric ruler, Mercury, but at its higher vibration. When she has attained a very advanced state of Soul evolvement, the hierarchical ruler, Jupiter, will become the predominating ruler. The love and wisdom that she can easily acquire through the energy of Jupiter will help her attain the harmony that her Ray Four Personality foreshadowed.

Her even-numbered Ray Four Personality is feminine supplemented by her Virgo Sun, which is also feminine, showing her personality to be introvertive and emotional as it concerns others. It is important to study thoroughly the Virgo information in Chapter Four in light of her personality expression. Generalizing, her Virgo Sun energy will stimulate the birth of the Christ consciousness to help solve her conflicts and those of others, thereby attaining harmony.

Step 7. Study the interaction of the Soul Ray supplemented by the Ascendant with the Personality Ray supplemented by the Sun sign, keeping in mind that the Soul Ray indicates her purpose in life and the Personality Ray indicates her way of expressing the Soul's purpose. Her Ray One Soul and Capricorn Ascendant show that her Soul's purpose is to abolish outworn ideas, concepts, and/or forms, and replace them with practical, workable ones for the good of all concerned. Her Ray Four Personality and Virgo Sun show that she can express her Soul's purpose by attaining harmony through resolving conflicts and by taking care of her physical body through good nutrition, sufficient exercise, sun, and fresh air.

Gender has specific meaning in a delineation. Using M for masculine gender of a Ray, F for feminine gender of a Ray, f and m for the Ascendant and Sun sign genders, and underlining the Soul's purpose to indicate its greater influence, we have the following formula: $\underline{Mf}Ff$. Not only three of the four genders, but both genders of the personality are feminine. This points strongly to sensitivity, psychic ability, and concern for others. These characteristics are a part of the feminine aspect of her being, associated with the "Yin" of the "I Ching" and the "anima" of Jung. These traits are strong in her personality, yet others may not see her personality as it truly is.

A Ray One Soul is very difficult to deal with until one has reached an advanced Soul state. Until that time the repressed power and will of the Soul occasionally overrides her personality traits, showing a driving force, a lack of love, and an arrogance that is not truly of her personality. There is a good balance of gender in her Soul's purpose which can therefore be very effective when the time is right to express it once she has overcome most of her character weaknesses.

Because her Soul's purpose is concerned with untold power, which if not used by a personality free of certain weaknesses, can do a great deal of harm when some of that energy welling up within her is released, there is a tendency to express it in a determined, self-centered way whether through forceful thoughts, words, and actions, or in a manipulative fashion for future gratification, without regard for the needs of others. To protect them and herself, her Soul holds the greater part of that power within her until it knows that such release is for the good of all. This may occur sooner than she expects if she is determined to overcome her weaknesses because her Capricorn Ascendant can provide discipline and persistence, and her Ray One Soul, the will and power to succeed.

The color that would help her most is pink, the vibratory energies of which enable one to feel more love toward others. Even though we all need to enhance our feelings of love, with Case 3 this enhancement should be of first importance. The will and power of her Ray One Soul supplemented by the coldness of her Capricorn Ascendant implies a need to feel more love toward others. When she has developed unattached love for All, it will be impossible for her to hurt another with the power at her command. Just by existing she either hurts or helps others greatly depending on the quality of love within her. Green, the color of relaxation, is of secondary importance to her. The discipline to restrain the power within her until she has overcome her weaknesses, though wise on a long-term basis, creates occasional short-term anxiety which can be relieved through the vibratory energies of green. The color of her Ray Four Personality is green, which helps her express her Soul's purpose in a more tension-free way. She should seldom use red or black. Red, the lowest vibratory color of the spectrum, would intensify her impulsiveness and tension. Black, the absence of all colors, is capable of absorption. Its use, when in the company of those of a low vibration at a time when she felt little love toward others, would cause her to receive negative thoughts and impressions and only add to her tenseness.

Step 8. Set up a Ray-Centered horoscope showing the inner Soul life and the outer personality life expressing the Soul's purpose (Horoscope 2). Use Chart 4 to find the esoteric rulers of the Ascendant and Sun sign. See natal Horoscope 1 for positions of the planets to be used in Horoscope 2.

To find the inner Soul life, use the natal Ascendant and all its esoteric planetary rulers. The primary esoteric ruler of the Capricorn Ascendant is Saturn which is in Aries; the esoteric ruler of Aries is Mercury which is in Libra; the esoteric ruler of Libra is Uranus which is in Capricorn.

To find the Soul-serving personality life, use the Sun and all its esoteric rulers. The primary esoteric ruler of the Virgo Sun is the Moon which is in Cancer. The esoteric ruler of Cancer is Neptune, which is also in Cancer.

Entering the Ascendant and Soul life planets and the Sun and the planets as personality expressions of the Soul life, each group with a different color into Horoscope 2, using the same cusps as in the natal Horoscope 1 and using different-colored lines to denote different types of aspects, produces a picture of Case Three's Soul life and Soul-serving personality life. The specific planetary energies designated for the Soul's purpose consonant with her Ray One Soul are shown. Those specific planetary energies designated for the personality expression of her Soul life consonant with her Ray Four Personality, which help her in her outer life to manifest her Soul's purpose, are also shown.

The interaction between these two groups is especially significant in pinpointing the planetary energies that are combined through aspects, and the identity of those aspects. She has four inner Soul life planets and three Soul-serving personality life planets. This indicates that her inner Soul urges are somewhat stronger than her personality serving the Soul.

In addition to the first house of the Soul and its purpose, four other houses are influential. Since none of the planets in this horoscope are influential for both the Soul life and the Soul-serving personality life, and since only one of the houses, the eighth, has a planet of both the Soul life and a planet of the personality serving the Soul, the eighth house is the area of contact between her Soul's purpose and its personality expression. It is the house of temptation, testing, and spiritual regeneration. This signifies that it is not easy for her to express her Soul's purpose, but with determination, nothing will stand in the way of Soul evolvement. This also indicates that her Soul's purpose for serving others cannot begin until she has made substantial progress in overcoming her weaknesses. Because the eighth house is a house of depth and power, she cannot begin her Soul's purpose until her personality is so perfected that her innate power will be used unselfishly. This statement, coupled with the power of her Ray One Soul, affords double strength to this interpretive knowledge.

CASE 3—HOROSCOPE 2

Indicates the Soul's Purpose and its Expression
Using Soul Life Planets and
Personality Planets Serving the Soul

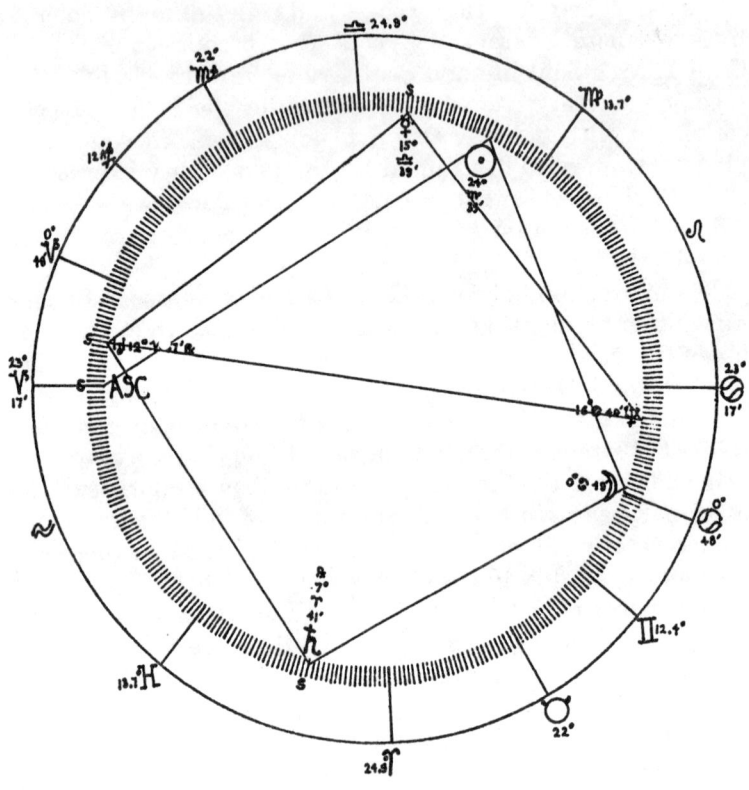

The next prominent house in this horoscope is the sixth, wherein two Soul-serving planets are found. This indicates that she will express her Soul's urges by aiding others to perfect themselves.

The twelfth and second houses each have one planet, both influential for the Soul's purpose. The planetary energy in the twelfth house shows that much energy is at her command for bringing to the conscious mind from the unconscious, repressed guilt feelings and character weaknesses to eradicate them. She must perform this task if she is to fulfill her Soul's purpose. If she does, help will be given from the spirit planes. The last influential house, the second, indicates that if she disciplines herself to change attitudes and values, she can attain illumination.

There is not much rapport between her Soul life planets and her personality expression of them. Aspectually, there are two squares, one opposition, and one trine between them. The trine between the Sun and Ascendant is in the earth element, and is the only element represented in both groups. Therefore it is mainly through practicality, the physical body, and material needs that the personality can express the Soul's purpose.

It is not easy for her to integrate the energies of her Soul's purpose or even to be aware of them. A T-square between three of her Soul planets creates obstacles until she learns to use these energies positively. A square between Mercury, a ruler of Ray Four of harmony through conflict in Libra in the eighth house, and Uranus, the ruler of Ray Seven of strong thoughts in Capricorn in the twelfth house, indicates a tendency toward strong thoughts to be used coldly and selfishly because of many temptations, yet at the same time there is a weighing in her mind of the outcome of such thoughts versus good ones, as well as indecisiveness. As a result, she experiences many conflicts until she becomes aware of the fact that the strong thoughts that are so necessary for her Soul's purpose, must be thoughts directed not toward self-centered ends but toward the good of All. The other square of her Soul planets is between Uranus, the ruler of Ray Seven of strong thoughts in Capricorn in the twelfth house, and Saturn, a ruler of Ray Three of the higher mind in Aries in the second house, giving a tendency to use strong thoughts of impulsiveness with a lack of love and concern for others, and to experience a conflict between freedom and responsibility.

Until she changes her attitudes and values and works hard and persistently on understanding the Oneness of All, and feels unattached love for them, her strong ego, coupled with her lack of rhythmic living, creates unpleasant tension and irritability. When she learns to use these energies together properly, her strong one-pointed powerful thoughts can be a pillar of strength to many.

Two of the planets influencing the personality expression of the Soul's purpose are square each other. They are the Sun, a ruler of Ray Two of love and wisdom in Virgo in the eighth house, and the Moon, a ruler of Ray Four of harmony through conflict in Cancer in the sixth house. This square indicates a temptation to be critical of others which creates conflicts. To bring harmony into her life she must learn to accept and love others as they are. Awareness that some people have lived more lives than others and therefore have had more opportunities to overcome weaknesses should help. When she has learned to use these two planetary energies together beneficially, love, wisdom, and harmony will be hers, enabling her to express her Soul's purpose.

Her Moon, a ruler of Ray Four of harmony through conflict, and Neptune, a ruler of Ray Six of idealism and devotion, are both in Cancer in the sixth house. These two planets of the Soul-serving personality indicate that she has great psychic capacity and the idealism to use it to nurture and serve others.

An aspect between a planet of the Soul's purpose, Mercury, a ruler of Ray Four of harmony through conflict in Libra in the eighth house, and a planet of the Soul-serving personality, Neptune, a ruler of Ray Six of idealism and devotion in Cancer in the sixth house, is a square. This indicates a conflict between the mind and the emotions. Her mind tries to weigh the benefits of manifesting on a Soul level of concern for others as against self-centered personality desires. Another part of her being desires to be guided by her sensitive emotions. When she learns to use the energies of these two planets together optimally by disciplining herself to be guided by her mind rather than her emotions, she will be freed of the conflict between them. After the original confusion is resolved, she can convert emotionalism into inspiration which can be used advantageously along with her mental capacities.

A second aspect between a planet of the Soul and a planet of the Soul-serving personality is a square between Saturn, a ruler of Ray Three of the higher mind in Aries in the second house, and Moon, a ruler of Ray Four of harmony through conflict in Cancer in the sixth house. This shows a conflict between her strong ego and her hypersensitivity, especially in matters of attitudes and values and in serving others. She can best use the energies of these two planets together when she allows the contemplation of her higher mind to change her own hypersensitivity to a sensitive perception of others' needs.

A third aspect between a planet influencing the Soul, Uranus, a ruler of Ray Seven of strong thoughts and rhythm in Capricorn in the twelfth house, and a planet influencing the Soul-serving personality, Neptune, a ruler of Ray Six of idealism and devotion in Cancer in the sixth house, is an opposition. This shows a tendency to harbor rebellious yet confused thoughts, not only in a repressed way but in the discharging of her duties. At the same time there is a Soul urge, which will be to her advantage to follow, to work hard and persistently with strong thoughts to raise her consciousness level and attain an ordered, rhythmic living pattern from an emotionally polarized personality.

The last aspect in Horoscope 2 is the only easy one. It is a trine between the Sun, a ruler of Ray Two of love and wisdom in Virgo in the eighth house, and the Capricorn Ascendant, signifying her Ray One Soul of will and power. It is fortunate that the only easy aspect is between the primary indicator of the Soul, the Ascendant, and the primary indicator of the personality aiding the Soul, the Sun. This shows physical vitality and the expectation of a long life to work on overcoming weaknesses and serving others. It also shows intense power, yet practicality in her Soul's purpose and in the expression of it with love and wisdom. Spiritual regeneration will not be as difficult as she might suppose it to be.

The planetary energies influential to the Soul life are one in the air element, one in fire, and two in earth. Those influential to the personality expressing the Soul's purpose are two in water and one in earth. As far as elements of the signs are concerned, because there is no air or fire in the Soul-serving personality planets, the Soul life is more powerful, fiery, and intellectual than is her personality to express her Soul's purpose which is more practical and sensitive.

The Soul life planets and the Rays they rule are: Ascendant—Ray One, Saturn—Ray Three, Mercury—Ray Four, and Uranus—Ray Seven. Rays Two, Five, and Six are not among her Soul life planets, which suggests that love, wisdom, the lower concrete mind, and idealism are not strong indicators of her inner nature. She must remember however, that every Ray has all seven Rays as sub-rays and that by having free will she can intensify any of these energy characteristics if she wishes. Love is the quality that she might best try to make stronger because it is the primary requisite for Soul evolvement in this solar system—the essence of the Ray Two Soul of our Sun.

Three of the four planets of the Soul are odd-numbered, giving her powerful energy, a strong mind, and confidence in her Soul life. Ray One gives her power and will, Ray Three gives a contemplative mind, and Ray Seven gives strong one-pointed thoughts conducive to rhythm and order. Her single, even-numbered Ray is Ray Four, confronting her Soul with conflicts until she achieves harmony through learning her needed lessons.

The Soul-serving personality planets and the Rays they rule are: Sun—Ray Two, Moon—Ray Four, and Neptune—Ray Six. These Rays are all even-numbered, showing that even though her Soul life planets indicate much power and confidence but a lack of love, her Soul-serving personality planets complement her Soul life in that they indicate love and concern for others, a magnetic personality, and a lack of self-confidence in expressing her powerful Soul urges. This lack of self-confidence on a personality level can be eliminated easily by going into the silence and contacting her Soul.

The only Ray activated in both groups is Ray Four of harmony through conflict, indicating many conflicts in both her inner life and its outer expression. Harmony cannot be hers until she develops better attitudes and values and expresses them in her outer world. There is little rapport between these two groups of planets, signifying that it may not be easy to express her Soul's purpose, yet the energies she lacks in her Soul life are found in her Soul-serving personality life and vice versa. An awareness of this fact and a determination to use these two groups of planets together for a common purpose will give her the necessary qualities for a self-fulfilled and Soul-elevating life. These two parts of her nature, so different, yet so helpful to each other, are analogous to marriage partners who are very different but need each other for complementation—this marriage relationship may prove difficult until an understanding develops as to the benefits each can receive from the other. So it is with these two parts of her nature.

Step 9. Set up another Ray-Centered Horoscope to find the main problem for this life as shown by the conflict between inner Soul aspirations and the self-centered personality desires. This is designated Horoscope 3. In this horoscope use the same house cusps as in Horoscopes 1 and 2. Insert the Ascendant and all its esoteric rulers as found in Step 8. The Ascendant and these planets depict the inner Soul life. From the natal chart, find the exoteric rulers of the Sun sign.

The exoteric ruler of the Virgo Sun is Mercury which is in Libra; the exoteric ruler of Libra is Venus which is in Leo; the exoteric ruler of Leo is the Sun which is in Virgo. In this horoscope insert the Sun, Mercury, and Venus which depict the self-centered personality desires. It would be advisable to (1) place the Sun, Mercury, and Venus in the horoscope in a different color from the Soul life planets, (2) enlarge the abbreviation, "Asc.," and the symbol for Saturn, the primary esoteric ruler, because they have more power than the other rulers of the Ascendant, (3) enlarge the symbols for Sun and Mercury because they have more power than Venus, the only other exoteric ruler of the Sun.

There are four planets very influential to the inner Soul life and only three that are very influential to the self-centered personality desires. This is fortunate in that more energy is thus available for the Soul life than for self-centered personality desires.

The self-centered personality planets and the Rays they rule are: Sun—Ray Two, Mercury—Ray Four, and Venus—Ray Five. It is to her advantage that twice as many planetary energies are even-numbered as are odd-numbered. This shows that not too much power has to be redirected to work out her prob-

CASE 3—HOROSCOPE 3

Indicates for this Life the Conflict Between Soul Life Planets and Self-centered Personality Planets and its Resolution

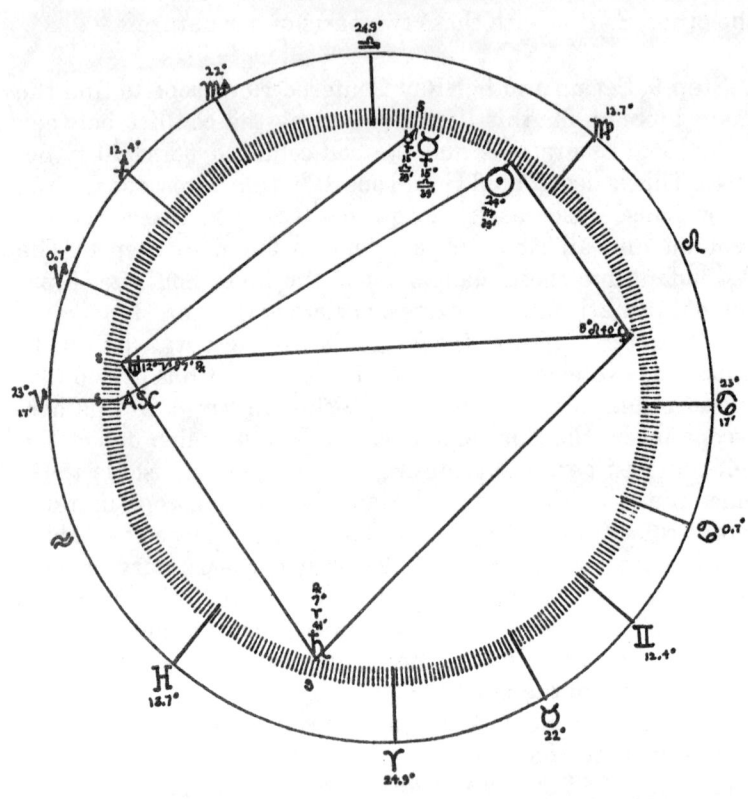

lems. However, two of these three planets are in masculine signs which endows them with a certain amount of power, but the higher cosmic origin of the Rays gives them more significance than the signs. Therefore there is a preponderance of feminine characteristics in her planetary energies for self-centered desires such as worry, indecisiveness, tension, and literal-mindedness.

In Step 8 we found the planets and the Ascendant and their Rays which influence the inner Soul life. They are: Ascendant—Ray One, Saturn—Ray Three, Mercury—Ray Four, and Uranus—Ray Seven. Three of these four Rays are odd-numbered (masculine), which indicates a strong predominance of power, will, and intellect over the feminine qualities of sensitivity, love, and concern for others.

In looking at Horoscope 3 and the personality self-centered desire planets, we see a semi-square between intercepted Venus, a ruler of Ray Five of the concrete mind in Leo in the seventh house, and Sun, a ruler of Ray Two of love and wisdom in Virgo in the eighth house. This aspect provides a wealth of information concerning self-centered desires which create problems for her. There is a tendency to display her accumulated knowledge in order to be the center of attention and to be critical of others' contributions. Because Venus is intercepted, the accumulated knowledge which could be instrumental in self-realization cannot be fully utilized until considerable Soul evolvement has occurred.

She has a close to partile fire sign trine from Venus to Saturn, a Soul planet retrograde in Aries, and a ruler of Ray Three of the abstract mind in the second house. This gives both her concrete and abstract mental faculties much energy, enthusiasm, and self-discipline in her inner life to change the energy use of the intercepted Venus to a less self-centered and more spiritual orientation. Because of a rapport between her logical and abstract minds, she has an opportunity to understand and change attitudes and values so that there will be a better seventh house relationship and a wise choice made between self-centered desires and spiritual aspirations, leading to a spiritual application of her stored knowledge. This easy flow of energy between the left and right hemispheres of the brain can result in self-realization through the ability to differentiate between karmic rewards and karmic difficulties which result from various thoughts, words, and actions. This will make it easier to discipline herself. This aspect indicates occult power coupled with stored knowledge and a facility with words, resulting in smooth communication.

A tri-septile from Venus to Uranus, a Soul planet and ruler of Ray Seven of strong thoughts in Capricorn in the twelfth house, confers the ability to develop strong logical and one-pointed thoughts in all newly acquired attitudes and values, and to work hard and persistently to make them a permanent part of her being in a compassionate way. All septile aspects are fated, that is, the Soul before coming into the present life impresses the mind to carry out its intention.

Her Uranus is square Saturn, a ruler of Ray Three of the higher mind in the second house, both being Soul life planets. This may present a problem in the use of the new inspirational ideas she may receive in contrast to her established habitual attitudes and values. The concept of the Oneness-of-All exemplified by Uranus in the twelfth house conflicts with her strong ego as exemplified by Saturn in Aries in the second house. She should make her new ideas workable before completely discarding established attitudes and values. If she does this, she will become aware of the advantage of being at One with others.

There is a square between Uranus and Mercury, a ruler of Ray Four of harmony through conflict. This aspect, though challenging, will mitigate the conflict between Uranus and Saturn. This mitigation could be accomplished when thoughts, strengthened by Uranus, are not of the highest and are manifested in an explosive temper. Instant lesson-teaching karma would result because the effect on others whose swift feedback would help change her established attitudes and values. She will then be more concerned about others than herself.

Because Mercury is in the eighth house and is the only planet which greatly influences both the Soul life and self-centered personality desires, it is a strong point of contact in which the self-centered desire energies can be transmuted to spiritual aspirations. Mercury, a ruler of Ray Four in Libra in the eighth house, gives her the ability to compare the benefits derived from using energy in self-centered desires with the energy used

in spiritual aspirations by noting whether the results are lesson-teaching karma or rewarding karma. Until she makes a
wise choice between the two, she will be subjected to many
temptations and testing.

She is fortunate in that she has an earth trine between the
Sun, a ruler of Ray Two of love and wisdom in Virgo in the
eighth house, and the Capricorn Ascendant, her Ray One Soul
of power and will. The practicality of her Virgo Sun and Capricorn Ascendant, and the strong will of her Ray One Soul,
can enable her to develop the love and wisdom needed to solve
her problems with the help of her Virgo analytical ability to
tune into her weaknesses and her Capricorn self-discipline to
overcome them. Because her eighth house has three times more
planetary energies than any other house, temptations and testing will be frequent but there is a potential for much spiritual
regeneration.

Step 10. From her natal horoscope (1), complete that part
of the delineation begun in Steps 8 and 9 referring to Horoscopes 2 and 3. Include in this delineation the Moon's Nodes
and all aspects not found in Horoscopes 2 and 3. Use the esoteric
meanings of the houses, their cuspal signs, the esoteric rulers
of the cuspal signs, and the meaning of the Ray each planet
rules.

She has a Finger-of-God aspect in which Pluto quincunxes
her Capricorn Ascendant and Scorpio Midheaven which sextile
each other. A Finger-of-God is a fated aspect—her Soul before
birth planned a spiritual mission consonant with this aspect.
Until it is begun, there will be much frustration in her life.
The focal point is Pluto, a ruler of Ray One of will and power
in Gemini in the fifth house, indicating intense power channelled toward the awareness of what constitutes self-centered
personality desires as opposed to spiritual aspirations. Both
Pluto and her Capricorn Ascendant, which form a quincunx,
give her Ray One energy of will and power. This aspect produces frustration of immense power until she decides to use
this energy to overcome her weaknesses through self-discipline
and persistence and to serve others through her communicative
ability. Pluto's quincunx to the Scorpio Midheaven produces
added frustration until she applies Pluto's power to a career

of serving others through her intense psychic capacity and communicative ability.

Because of a very close square between Pluto and the Sun, a ruler of Ray Two of love and wisdom in Virgo in the eighth house, she tends to force her opinions on others in a critical way. Until this weakness is overcome, it is impossible for her to carry out her spiritual mission. This square and her South Node in Capricorn in the twelfth house show that she had developed power and control in past lives but has not yet learned to use them beneficially. Until she does, this self-centered power will come back strongly and quickly to teach her needed karmic lessons.

Although most charts approximate a square between Midheaven and Ascendant, hers has a close sextile showing that her Soul and career can easily be in rapport. The successful completion of her mission results from the combination of the resourcefulness and the intense psychic capacity of Scorpio with the discipline, hard work, calmness, and practicality of Capricorn. It is no coincidence that her Ascendant is not only one point of this aspect, but more importantly, it is the indicator of her Ray One Soul; and that her Midheaven is not only another point of this aspect, but more importantly is the sign in which only one Ray enters, namely Ray Four of harmony through conflict, her Personality Ray, and thirdly, the focal point is Pluto, a ruler of Ray One, her Soul Ray. Her Ray One Soul of will and power and its purpose is the crux of this Finger-of-God aspect which can be expressed through her Ray Four Personality of harmony through conflict. It is unusual that a Finger-of-God aspect is tied so closely to one's Soul Ray and Personality Ray as in this case, giving her strong urges and immense power and energy to accomplish her life purposes. The release point of the Finger-of-God aspect is in Sagittarius in the eleventh house, meaning that her spiritual mission will be carried out with universal truths in the service of humanity using Aquarian Age philosophies. It is not only interesting but fortunate for her that the release point closely conjuncts the Midheaven of her marriage partner whose career is associated with her Soul's purpose.

A sesquiquadrate of the Midheaven to Saturn, a ruler of intellectual activity in Aries in the second house, has unusual significance—Saturn is the esoteric ruler of her Capricorn Ascendant signifying the Soul, and this aspect indicates a tendency to a strong ego, making it difficult not only for Soul evolvement but also career fulfillment until she changes her attitudes and values.

A trine from Midheaven to Neptune, a ruler of Ray Six of idealism and devotion in Cancer in the sixth house, gives idealism and inspiration to learn quickly from the temptations and testing her Scorpio Midheaven threatens. The esoteric ruler of the tenth house cusp, Scorpio, is Mars, also a ruler of Ray Six. Mars is in Virgo in the eighth house, reinforcing the testing and temptations she will experience emotionally, tied in with criticism of others' weaknesses. Even though this aspectual energy is not easy to live with, it gives her the impetus toward a high degree of spiritual evolvement.

The Gemini cusp of the fifth house, indicating an awareness of her self-centered personality desires and her spiritual aspirations, is necessary for self-realization. The esoteric ruler of Gemini is Venus, the ruler of Ray Five of the logical mind. This implies that reasoning and logic are necessary to both her spiritual mission and self-realization. Her self-realization is dependent on her accumulation of knowledge and the expression of that knowledge. An obstacle presents itself because Venus in Leo in the seventh house is intercepted. It has been my experience that the energies of intercepted planets are not manifested until one begins to work toward Soul evolvement. Therefore, she should be working toward Soul evolvement in order to free her logical reasoning mind from its intercepted condition.

The strongest house is her eighth, being tenanted by four planets—the Sun whose aspects have already been interpreted, Mars, Mercury, and Vulcan. Much energy is used for testing by temptation. Successfully meeting her varied temptations is conducive to rapid Soul growth. Her Sun in this house reveals the close linking of her personality with testing and Soul evolvement through love and wisdom. Here Mars shows deep emotional involvement with eighth house matters.

Mars, a ruler of Ray Six of idealism, devotion, and emotionalism in Virgo, is semi-square the Moon, a ruler of Ray Four of harmony though conflict in Cancer in the sixth house, revealing a tendency toward easily hurt feelings followed by unkind criticism resulting in conflicts. When she becomes aware that others wrong her so that she may learn needed lessons, she will no longer hurt, and no longer criticize them.

Mars sextile Neptune, a ruler of Ray Six of idealism and devotion in Cancer in the sixth house, indicates not only an urge for idealistic behavior leading to perfection, but also courage and a deep psychic capacity to aid in this undertaking.

Mars trine Uranus, a ruler of Ray Seven of strong thoughts and order in Capricorn in the twelfth house, shows a potential for analytical research in occult work and the ability and persistence to substitute desirable for undesirable thoughts.

Vulcan, a ruler of Ray One of will and power in Libra, gives her the power to easily crystallize her unconscious guilt feelings and buried wrong thoughts, bring them to the surface to eradicate them with the help of the strong thoughts produced by the trine of Mars and Uranus.

Her Mercury, a ruler of Ray Four of harmony through conflict in Libra, shows that she can clearly weigh the benefits of manifesting on a Soul level versus manifesting on a self-centered personality level. In addition to an aspect to Uranus previously interpreted, Mercury has two other aspects. One, a semi-square to Jupiter, a ruler of Ray Two in Virgo in the seventh house, indicates a tendency to talk more than is necessary for effectiveness which is often done critically. Two, Mercury's bi-septile to North Node in Cancer in the sixth house is its last aspect. While most aspects show only tendencies to use the combined energies in a wise or unwise manner, I have found the septile and also the quincunx to be more than a mere tendency. In my astrological counselling experience, I have found that the energies of these two aspects seem to be fated to result in a wise use. Fate in this case does not negate free will in toto. What it does is block conscious free will in this life solely in these aspects because of a strong-willed desire either in a past life or in the spirit plane before birth. This desire expresses its strength on an unconscious level which is interpreted as fate. The bi-septile of Mercury to North Node in Cancer in the sixth house indicates that she will attain a certain degree of harmony through a concerned nurturing of those who need help. In contrast, South Node in Capricorn in the twelfth house indicates an undue concern for herself and a coldness toward others, which weakness she will transmute into concern and help for others as noted above.

Virgo is on the eighth house cusp, implying a deep urge to perfect herself. The esoteric ruler, the Moon, a ruler of Ray Four of harmony through conflict in Cancer in the sixth house, is conjunct North Node showing that spiritual regeneration (eighth house) is closely tied with serving others (Virgo and sixth house) who need nurturing (Cancer).

The second strongest house is the sixth with two planets and North Node in the cuspal sign, Cancer. The esoteric ruler of Cancer, Neptune, a ruler of Ray Six of idealism and devotion, is one of these planets. This indicates that much psychic capacity is at her command for serving others caringly and idealistically.

In addition to Neptune's square to Mercury and sextile to Mars already interpreted, there are three other aspects. An opposition to Uranus, the ruler of Ray Seven of strong thoughts in Capricorn in the twelfth house, indicates a tendency toward strong thoughts coming into her consciousness unexpectedly from her unconscious mind causing some confusion. The semi-square from Neptune to Jupiter, a ruler of Ray Two of love and wisdom in Virgo in the seventh house, indicates a tendency to an imagination that often plays tricks on her. However, a trine from Neptune to the Scorpio Midheaven indicates that once her psychic capacity is channelled toward a career of helping others in a concerned, nurturing manner, her strong thoughts and highly imaginative nature, instead of causing problems, will be a source of help to those she serves.

The Moon/North Node conjunction is square Saturn, a ruler of Ray Three of the abstract mind in Aries in the second house. Any aspect square to the Nodes makes it potently karmic. With her Moon conjuncting the North Node, the karmic potency is increased, yet the orb is not small. This means that she will attract to herself someone who is both critical of her weaknesses and egotistical to aid in her karmic lesson learning.

The North Node/Moon conjunction is sextile Jupiter, a ruler of Ray Two of love and wisdom in Virgo in the seventh house, giving her the ability to analytically and wisely distinguish between benefits derived from self-centered desires and spiritual aspirations for herself and for those she serves. The Cancer seventh house cusp indicates a capacity for nurturing, when necessary, in close relationships. It also reveals a sensitivity in distinguishing between the benefits of manifesting on a self-centered personality level or on a Soul level. The esoteric ruler of Cancer, Neptune, a ruler of Ray Six in Cancer in the sixth house, enables her to better serve others and perfect herself because of her psychic and inspirational capacity.

Leo intercepted in the seventh house gives her the potential for self-realization and Soul evolvement through a close relationship. The esoteric ruler of Leo, the Sun, a ruler of Ray Two of love and wisdom in Virgo in the eighth house, gives her the ability to analyze thoroughly the benefits of self-centered personality manifestation versus Soul manifestation. Because Venus, the ruler of Ray Five of the concrete mind in Leo in the seventh house, is intercepted, its energy for logical reasoning so necessary for self-realization is not released in her outer life until she begins to get in touch with her Soul.

A second planet, Jupiter, a ruler of Ray Two of love and wisdom in Virgo, tenants the seventh house. The Virgoan Jupiter urges her to perfect herself and serve others, aided by an analysis of the benefits of Soul manifestation as compared with self-centered personality manifestation. Because Jupiter is not found in Horoscopes 2 or 3, its aspects were not interpreted in Steps 8 and 9. Jupiter semi-square Mercury, a ruler of Ray Four of harmony through conflict in Libra in the eighth house, indicates a tendency toward indecision and superfluous speech, especially in close relationships.

A semi-square from Jupiter to Neptune, a ruler of Ray Six of idealism, devotion, and emotionalism in Cancer in the sixth house, indicates some confusion in trying to perfect herself because of a tendency for her feelings to be hurt easily and to criticize others' faults.

The following three easy aspects to Jupiter give her the needed energy to overcome these weaknesses. The first, Jupiter bi-septile Saturn, a ruler of Ray Three of the higher mind in Aries in the second house, gives her intuition, enthusiasm, and wisdom to perfect herself by changing certain attitudes and values. Second, a sextile to the Moon, a ruler of Ray Four of harmony through conflict in Cancer in the sixth house, gives her energy to attain harmony through sensitively serving others. Third, a sextile to the North Node in Cancer in the sixth house gives added energy to the preceding aspect.

The Capricorn twelfth house cusp indicates the advisability of becoming aware of certain past lives in order to understand present conditions and to make progress in Soul evolvement. The Capricorn South Node so closely conjunct the cusp indicates a coldness and lack of concern for others which should be transmuted into its Cancer polarity of sensitive concern and nurturing capacity. Her unconscious gives her subtle lesson-teaching experiences of which she may be only dimly aware until she reverses the energies of her Capricorn South Node of undue concern for self to becoming interested in the lives of others. She will understand that unless she allows others to hurt her, they cannot do so. She will not allow them to hurt her after she understands that when others wrong her, she has lessons to learn in that area of her life. The esoteric ruler of Capricorn is Saturn, a ruler of Ray Three of intellectual activity in Aries in the second house, indicating the desirability of changing certain attitudes and values in order that Soul evolvement takes place. Uranus, the ruler of Ray Seven of strong thoughts is in Capricorn in the twelfth house, signifying strong thoughts coupled with inspirational ideas, both of which can be used with discipline and persistence to change unwise attitudes and values to better usage.

The Pisces second house cusp gives her the psychic capacity to become aware of attitudes and values that are better than her own. Pluto, the esoteric ruler of Pisces and a ruler of Ray One of will and power, is in Gemini in the fifth house. This suggests a strong will to attain self-realization which can be accomplished through an awareness of and a communication to others of the difference between self-centered desires and spiritual aspirations. One of the planets tenanting the second house, the Earth, a ruler of Ray Three of the higher mind in Pisces, is square Pluto. This aspect indicates a need for difficult karmic experiences in order to learn compassion, kindness, and right attitudes before the energy of Pluto can be used for self-realization and as the focal point of her Finger-of-God aspect. The Earth and the Capricorn Ascendant indicate that Soul progress can be made using discipline and persistence in overcoming certain weaknesses of which she has or will become aware through difficult karmic experiences. The other planet in the second house is Saturn in Aries. Both planets tenanting the second house are rulers of Ray Three, enhancing the effectiveness of the contemplative, abstract mind in changing attitudes and values that need changing.

Of Saturn's many aspects, the only one not yet interpreted is the bi-quintile to Jupiter, a ruler of Ray Two of love and wisdom in Virgo in the seventh house. This shows the possibility of acquiring love and wisdom by enthusiastically trying to perfect herself by analyzing those facets of her being that are manifesting on a self-centered level and those manifesting on a Soul level, and wisely weighing the benefits of both.

The remaining four houses have no planets. Though the Aries third house cusp signifies a mind with original ideas, the esoteric ruler, Mercury, a ruler of Ray Four of harmony through conflict in Libra in the eighth house, indicates that her mind also has the capacity to compare on a deep level all the various facets of her new ideas to those that are already established. When she communicates ideas that are not for the good of others, instant karma results in conflicts through which learning and harmony ultimately ensue.

The Taurus fourth house cusp indicates that as she becomes aware of the depth of her Soul and changes certain attitudes and values, spiritual illumination will be given her. The esoteric ruler of Taurus, Vulcan, a ruler of Ray One of will and power in Libra in the eighth house, gives her the will and the power to delve deeply into her unconscious to crystallize that which is not for her good and bring it to her conscious mind to eradicate.

The Libra ninth house cusp gives the ability to compare the advantages of certain religions, philosophies, and concepts. The esoteric ruler of Libra, Uranus, the ruler of Ray Seven of strong thoughts in Capricorn in the twelfth house, is a powerful aid in carrying out this ability because of its thought-enhancing capacity.

The Sagittarius eleventh house cusp indicates strong goals directed toward serving humanity in the light of Aquarian Age philosophies. The esoteric ruler of Sagittarius, the Earth, a ruler of Ray Three of intellectual activity, is in Pisces in the second house. Many karmic experiences lie between her and her goals. They will teach her the compassion for and kindness toward suffering humanity as her attitudes and values change and she accepts the reality of the Oneness of All.

Step-11. Find the planet nearest the zenith in the natal horoscope and the Ray it rules. Because this is the last planet her consciousness was on before this life, explain the abilities derived there to be presently applied. Mercury, a ruler of Ray Four of harmony through conflict, was her last planet of occupancy before this life. She learned there that to attain harmony, one must experience conflict in the areas of character weaknesses until those weaknesses are overcome through learning the lessons those difficult karmic experiences are meant to teach. That Mercury is a ruler of Ray Four which is her Personality Ray suggests that the abilities learned on Mercury are the same as those to be used by her personality in expressing her Soul's purpose. In addition to understanding the Laws of Reincarnation and Karma, her Mercury abilities include such skills as speaking, writing, and analyzing. Note in Horoscope 3 that Mercury is the only planet which is both a Soul life planet and a planet of self-centered personality desires. This creates a conflict as to whether she should use her excellent Mercurian capacities for her Soul's purpose or for self-centered desires. When used for self-centered desires, she will experience lesson-teaching karma and will easily learn that to attain the harmony she so strongly desires, she must use this energy for her Soul's purpose instead.

Step 12. Find the planet or planets in the natal horoscope that are most influential in an all-encompassing way. Use Chart 28 showing all signs each planet rules. A planet is influential by virtue of having three planets or important points in the sign or signs it rules. Interpret the functions of these planets, the functions of the Rays they rule, and the specific influence of each that relate to the Soul's life, the personality serving the Soul, the self-centered personality desires, or none of these specific influences.

While five planets are especially influential, none is influential in all three areas of her life. Only one, Mercury, is inflüential in any two areas. Even though there are seven planets in the signs the Moon rules, and six in the signs Mercury rules, Mercury is considered the most influential planet in her natal horoscope for the following reasons: (1) It is the only planet influential in two areas of her life (found in Horoscopes 2 and 3), and (2) it is the nearest planet to the zenith in her natal horoscope. Mercury, a ruler of Ray Four of harmony through conflict, is the only one of the five most influential planets which is a Soul planet (shown in Horoscopes 2 and 3). Her intellect and her communicative abilities are paramount to Soul evolvement which takes place by attaining harmony through lessons learned from difficult karmic experiences. Because Mercury is influential not only in her Soul life but also in her self-centered personality desires, this creates a conflict as to which of these areas will receive her Mercury energy. This fact, coupled with Mercury's true essence, being a ruler of Ray Four conveying harmony through conflict, indicates many lesson-teaching experiences. Looking at this from the Soul angle, this is not undesirable. It shows a potential for much Soul evolvement.

The Moon, the second most influential planet, is also a ruler of Ray Four. This, added to the fact of her Ray Four Personality, reinforces the experiencing of difficult karma which her Mercury suggests, and strengthens them in number and intensity. Because the Moon which deals with her emotions and her imaginative capacity is influential (Horoscope 2) in only one area of her life—the personality serving the Soul—her feelings resulting from karmic learning experiences are paramount in attaining harmony and in serving her Soul.

Neptune, a ruler of Ray Six of idealism and devotion, is the third most influential planet. Like the Moon, it is influential in the personality serving the Soul. Both Neptune and the Moon are important in this area of her life and suggest great psychic capacity, especially because both are in Cancer. Neptune gives her the idealism and the inspiration to use her personality for her Soul's purpose.

The fourth most influential planet is Venus. Because it is a ruler of Ray Five of the concrete mind, because it is intercepted, because it is in Leo, because it is the only planet that is influential solely in the area of self-centered desires, and because the essence of the planet itself is the desire nature and the affections, the energies of this planet create more problems for her than any other single planet. She has strong desires to use rationalization and other facets of her concrete mind in order to be the center of attention. Until she begins to work on her Soul evolvement, most of the higher energies of Venus, love and a logical reasoning mind, remain dormant. Pink, a color whose vibration helps one feel more love and concern for others, is highly recommended in her clothes and surroundings. When, through the help of this interpretation and through meditation, she is able to raise the lower vibration of Venus energies to a higher level, her newly discovered love will be the instigating factor for self-realization.

The fifth most influential planet is Jupiter. Both Venus and Jupiter have three planets and important points in the signs they rule, but because Jupiter is not influential in any of the three important areas of life, of the five planets it is rated last in influence. It is a ruler of Ray Two of love and wisdom, which qualities, though not influential in the three important areas of her life at the time of birth, can be made to be influential in all areas if she works diligently on her Soul evolvement. Because only one of the five most influential planets is a ruler of an odd-numbered Ray, she is influenced greatly by her sensitivity and strong psychic capacity.

Step 13. Every seventh year in one's life there is a significant change, a possible crisis, and a good chance for opportunities. Find her age when the last opportunity year occurred and when the next one will occur. She can then look back to assess how she handled it and contemplate how she might have handled it better so that she can take full advantage of the next year of opportunity. Her age during the last year of opportunity was seventy in 1978, and the next will be seventy-seven in 1985.

Step 14. Determine the general tendencies of each fourteen-year period to age eighty-four. Using a day for a year, find the exact major aspects (conjunction, opposition, square, trine, and sextile) of all progressed planets, except the progressed Moon, to natal planets for each period. From this information, compare the number of total aspects in the various periods, the number of easy versus challenging aspects, the Ray each planet making an aspect rules, and the number of times each Ray is activated. From this comparison, indicate the general trend of thoughts and activities in the various periods of her life. Exact aspects provide extra energies of the Rays, planets, and signs involved. Because this step is not detailed, but is a general overview, and because Ray-Centered Astrology and the progressions are concerned mostly with the inner Soul life, the progressions and the Rays ruled by the aspecting planets are stressed.

Ray Five of the concrete mind is the most prominent energy she receives from aspects through the six periods as a whole, indicating that logic, science, and the accumulation of knowledge are very important to her. This explains why she was a scientist for a greater part of her life and why she is often referred to as a "walking encyclopedia." Ray Four of harmony through conflict is of secondary influence among the energies she receives from partile aspects. Her Personality Ray is also Four which energy when added to that of the Ray Four from partile aspects makes it the most important single Ray. This reveals that this life is not an easy one because of many karmic lessons to be learned, but an appreciable degree of spiritual evolvement can be attained as she becomes familiar with and understands the Universal Laws of Reincarnation and Karma, becomes aware of her weaknesses, and uses visualization and discipline to transmute them into strengths. To actualize this potential, the abundant Ray Five energy urges her to acquire the necessary knowledge and to use logic to make this knowledge productive, her Ray One Soul gives her the will power to apply it, and her Capricorn Ascendant gives her the persistence to continually apply it in diciplining herself. Since her easy aspects are far more numerous than her challenging ones, she receives much help throughout her life in learning her karmic lessons.

The period from birth to age fourteen finds Ray Four of harmony through conflict to be the strongest, a time of many karmic responsibilities and lesson-teaching experiences. Of all six periods, this is by far the most sensitive, emotional, and insecure because the even-numbered Rays denoting the feminine characteristics were much stronger than the odd-num-

AGE—0 to 14 years for Case 3

Progressed Planets' Positions	Partile Aspects	Easy	Challenging	Rays Planets Rule
☉ 24 ♍ 39--8 ♎ 23	P ☉ □ ☽		×	2, 4
☊ 1 ♋ 19--29 ♊ 31	P ☉ □ ☊		×	2
☿ 15 ♎ 39--3 ♏ 39	P ☉ ☍ ♄		×	2, 3
♀ 8 ♌ 40--23 ♌ 12	P ☉ □ ♇		×	2, 1
♂ 15 ♍ 44--24 ♍ 42	P ☊ ☌ ☽	×		4
♃ 1 ♍ 10--4 ♍ 1	P ☊ ✳ ♃	×		2
♄ 7 ♈ 41 R--6 ♈ 36 R	P ☿ □ ♆		×	4, 6
♅ 12 ♑ 57 R--12 ♑ 58	P ☿ △ ☽	×		4, 4
♆ 16 ♋ 49--17 ♋ 1	P ☿ △ ☊	×		4
♇ 25 ♊ 50--25 ♊ 51 R	P ♀ ✳ ☿	×		5, 4
	P ♂ ✳ ♆	×		6, 6

7 Rays	# Found		7 Rays	Frequency
1	-- 1		4	-- 7
2	-- 5		2	-- 5
3	-- 1		6	-- 3
4	-- 7		1 & 3 & 5	-- 1
5	-- 1		7	-- 0
6	-- 3			
7	-- 0			

AGE—14 to 28 years for Case 3

Progressed Planets' Positions	Partile Aspects	Easy	Challenging	Rays Planets Rule
☉ 8♎23--22♎13	P☉ ✶ ♀	x		2, 5
☊ 29♊31--28♊20	P☉ □ ♅		x	2, 7
☿ 3♍39--13♍37	P☉ ☌ ☿	x		2, 4
♀ 23♌12--8♍38	P☉ □ ♆		x	2, 6
♂ 24♍42--3♎42	P☿ □ ♀		x	4, 5
♃ 4♍1--6♍41	P☿ ✶ ♅	x		4, 7
♄ 6♈36R--5♈32R	P♀ ✶ ♇	x		5, 1
♅ 12♑58--13♑10	P♀ △ ♄	x		5, 3
♆ 17♋1--17♋7	P♀ ✶ ☿	x		5, 4
♇ 25♊51R--25♊47R	P♀ ✶ ☽	x		5, 4
	P♀ ✶ ☊	x		5
	P♂ ☌ ☉	x		6, 2
	P♂ ✶ ♆	x		6, 6
	P♂ □ ☽		x	6, 4
	P♂ □ ☊		x	6
	P♂ □ ♇		x	6, 1

7 Rays # Found		7 Rays Frequency
1 — 2		5 & 6 — 7
2 — 5		4 — 6
3 — 1		2 — 5
4 — 6		1 & 7 — 2
5 — 7		3 — 1
6 — 7		
7 — 2		

AGE—28 to 42 years for Case 3

Progressed Planets' Positions	Partile Aspects	Easy	Challenging	Rays Planets Rule
⊙ 22♎13--6♏10	P ⊙ △ ☽	×		2, 4
☊ 28♊20--27♊2	P ⊙ △ ☊	×		2
☿ 13♏42--3♏11R	P ⊙ ✶ ♃	×		2, 2
♀ 8♏38--24♏45	P ⊙ △ ♇	×		2, 1
♂ 3♎42--12♎43	P ☿ □ ♀		×	4, 5
♃ 6♏41--9♏5	P ☿ ✶ ♅	×		4, 7
♄ 5♈32R --4♈35R	P ♀ ☌ ⊙	×		5, 2
♅ 13♑10--13♑32	P ♀ ☌ ♂	×		5, 6
♆ 17♋7--17♋6R	P ♀ △ ♅	×		5, 7
♇ 25♊47R --25♊59R	P ♀ ✶ ♆	×		5, 6
	P ♂ ✶ ♀	×		6, 5
	P ♂ ☌ ♄		×	6, 3

7 Rays ☿ Found		7 Rays Frequency	
1 — 1		2 & 5 — 6	
2 — 6		6 — 4	
3 — 1		4 — 3	
4 — 3		7 — 2	
5 — 6		1 & 3 — 1	
6 — 4			
7 — 2			

AGE—42 to 56 years for Case 3

Progressed Planets' Positions	Partile Aspects	Easy	Challenging	Rays Planets Rule
☉ 6 ♍10--20 ♍13	P ☉ □ ♀		x	2, 5
☊ 27 ♊ 2--26 ♊ 25	P ☉ ✱ ♂	x		2, 6
☿ 27 ♎ 52--3 ♍11	P ☉ ✱ ♅	x		2, 7
♀ 24 ♍ 45--11 ♎ 19	P ☉ △ ♆	x		2, 6
♂ 12 ♎ 43--21 ♎ 48	P ☿ △ ☽	x		4, 4
♃ 9 ♍ 5--11 ♍ 8	P ♃ △ ☊	x		4
♄ 4 ♈ 35℞ --3 ♈ 52℞	P ♃ ✱ ♃	x		4, 2
♅ 13 ♑ 32--14 ♑ 2	P ♀ □ ☽		x	5, 4
♆ 17 ♋ 6℞ --16 ♋ 58℞	P ♀ □ ☊		x	5
♇ 25 ♊ 39℞ --25 ♊ 27℞	P ♀ ✱ ♀	x		5, 5
	P ♀ ⚻ ♄		x	5, 3
	P ♀ □ ♇		x	5, 1
	P ♂ □ ♅		x	6, 7
	P ♂ □ ♆		x	6, 6

7 Rays / Found	7 Rays Frequency
1 — 1	5 — 7
2 — 5	2 4 4 4 6 — 5
3 — 1	7 — 2
4 — 5	1 & 3 — 1
5 — 7	
6 — 5	
7 — 2	

AGE—56 to 70 years for Case 3

Progressed Planets' Positions	Partile Aspects	Easy	Challenging	Rays Planets Rule
☉ 20 ♍ 13--4 ♐ 22	P ☉ ⚹ ☉	x		2, 2
☊ 26 ♊ 25--26 ♊ 0	P ☉ ⚹ ♃	x		2, 2
☿ 1 ♍ 5--19 ♍ 39	P ☿ △ ☊	x		4
♀ 11 ♎ 19--28 ♎ 14	P ☿ □ ♀		x	4, 5
♂ 21 ♎ 48--0 ♍ 55	P ☿ ⚹ ♂	x		4, 6
♃ 11 ♍ 8--12 ♍ 47	P ☿ ⚹ ♃	x		4, 2
♄ 3 ♈ 52℞--3 ♈ 28℞	P ☿ ⚹ ♅	x		4, 7
♅ 14 ♑ 2--14 ♑ 39	P ☿ △ ♆	x		4, 6
♆ 16 ♋ 58℞--16 ♋ 45℞	P ♀ ☌ ☿	x		5, 4
♇ 25 ♊ 27℞--25 ♊ 13℞	P ♀ □ ♅		x	5, 7
	P ♀ □ ♆		x	5, 6
	P ♀ △ ♇	x		5, 1
	P ♆ ☌ ♆	x		6, 6
	P ♂ △ ☽	x		6, 4
	P ♂ △ ♇	x		6, 1

7 Rays	# Found		7 Rays	Frequency
1	2		4	8
2	5		6	7
3	0		2 & 5	5
4	8		1 & 7	2
5	5		3	0
6	7			
7	2			

AGE—70 to 84 years for Case 3

Progressed Planets' Positions	Partile Aspects	Easy	Challenging	Rays Planets Rule
☉ 4 ♐ 22--28 ♐ 34	P ☉ ⚹ ☿	×		2, 4
☊ 26 ♊ 0--25 ♊ 55	P ☉ △ ♀	×		2, 5
☿ 19 ♍ 39--11 ♐ 16	P ☉ □ ♂		×	2, 6
♀ 28 ♎ 14--15 ♏ 23	P ☉ △ ♄	×		2, 3
♂ 0 ♏ 55--10 ♏ 5	P ☿ ⚹ ☉	×		4, 2
♃ 12 ♏ 47--13 ♏ 55	P ☿ △ ♀	×		4, 5
♄ 3 ♈ 28℞ --3 ♈ 22	P ☿ □ ♃		×	4, 2
♅ 14 ♑ 39--15 ♑ 23	P ☿ △ ♄	×		4, 3
♆ 16 ♋ 45℞ --16 ♋ 26℞	P ♀ △ ☽	×		5, 4
♇ 25 ♊ 13℞ --24 ♊ 57℞	P ♀ △ ☊	×		5
	P ♀ □ ♀		×	5, 5
	P ♀ ⚹ ♃	×		5, 2
	P ♀ ⚹ ♅	×		5, 7
	P ♂ △ ☊	×		6
	P ♂ □ ♀		×	6, 5
	P ♂ ⚹ ♃	×		6, 2
	P ♃ △ ♅	×		2, 7

7 Rays	# Found		7 Rays	Frequency
1	— 0		2 & 5	— 9
2	— 9		4	— 6
3	— 2		6	— 4
4	— 6		3 & 7	— 2
5	— 9		1	— 0
6	— 4			
7	— 2			

SUMMARY OF RAY ACTIVATION
FOR CASE 3
Derived from 6 Age Period Charts

Age Period	Total	Easy	Challenging	10	9	8	7	6	5	4	3	2	1	0
		Aspects					Frequency per Ray per Period							
0 to 14	11	6	5				4		2		6	1 3 5	7	
14 to 28	16	10	6					5 6	4	2		1 7	3	
28 to 42	12	10	2					2 5		6	4	7	1 3	
42 to 56	14	7	7					5	2 4 6			7	1 3	
56 to 70	15	12	3			4	6		2 5			1 7		3
70 to 84	17	13	4	2 5					4		6	3 7		1

bered Rays denoting masculine characteristics. This period is very interesting and unusual in that the feminine Rays, Four, Two, and Six were found respectively seven times, five times, and three times, while of the remaining Rays which are masculine, Rays One, Three, and Five were found only once and Ray Seven was missing entirely. The missing Ray Seven reveals a lack of rhythmic living. In this period the smallest number of aspects are found, which means that it was the least energetic, yet the second most challenging period of the six.

Age fourteen to twenty-eight differs from the first period in two significant respects. There is a decided increase of aspects affording her a much higher energy level. The strength of influence of Ray Five of concrete knowledge increased surprisingly from its level in the first period. This results in a strong interest in the acquisition of knowledge and in science. Period Two as well as the two succeeding ones have no missing Rays, revealing sufficient inflow of diversified energies.

The third period from age twenty-eight to forty-two is the easiest of all periods because it has the highest ratio of easy to challenging aspects, and the karmic Ray Four energy is greatly diminished. This is also a period of decreased activity from the previous period because the number of aspects is appreciably lower. Though Ray Five energy has decreased somewhat from the previous period, it is still the strongest Ray, equal to Ray Two of love and wisdom, which explains why she continued in her scientific profession and why she married during this period.

The fourth period from age forty-two to fifty-six is the most challenging of all six periods. This period has the same number of easy as challenging aspects while in each of the other periods there are more easy than challenging aspects. This time is especially difficult, not only because of the many karmic responsibilities and lesson-teaching experiences, but because it follows the easiest of all periods. Ray Five is still the strongest Ray, indicating a continued interest in the accumulation of knowledge and in science.

The fifth period from age fifty-six to seventy shows, like the first period, Ray Four to be the strongest. This indicates many karmic lessons to be learned. This period is again similar to the first period in that these are the only two periods in which Ray Five is not the strongest. A decrease in Ray Five energy of the concrete mind, the omission of Ray Three of the abstract mind, and the increased strength of Ray Four of harmony through conflict suggest a tendency to allow her emotions, rather than her mind, to guide her, resulting in many conflicts. Unlike the first period where the ratio of easy to challenging aspects was six to five, in this period it is twelve to three, revealing not only a greater energy level but also much help in learning her lessons easily.

The sixth period from age seventy to eighty-four has the highest energy level of all periods because it has the most aspects. The ratio of easy to challenging aspects is almost as high as that of the previous period, but Ray Four is relegated to a reduced strength, so this is not a too difficult period as far as karmic lessons are concerned, but is one in which much time and energy is available for serving others. Ray Five for the fourth time is the strongest Ray, yet equal to Ray Two—which indicates a possibility of a lifetime accumulation of knowledge being used with love and wisdom. It also indicates a potential for logical understanding of certain Universal Laws and the application of this understanding in a loving and wise way in serving others. This is especially true in this period because it is the only one in which Ray One of will and power is missing. She has a Ray One Soul, the most difficult Ray to have until one is highly evolved because until that time there would be a tendency to force one's will on others. The absence of Ray One from aspects in this period for mitigating the authoritative nature, shows that she is more able to serve others with love.

Step 15. Because each person is influenced greatly by the four signs of the cross the Sun was in at his birth, elucidate the specific opportunities during the four periods. Include for each sign the meaning and esoteric planetary ruler, the Ray that planet rules, and the house or houses that sign tenants. (1) During the last week of August and the first three weeks of September, the Sun is in Virgo in her seventh and eighth houses. The esoteric ruler of Virgo is the Moon, a ruler of Ray Four of harmony through conflict. The first half of this period is a good time for Soul growth by learning lessons from difficult karmic experiences that result from close relationships, and is an auspicious time for helping those close to her. The last half of the period is a time of temptation and testing in which there are strong tendencies to criticize the weaknesses of others. If she is able to transmute the energy for these tendencies by helping others, Soul progress on a deep level can be attained and harmony can be achieved. (2) During the last week of November and the first three weeks of December, the Sun is in Sagittarius in Houses ten and eleven. The esoteric ruler of Sagittarius is the Earth in Pisces, a ruler of Ray Three of intellectual activity. The first twelve days of that period are advantageous for extra thought and time spent on her career because there is enthusiasm in that area in which her motivation is to help the suffering through compassion and contemplation. The rest of that period is a time in which empathetic experiences and her contemplative capacity can be combined optimally in serving humanity through unattached love and the actualization of other Aquarian Age concepts. (3) During the last week of February and the first three weeks of March, the Sun is in Pisces in houses one and two. The esoteric ruler of Pisces is Pluto, a ruler of Ray One of will and power. During the first two weeks of this period there is much power for Soul expression and self-realization through communication if these are done in a kind and compassionate way. The last half of this period is an excellent time for meditation. There is power then to get in touch with her Soul and her spiritual teachers, which may result in illumination and spiritual growth. (4) During the last week in May and the first three weeks in June, the Sun is in Gemini in houses four and five. The esoteric ruler of Gemini is Venus, the ruler of Ray Five of the concrete mind. During the first twelve days of this period, she could do well by using her logical reasoning mind to become aware of her self-centered desires, her spiritual aspirations, and the results of each. Stored knowledge will surface easily at this time. During the rest of this period, her stored knowledge, coupled with her logical mind, is a potent combination that can lead to self-realization.

Step 16. When she has formulated a plan for her life work, she should reassess it periodically in terms of her motivation because lasting success is not possible without proper motivation. If her plan is not to serve others to the best of her ability because of her love and concern for them, she had best spend time becoming aware of her weaknesses as elucidated in this delineation, endeavoring to transmute them into strengths, especially those strengths of her Ray One Soul and Ray Four Personality, as found in Chapter Three. If her motivation is right and strong, she can expect success and joy in her work as she follows these steps in carrying out her life plan:

1. A strong intention to carry it through by focusing her ideas.
2. Visualization by imagination and impressing on her mind what she wants to do.

3. Projection, which is the willing of her plan by thought, because energy follows thought. This projection must be carried out in a way that is consistent with her Soul and Personality Rays. From Chart 29 we find that her Ray One Soul predicates the assertion of the intent of her life plan because of knowledge, conviction, and love. Her Ray Four Personality indicates that she should concentrate on merging her personality and Soul in order to achieve her life plan.

The natal horoscopes of three persons were chosen for complete delineations in order to illustrate the complexity of any horoscope. The techniques involved in the Ray-Centered delineation rise far beyond the "key-word" usages that too often cloud the traditional delineation. The three cases offer the opportunity to become familiar with the specific techniques upon which Ray-Centered Astrology is founded. These techniques are not "cook-book" inventions, but are the results of the synthesis of certain truths which have their origin in the Ancient Wisdom.

Chapter Ten

CONCLUSION

For century upon century, the Seven Rays have been flowing from their distant starry sources to the Sun of our solar system and pouring down upon the earth. Eventually they became recognized as having colors and the beauty of the colors touched all who looked upon the world with joy and wonder.

Only those few at any one time who were aware that something was touching them from above and urging them to seek their Soul and use their personality as an aid in the search—only these few were benefiting in a knowing way from the Rays. It is true that in the days of the Ancient Wisdom, the Astrology of the Rays was known by a few but like so many other wisdoms it became tangled in the threads of time and forgotten. Later, certain Masters of Knowledge rediscovered parts of it and dropped them like little jewels here and there throughout their writings. From these, after arduous study, the synthesis of a workable system was accomplished as Ray-Centered Astrology.

In his volume on Esoteric Astrology, the Tibetan Master Djwahl Khul stated, "In the discussion upon the zodiac and its relation to the Seven Rays, the signs and their effects, the new and deeply esoteric astrology will gradually supersede the present mundane astrology. By the end of this century it will have won its rightful place in human thoughts."* He further stated, "I have shifted the approach of the astrological student away from the world of tangible happenings, precipitated events, and personal characteristics (which are distinctive of exoteric modern astrology) into the world of conditioning energies, controlling incentives, impulses and causes and have laid down the basis of an inner esoteric astrology which must govern this ancient science in the future. In the latter part of this century what I have given to you will be demonstrated to be true."**

Changes were bound to come about in Astrology as in other fields of learning with the dawning of the Aquarian Age. All

*Bailey, Alice A., *Esoteric Astrology*, p. 579.
**Bailey, Alice A., *Esoteric Astrology*, pp. 496 498.

functions of the cosmos are cyclic. There are therefore certain auspicious times for change to take place in all areas of life. Such a time in the cycle of the precession of the equinoxes occurred, according to the Master Djwahl Khul, in 1945 with the opening of the Aquarian Age. The Master D. K. stated, "In June, 1945, at the time of the full moon (so significant a day in the spiritual experience of the Christ) He definitely and consciously took over His duties and responsibilities as the Teacher and Leader during the Aquarian solar cycle."*

In 1945 there were a number of unusual happenings heralding the New Aquarian Age, some of which were: (1) The Organization of the United Nations was established and began its ongoing work to bring about better relations between nations and peace in the world through universality, brotherly love, and service to humanity for which Aquarius stands. (2) The finding of the Dead Sea Scrolls and the continuing study resulting therefrom is pouring new light on the writings and beliefs of that period preceding and following the coming of the Christ. They were not found by a carefully organized group looking for them but accidentally by a shepherd boy, which is characteristic of the unplanned, sudden, and unexpected qualities of Uranian-ruled Aquarius. (3) The Master D. K. in his volume on the "Reappearance of the Christ" said, "The agony of the war and the distress of the entire human family led Christ, in the year 1945, to come to a great decision—a decision which found expression in two most important statements. He announced to the assembled spiritual Hierarchy and to all His servants and disciples on Earth that He had decided to emerge again into physical contact with humanity if they would bring about the initial stages of establishing right human relations; secondly, He gave to the world one of the oldest prayers ever known, but one which hitherto had not been permitted to be used except by the most exalted, spiritual Beings."**

"The Great Invocation," as He named it, follows:

From the point of Light within the Mind of God
Let Light stream forth into the minds of men
Let Light descend on Earth.

*Bailey, Alice A., *Reappearance of the Christ*, p. 82.
**Bailey, Alice A., *Reappearance of the Christ*, pp. 30, 31.

From the point of Love within the Heart of God
Let love stream forth into the hearts of men
May Christ return to Earth.

From the centre where the Will of God is known
Let purpose guide the little wills of men—
The purpose which the Masters know and serve.

From the centre which we call the race of men
Let the Plan of Love and Light work out
And may it seal the door where evil dwells.

Let Light and Love and Power restore the Plan on Earth.

We are now in the dawning of the Age of Aquarius which brings with it new energies to accelerate the evolvement of humanity. It is the nature of humanity to evolve as time goes on and Ages pass. People are beginning to feel the urge to create their own environment by thoughts, words, and actions, and are struggling for the freedom to do so.

People are benefiting less and less from the prediction of events by Traditional Astrology and are becoming more aware that it is character weaknesses and strengths that precipitate difficult or rewarding experiences—that difficult events will not happen when certain weaknesses shown in their horoscopes are overcome by learning to use the energies of a challenging aspect beneficially. Weaknesses can seldom be transmuted into strengths by one attempt of the individual. Repeated evidences of the existence of the weakness are usually found to be concurrent with the occurrence in the horoscope of a challenging aspect formed by transitting or progressed planets. If each time such a congruence of challenge by aspect and weakness by thought, speech, or behavior takes place, the individual makes, through the use of the will, beneficial use of the challenging aspect, the anticipated difficult experience will not happen. As a result of the repetition of this use of the challenging aspect, the weakness will in time be transmuted into a strength or strengths.

Every Age brings into the consciousness of humanity the types of energies necessary for the evolvement of its people at that particular period. In this Age, the Aquarian energies flooding our beings urge us to understand ourselves, to be guided by our minds rather than our emotions, to know the reasons we are on Earth, to be what we inherently are, and to serve others in a spirit of universal love and brotherhood. Through the understanding and use of Ray-Centered Astrology, these goals can be met. The result of serving others with love is expressed beautifully in the poem by Leigh Hunt:

Abou Ben Adhem (may his tribe increase!)
Awoke one night from a deep dream of peace,
And saw within the moonlight in his room,
Making it rich like a lily in bloom,
An Angel writing in a book of gold.
Exceeding peace had made Ben Adhem bold,
And to the presence in the room he said,
"What writest thou?" The vision raised its head,
And, with a look of all sweet accord,
Answer'd, "The names of those who love the Lord."
"And is mine one?" said Abou. "Nay, not so,"
Replied the Angel. Abou spoke more low,
But cheerily still; and said, "I pray thee, then,
Write me as one that loves his fellow men."
The Angel wrote, and vanish'd. The next night
It came again, with a great wakening light,
And show'd the names whom love of God had blest—
And, lo! Ben Adhem's name led all the rest!"

The new Aquarian energies bring new needs and new urges to mankind that must be met and fulfilled by newer and more advanced disciplines. Humanity is ever-evolving, but changes are more pronounced at the ending of one Age and the beginning of the next, as the New Age energies replace those of the Old Age. Such a time is now—in the dawning of the Aquarian Age. In the lives we lived in the Piscean Age, in which personality desires of this emotional water sign were uppermost for most of us, we did not find the happiness we sought. The Aquarius air sign is intellectually stimulating, impelling us to become aware that our emotional desires bring suffering, and urges us to change our long-standing personality desires to Soul aspirations.

Just as humanity ever evolves, the disciplines that serve it must also evolve. For the disciplines to survive, they must keep up with evolving humanity. Even though this is true at any time, it is truer at the beginning of every New Age which produces revolutionary discoveries and methods. The New Age releases new energies consonant with the needs that evolving humanity has developed as the Old Age energies diminish.

Ray-Centered Astrology was synthesized from the study of those fragments of the Ancient Wisdom found in the writings of certain Masters who deemed it time for a technique to be presented that was compatible with the ongoing Aquarian Age. As the Age progresses, it can thus grow to become the method by which the seeker contacts his Soul, identifies its purpose, discovers his weaknesses, and learns how to turn them into strengths so that he may fulfill his Soul's purpose in this life in the Aquarian Age.

As the Earth enters a New Age because of the precessing equinox, change becomes inevitable, and if the sign of the Age is a guide to its character, Aquarius will produce revolutionary, deep, and sweeping alterations in all activities and disciplines; and contrary to its predecessor, the Piscean Age of the water element whose energies focused on the emotions and the self-centered personality, the Aquarian Age energies of the air element focus on the mind leading to the Soul. Such change can be fostered and encouraged by Ray-Centered Astrology.

Ray-Centered Astrology provides enlightenment through awareness of and optimal use of the true sources of all energy, the Seven Rays. It fosters universal love and humanitarian service through the knowledge and stimulation necessary for upliftment. It can be deeply meaningful to the ever-increasing number of those who are becoming attuned to the New Age energies in that it reveals to them the real essence of their beings. It stresses the uniqueness of each individual's contribution to the overall evolution of humanity. We came to this earth for a special purpose consonant with what we were, what we are, and what we can be. Each of us has had different types of past lives with many different kinds of relationships and experiences, and with the development of certain kinds of abilities. The sum total of these relationships, experiences, and abilities is what makes each of us unique. Each of us belongs here and has an important function for the continued evolvement of the race. In God's Plan there is a special place for each of us to shine and serve. Ray-Centered Astrology helps us find that place.

The uniqueness of the individual implies neither separativeness nor arrogance, but is the key to the use of his special abilities consonant with his stage of evolvement and awareness of the equal importance of all other beings. As a result, the essence of existence in the Aquarian Age is the working together of all in a diversified yet unified way for the successful evolvement of all humanity, leading to universality, humility, and a feeling of Oneness-with-All.

Just as an individual's character is not a summation of his various traits, but each trait in relation to the whole of his being, so is humanity not a summation of the manifestation of the uniqueness of all its members, but the uniqueness of each member in relation to all others. It is only in becoming aware of our unique quality that we can contribute to the evolution of humanity. Diversity in unity is the hallmark of the Aquarian Age, and is an important though subtle concept of this New Age Astrology.

The astrologer is not apart from this diversity in unity. He has his own uniqueness. Before an astrologer decides to use Ray-Centered Astrology professionally, he should do his own Ray-Centered delineation as a test of its validity, and to find his own uniqueness as a technique for reaching his Soul. Having thus satisfied himself, he can then help his clients apply the same technique.

Ray-Centered Astrology has its origin in the Ancient Wisdom, yet is consonant with the New Aquarian energies. In each Age, part of the Ancient Wisdom needed for that particular stage of development is released by certain Masters, and used through the energies of that Age.

There is a strong parallel between Ray-Centered Astrology and the New Aquarian energies—both are concerned with understanding and enlightenment, and both are aimed toward Soul manifestation. Because of this parallel, the use of Ray-Centered Astrology can help us tune in to the New Age energies for optimal usefulness; and the New Aquarian energies will urge us to accept Ray-Centered Astrology. It is important at our present level of evolvement to develop understanding and enlightenment. True understanding enables us to become aware of our weaknesses, and enlightenment gives us the impetus to change them. As this upliftment takes place, we become more knowledgeable of the Soul's purpose of serving others. As the years pass, Ray-Centered Astrology and Aquarian Age energies, through understanding and enlightenment, can help us develop for ourselves and for others, tolerance, acceptance, patience, and love that together will be the elixer of joint living which will in time make the word "weakness" no longer useful and the word "strength" superfluous because it will belong to All.

Aquarian Age energies induce Soul evolvement, unattached love, universality, service to humanity, and the freedom to be guided by one's conscience, the same traits fostered by Ray-Centered Astrology.

Everything in the Universe is energy. The cosmos is simply and totally energy being manipulated by time, stress, space, and motion. We do not yet know in detail how the Seven Ray energies in all their ramifications manifest in the cosmos of which we are a small part.

Though intelligence or wisdom are attributed to some of the Seven Rays, being energy, they do not possess intelligence or wisdom but induce one or the other in those to whom the particular Rays are assigned by the nature of their natal horoscopes. The same is true of such characteristics as love, power, will, and idealism.

The exoteric, traditional, personality-centered astrology served the needs and urges of astrologers and their clients well during the Age of Pisces. The change of Piscean Age energies to those of Aquarius does not mean merely a change from faith to reason, but a change from blind faith of the emotions to understanding through both the logical reasoning and the abstract intuitional levels of the mind.

Because Aquarian concepts have not yet been introduced into organized religions, many people are leaving the churches, seeking a spirituality that is in rapport with the urges and needs of the Aquarian Age and the Seven Ray energies. Ray-Centered Astrology can fill those needs because it not only teaches self-understanding on both a logical and deep intuitive

level, but is an esoteric astrology of the Soul. The understanding mind is the bridge from the personality to the Soul, and
because the Seven Rays are involved, it is often called the
rainbow bridge.

It is through the wise use of the mind on all its levels that
one will choose either self-centered personality desires or Soul
aspirations. When one has suffered enough from karmic experiences resulting from self-centered desires, he will be guided
by his mind more than by his emotions and will substitute Soul
evolvement for self-centered desires to attain the peace, success, and joy he seeks.

When one is aspiring to Soul evolvement, joy becomes a part
of his life. Ray-Centered Astrology can help to make joy a
reality by helping us get in touch with our Souls. It is in pro-
jecting self-centered personality desires that troubles and conflicts beset us. When the majority of us manifest on a Soul level
on which we become aware of our weaknesses and make efforts
to transmute them into strengths and at the same time become
aware of our Soul's purpose for serving others and we work
toward this end, then that joy will no longer be an ideal to
strive toward, but a common experience of life on earth. Ray-
Centered Astrology can be the key to achieving this end because it is in rapport with the New Aquarian Age energies. It
is an Astrology of the Soul, using the personality-centered Traditional Astrology of the past and present as the base upon
which the deeper levels of a Soul-centered Astrology which this
New Age demands can be built.

There is always a period of transition from one Age to the
next in which their energies intermingle until the old Age
energies vanish with the passing years. We are now in that
transition period.

To be in harmony with the ever-increasing Aquarian energies, changes in disciplines and ways of life must keep pace
with the influx of new energies. The intermingling of the two
Age energies will result in the practice of two kinds of Astrology—the present exoteric Traditional Astrology of the personality which the Piscean Age energies foster, and the esoteric
Ray-Centered Astrology of the Soul that is induced by Aquarian Age energies.

Even with this fusion of the old with the new, for many years there will be some individuals who are not ready for Esoteric Astrology. But they will be exposed more and more to it through friends who have benefited from it, by attending lectures, and by finding more and more new books in libraries and book stores. Eventually they will begin to question themselves and make the transition from self-centered desires to Soul aspirations. They will then be self-conditioned to accept Ray-Centered Astrology.

As Piscean Age energies decrease and Aquarian Age energies increase, Traditional Astrology will fill the needs of fewer people, and the esoteric Astrology of the Rays will fill the needs of more and more.

The understanding and sensitive astrologer will realize that more of his clients are moving in thought and feeling in a new direction. It would profit both the astrologer and the client if the astrologer can sense the direction in which the client is moving and guide him from wherever he is to where he is ready to go. This would probably require an initial interview during which the astrologer endeavors to learn what brought the client to him, the nature of his problems, the range of his understanding of the essense of esotericism—awareness of his Soul, awareness that he has potentials to be explored, weaknesses to be overcome, strengths to be relied on, love to be given to All, and a willingness to share all that he is. If the interview is sufficiently productive, the astrologer can begin to lead the client toward self-change which may ready him for a Ray-Centered Astrology delineation.

On the other hand, if the interview is not sufficiently productive to warrant the acceptance of the client for a Ray-Centered delineation, the astrologer would be wise to suggest a deeply delineated Traditional horoscope with a consequent further interview as a stepping stone toward the client's upward progress. In any case, the relationship with the client should not be terminated, as he may one day return to ask for help in knowing more about who he is, where he is, and where he ought to be.

Ray-Centered Astrology is for those who desire to get in touch with their Souls, those who welcome the opportunity to see their weaknesses, strengths, and abilities, those who, when they become aware of their problems, will have the courage to face themselves honestly, and the wisdom and self-discipline to change, and those who have an urgent need to be what they are capable of being.

When one is no longer satisfied to manifest on a self-centered personality level, he then begins to search for something better. The Ray-Centered Astrologer can make it possible for him to discover the Path which leads to self-realization, to a zest for living, a feeling of his contributing to the welfare of others consonant with his uniqueness, and the joy of Soul evolvement.

Manifesting on a Soul level more than on a self-centered personality level does not mean negating the personality. When integrated, aspiring to Soul growth, and freed of self-centeredness, the personality enables us to reach and express the Soul's purpose. An integrated personality is one which uses the physical body, the emotional body, and the concrete mind to achieve self-realization. An integrated personality is necessary for expressing the Soul Ray's purpose. Because the integrated personality is controlled by the mind, it is through the mind that contact is made with the Soul.

The mind of man is an immense storehouse and power plant because when it chooses to reside in the brain it utilizes electrical energy of the brain for its purposes which are enhanced, directed, motivated, and their goals accomplished through the aid of the Rays and sub-Rays that flood it.

When one is aware of weaknesses and tries to transmute them into strengths, while serving others consonant with his Soul and Personality Rays, he will find that the exoteric rulers of all the signs begin to affect him more positively, and the esoteric rulers begin to give him additional beneficial energies. In time he will also receive greater beneficial energies from the hierarchical rulers. Simultaneously he will note that the adverse effects of the difficult aspects from his progressions and transits are diminishing, and he will later find the energies from his difficult aspects will begin to affect him beneficially.

It is conceivable that all people will not be able to reap the benefits of the hierarchical rulers during this incarnation. It must be kept in mind that we are not only concerned with the Soul manifestation in this life, but with the Soul as a continuing entity from this life to an After-life, and then perhaps another earth life.

Is it not true that you are convinced that the "real you" will livë forever? And if you are so convinced, then it would be wise to consider the unchanging process by which the Soul relinquishes existence on the earth plane, passes through the veil to the Afterlife, grows there in wisdom and in understanding until those Souls who guide it agree with it that the Universal Law called, Reincarnation, should apply. One reason is that having grown on the spirit plane, the Soul is ready to return to an earth life to further its purpose and continue its growth. This reason is a matter of choice on the part of the Soul involved. The second reason is not a matter of choice, but having grown sufficiently on the spirit plane, is another step in the fulfillment of that Universal Law known as Karma which necessitates a return to earthly life to learn through experience those yet-unlearned lessons, the necessity for which the Soul itself created through certain misuses of its abilities and powers in previous life-times. This fulfillment of the second reason may require more than one life cycle, the After-life for a time, and a return to what Gautama, the Buddha, so aptly called, "The Wheel of the Law." The Soul and the mind continue from earth life to the After-life, and from the After-life to a successive earth life.

In a successive earth life we might well ask, as did Talbot Mundy in his book, *Om,* "For what purpose are we in the world? The purpose lies in front of each of us and is never more than one step in advance, and whither it leads none knows but the Soul. It is the best that we can do at any moment that is required of us, and if we do our best each moment, we live as long as we are useful and as long as it is good for us to live. Thereafter we die, which is another form of living, even as ice and water are the same thing in different aspects."

Mundy further states, "Men think they work for money or some other momentary need, but they deceive themselves, it being curious to witness how unanimously human beings substitute the shadow for the truth—which truth is, that no other impulse governs us than the necessity for growth." This impulse for spiritual growth has led to the synthesis of Ray-Centered Astrology and can lead astrologers to the Ray-Centered delineation of themselves and their clients.

Just as the Soul of each of us chose, with the help of more

advanced Souls, the parents and time of birth consonant with the level of Soul evolvement at that time, so will the Soul choose, after the death of the physical body, the parents and time of birth for the next life consonant with the then level of Soul evolvement.

To attain a higher level of Soul evolvement, we must not only change weaknesses into strengths, but we must work on our Soul's purpose in serving others. Ray-Centered Astrology can aid one's Soul through the mind to find its true purpose in this lifetime. After having found it and working at it with love and wisdom, reaping the deserved benefits of success, better physical health, and joy, he can easily continue his Soul's purpose in the After-life through serving and learning. The Soul then, having found its way, its purpose for existing, will suffer no confusion. There will be only increasing joy and success in serving others in the After-life because there will be no dense physical body with all its needed care and requirements for sustenance.

The Soul Ray not only indicates one's purpose of serving others for this life, but also the After-life purpose. When one benefits from the study of his Soul Ray and begins to serve others according to his Soul's purpose, at the death of his physical body he will be welcomed to the higher planes as a developed Soul to continue his Soul Ray's purpose. A Ray-Centered delineation can help in his Soul evolvement so that he can not only reap the benefits he deserves in this life, but also in the After-life.

It is enlightening that a function of Universal Law and a Ray-Centered delineation can both reach the same goal in one individual. It occurs thus: (1) A function of Universal Law is that the Soul in each existence on the earth plane and in the After-life reaches ever-higher evolvement with the result that the conditions of being become better on both planes. Both on the earth and in the After-life, a higher level of Soul evolvement gives an enhancement of peace, joy, creativity, and greater opportunity for additional growth. (2) A Ray-Centered delineation that is used conscientiously not only helps a person experience a more fulfilled and joyful present life, but continues to give a better After-life and better future incarnations.

Ray-Centered Astrology can be revolutionary in scope through helping a person understand why and how he is impelled or privileged, depending on his level of consciousness, to pursue his course through a given incarnation. A person's course in a given incarnation, that is his Soul's purpose, depends on the progress made in past lives, and his course in the next incarnation depends on how wisely he spends the time allotted to him now. Talbot Mundy says, "We live in the eternal Now and it is Now that we create our destiny. It follows, that to grieve over the past is useless. There is only one ambition that is good and that is so to live now that none may weary of life's emptiness and none will have to do the task we leave undone."

The plans that each Soul made before the birth of his physical body for its present incarnation can be found in a Ray-Centered delineation. When a person's will during an incarnation is contrary to his Soul's purpose because of strong self-centered desires, then frustration, unhappiness, and a lack of self-realization result. Mundy states, "Stars do not limit their light to certain individuals. One learns more about them than another. Selfishness prevents discovery of anything worthwhile. Selfishness makes people mentally blind."

Selfishness and mental blindness make it difficult for one to be aware of his Soul's purpose. The Soul's purpose and one's weaknesses and strengths can be delineated by Ray-Centered Astrology. If a person begins to work toward his Soul's purpose and at the same time works toward transmuting his weaknesses into strengths, he will attain the self-realization and joy which are his heritage. Again from Mundy: "You have first to prove that you are fitted to discover what you seek; and there is no way to prove that except by doing it. Only those who have the character pertaining to the path they choose can succeed in the end."

It is our hope that Ray-Centered Astrology will stimulate the minds and hearts of dedicated spiritual seekers to a higher level of consciousness through inspiration, encouragement, and additional astrological knowledge from the Ancient Wisdom so that their lives may become more fulfilling, successful, and joyful—then the freedom to be what one is supposed to be and the unattached Love toward All which the Aquarian Age promises, can sooner become realities.

Appendix A

THE EARTH'S PLACEMENT IN THE CHART

In Ray-Centered Astrology it is necessary to place the Earth's position in the chart because the Earth is the esoteric ruler of Sagittarius and the hierarchical ruler of Gemini. Perhaps in the future the Earth will be considered the exoteric ruler of Taurus at the time a new exoteric ruler of Virgo or Gemini is accepted by astrologers, allowing every planet to be a ruler of only one sign.

Even though the Earth's placement in the chart is necessary for Ray-Centered Astrology, there is no definite answer as to where it should be placed. Yet there are certain matters for which there are reputed answers, known as conventions, that are accepted by all even though they are known to be false. They are accepted because they project the correct ideas and implications even though they are not accurate. An example is, "the Sun rises in the east." We all know this is not true, yet the idea and the implications of this statement are accurate in that the Sun *appears* to rise in the east rather than the west, north, or south.

There are also conventions in astrology which, though inaccurate, help to simplify and project accurate thoughts. One is that we use geocentric calculations in our heliocentric universe. We astrologers achieve amazing ends through the amount of information we place in the circle of the chart, and thus assume astounding accuracy by doing so.

Another convention is that the Earth is regarded as opposite the Sun as pictured in certain forms of heliocentric charting.

In geocentric astrology, by convention, we place the Earth either in the center of the chart or opposite the Sun, giving two conventional placements for the Earth in the chart, both of which are accepted by most astrologers. In Ray-Centered Astrology, the Earth's conventional placement opposite the Sun is used.

Appendix B

FINDING RAYS FOR UNKNOWN BIRTH TIME

In determining the accuracy of one's Rays when the clock-time of birth is inaccurate or unknown, there is a strong possibility that the calculated Personality Ray will be accurate. Because the Personality Ray is determined by a person's Sun sign, unless he was born on the single day of the month during which the Sun changes signs, the Personality Ray will be accurate. However, there is a possibility of inaccuracy if one is born between the nineteenth and twenty-fifth of any month. This can be checked in the ephemeris for the year of birth to see if the birthday coincides with the day the Sun sign changes.

If a person is not sure of his clock-time of birth and was born on the one day the Sun changed signs, it would be advisable to study Charts 4 and 5 to find the Personality Ray for each of the two Sun signs. The information in Chapter Three and Chapter Four should be reviewed in order to determine which combination of Sun sign and Personality Ray fits best.

To find the Soul Ray it is imperative to know the true Ascendant. To accomplish this, a person can eliminate those signs which ascended during that portion of the day the Sun was not in the sign of his birth. The drawing of three horoscopes is required—one for zero hours local mean time of the day of birth at the birthplace, a second for zero hours local mean time of the day after birth at the birthplace, and a third for the local mean time that the Sun entered the next sign at the birthplace.

For the first two horoscopes, it is only necessary to find the Ascendants and the Suns, and for the third horoscope it is only necessary to find the Ascendant.

The information required to set up the third horoscope consists of: (1) the movement of the Sun from zero hours local mean time of the birthday at the birthplace to zero hours local mean time of the next day at the birthplace, and (2) the Sun's movement from zero hours local mean time at the birthplace until it entered the next sign. To find the time for this horoscope, divide the Sun's movement from zero hours local mean time at the birthplace until it entered the next sign by the

Sun's movement during the 24 hours of the date of birth at the birthplace and multiply by 24. This is the local mean time to be used for setting up the third horoscope.

Noting the Ascendants of all three horoscopes, it can be determined easily which signs ascended during the time the Sun was in the old sign, and which ascended when the Sun was in the new sign. Having previously determined the Sun sign, it is now possible to select the only possible Ascendants rising by studying these three horoscopes. By referring to Chart 6, the possible Soul Ray or Rays for each of these Ascendants can be found. To determine which Ascendant and Soul Ray combination is most suitable, the two constants, the Sun sign and the Personality Ray, should be combined with each Ascendant and Soul Ray combination compatible with its Sun sign to help find which Ascendant fits best. With two constants and one detailed variable, the astrologer has adequate help in this determination. The following example is illustrative.

If a person was born on September 23, 1942 in Batavia, New York, clock-time unknown, what are his Personality and Soul Rays? The reference used in the following steps were: *Longitudes and Latitudes in the United States* by Eugene Dernay, *Table of Houses* by Joseph Dalton, *The American Ephemeris for the Twentieth Century* by Neil Michelsen, and *Tables of Diurnal Planetary Motion* by American Federation of Astrologers.

Step 1. Set up a horoscope for the local mean time of zero hours at Batavia, New York on September 23, 1942 to find the Sun's exact placement and to find the Ascendant, omitting minutes unless Ascendant is zero degrees or twenty-nine degrees fifty-nine minutes of a sign.

	Hours	Minutes	Seconds
a. local mean time	0	00	00
b. Greenwich sidereal time	0	04	50

c. correction of 10″ for
   each hour of difference
   from Greenwich mean
   time   00   52
d. sidereal time at
   Batavia   0   5   42

This sidereal time indicates the Ascendant to be 21° Cancer at
43° North, the latitude of Batavia. The Sun moved 58′43″ at
Greenwich on September 23, 1942. Using this motion, together
with the distance of Batavia from Greenwich which *Longitudes
and Latitudes* gives as 5 hours 12 minutes 44 seconds, we calculate the Sun's motion beyond its placement at Greenwich,
using *Tables of Diurnal Planetary Motion* and find it to be
12′46″. Adding this motion to the Sun's placement at zero hours
at Greenwich which is 29° Virgo 20′11″, the result is 29° Virgo
32′57″ which is the Sun's placement at zero hours, local mean
time, at Batavia, September 23, 1942.

Step 2. Set up a horoscope similar to Step 1 for zero hours
local mean time, September 24, 1942 at Batavia to find the
Sun's exact placement and to find the Ascendant, omitting
minutes unless Ascendant is zero degrees or twenty-nine degrees fifty-nine minutes of a sign.

	Hours	Minutes	Seconds
a. local mean time	0	00	00
b. Greenwich sidereal time	0	08	47

c. correction of 10″ for
   each hour of difference
   from Greenwich mean
   time
		00	52

d. sidereal time at Batavia	0	9	39

315

The above sidereal time indicates the Ascendant to be 22° Cancer at 43° North, the latitude of Batavia. The Sun moved 58′45″ at Greenwich on September 24, 1942. Using this motion, together with the distance of Batavia from Greenwich which *Longitudes and Latitudes* gives as 5 hours 12 minutes 44 seconds, we calculate the Sun's motion beyond its placement at Greenwich using *Tables of Diurnal Motion* and find it to be 12′47″. Adding this motion to the Sun's placement at zero hours at Greenwich which is 0° Libra 18′54″, the result is 0° Libra 31′41″ which is the Sun's placement at zero hours, local mean time, September 24, 1942 at Batavia.

Step 3. Find the local mean time at Batavia, September 23, 1942 when the Sun entered Libra.

Sun's place at Batavia at zero hours local mean time September 24, 1942	0° Libra 31′41″
From this we subtract the Sun's place at Batavia at zero hours local mean time September 23, 1942	29° Virgo 32′57″
	58′44″

58′44″ is equivalent to 3524″—the Sun's movement at Batavia in the 24 hours of September 23, 1942.

Sun entered new sign	0° Libra 00′00″
From this we subtract the Sun's place at Batavia at zero hours local mean time September 23, 1942	29° Virgo 32′57″
	27′03″

27′03″ is equivalent to 1623″—the Sun's movement at Batavia from zero hours local mean time until it entered Libra.
1623 ÷ 3524 × 24 = 11.053348 hours = 11 hours 3 minutes 12 seconds local mean time at Batavia when the Sun entered Libra.

Step 4. Set up a horoscope using the local mean time calculated in Step 3. Find the Ascendant at Batavia when the Sun
entered Libra September 23, 1942. Unless the Ascendant is 0°
or 29° 59′, omit the minutes.

	Hours	Minutes	Seconds
a. local mean time	11	03	12
b. Greenwich sidereal time	0	04	50
c. correction of 10″ for each hour of local mean time past zero hours			111
d. correction of 10″ for each hour of difference from Greenwich mean time			52
e. sidereal time at Batavia	11	10	45

This sidereal time gives an Ascendant at 43° North latitude at
Batavia of 29° Scorpio.

Step 5. Find all possible Ascendants when the Sun was in
Virgo and all possible Ascendants when the Sun was in Libra
on September 23, 1942 at Batavia, New York.

    A. From Step 1 we found the Ascendant at zero hours on
September 23 to be *21° Cancer.*
    B. From Step 4 we found the Ascendant when the Sun
entered Libra to be *29° Scorpio.*
    C. From Step 2 we found the Ascendant at zero hours on
September 24 to be *22° Cancer.*

Therefore the possible Ascendant signs when the Sun was in
Virgo were Cancer, Leo, Virgo, Libra, and Scorpio. The possible
Ascendant signs when the Sun was in Libra were Scorpio, Sagittarius, Capricorn, Aquarius, Pisces, Aries, Taurus, Gemini,
and Cancer.

Step 6. Find the possible Soul Ray or Rays for each Ascendant sign by referring to Chart 6 and find the Personality Ray for each of the two Sun Signs by referring to Charts 4 and 5.

Ascendant Sign	Possible Soul Rays	Sun Sign	Personality Ray
Cancer	3, 7	Virgo	4
Leo	1, 5	Virgo	4
Virgo	2, 6	Virgo	4
Libra	3	Virgo	4
Scorpio	4	Virgo	4
Scorpio	4	Libra	5
Sagittarius	4, 5, 6	Libra	5
Capricorn	1, 3, 7	Libra	5
Aquarius	5	Libra	5
Pisces	2, 6	Libra	5
Aries	1, 7	Libra	5
Taurus	4	Libra	5
Gemini	2	Libra	5
Cancer	3, 7	Libra	5

Step 7. From Step 6, determine which combination of Ascendant Sign, Soul Ray, Sun Sign, and Personality Ray best suits the client.

This concludes the example.

This system can also be used to find the Soul Ray for one who was born on a day when the Sun did not change signs. Use the Chart in Step 6, substituting the person's Sun for the Virgo and Libra Suns of the example. Having determined the Ascendant sign for a person born under either of these two Sun sign behaviors, the Soul Ray is calculated by steps given in the text. Finally, it may be remarked that this method of Soul Ray determination can, with study and application, achieve birth-time rectification within a two-hour accuracy.

Erratum, p. 317: In the column headed, "Personality Ray," each of the nine digits adjacent to "Libra" should be 7 instead of 5.

Appendix C

RAY-CENTERED ASTROLOGY
EMPHASIZES UNIQUENESS OF EACH INDIVIDUAL

Because there are only seven Rays, some people may suppose that the uniqueness of the individual, which Ray-Centered Astrology supports, can be questioned. Yet this supposition is far from true. By random selection, every forty-ninth person would have the same Soul and Personality Rays. The fact is, however, that these hypothetical forty-ninth persons have many dissimilarities in their horoscopes, establishing the uniqueness of every individual.

Of the probable dissimilarities, foremost is the Ascendant sign. The chances are only one in three that two people with the same Soul Ray would have the same Ascendant sign. It is also possible that two people with the same Ascendant sign would not have the same Soul Rays; in fact it is not only possible but highly probable with the following seven signs: Aries, Cancer, Leo, Virgo, Sagittarius, Capricorn, and Pisces. Two people who share one of these Ascendant signs have the possibility of different Soul Rays. With Aries, Cancer, Leo, Virgo, and Pisces, the chances are one to one, and with Sagittarius and Capricorn, the chances are two to one that they would have different Soul Rays.

Second in importance of the probable dissimilarities between the randomly selected forty-ninth person is the possibility of different Sun signs. While all those forty-ninth persons with a Ray Five Personality have the same Sun sign and all those with a Ray Seven Personality have the same Sun Sign, all other forty-ninth persons with any of the other Personality Rays may have different Sun signs. These are just two examples by which Ray-Centered Astrology defines the uniqueness of the individual in ways that Traditional Astrology cannot do.

Even for two persons with the same Soul and Personality Rays who have the same Ascendants sign and Sun sign, Ray-Centered Astrology finds myriad differences to prove the uniqueness of every person. Ray-Centered Astrology uses the same differences as Traditional Astrology, but uses them in a deeper connotation and uses additional dissimilarities as found in this book which Traditional Astrology does not use.

Appendix D

HOW TO ALTER EXPERIENCES
DURING CHALLENGING ASPECTS

Difficult experiences are the karmic results of weaknesses not yet transmuted into strengths. Weaknesses are self-centered desires which in some life do come to fruition unless a stronger aspiration is substituted for the original desire. Difficult experiences recur as the planets which signify a person's weaknesses make challenging partile aspects in the transitting, progressed, or natal mode unless the substitution of aspiration for self-centered desire has been made and the weaknesses have been transmuted into strengths. By examining the natal horoscope, one can determine the weaknesses and their intensity brought from a past life and how they might be changed into strengths.

If, for example, one has a close square between Uranus and Mars natally, and has not yet transmuted the weakness that it indicates, he would have a tendency toward an explosive temper. The energies of Uranus and Mars would not only be intense in his being, but they would be manifesting together. By being aware that this planetary energy combination will always be strong in his life, he can change the unwise use of it to a wise use, thus transmuting the difficult karmic experiences into rewarding ones. In this example, intuition and creativity can be substituted for anger. If a person comes to understand the Universal Laws of Reincarnation, Karma, and the Oneness-of-All, certain spiritual concepts will become a part of his being to help him in time of need. Then when someone wrongs him, the intuitive flashes Uranus provides will recall helpful learned concepts such as, "We are our own creators because of past thoughts, words, and actions," "No one can hurt us unless we allow them to," "We will benefit if we accept and love others in spite of their weaknesses," and "If we allow anger to happen we must suffer its results." The strong energy of Mars can provide the courage and immediacy to adopt these concepts and make them work for him in the face of which anger cannot exist. The Mars-Uranus energies can then give him original ideas which lead to creative projects.

319

As he successfully practices this technique on this particular weakness, he will find that success breeds success and he will be led to practice it on other weaknesses. He will then discover that when these challenging aspects, from which he has learned to use the energy wisely, appear in his chart, he need not fear them, but will enjoy the rewarding karmic experiences he deserves.

As a person applies this process, he will find that the Traditional Astrological predictions of undesirable experiences become more and more inaccurate until they are practically nonexistent. He will then be the master of his fate.